THE *Good Beer* GUIDE TO NEW ENGLAND

★

Published by University Press of New England,
One Court Street, Lebanon, NH 03766
www.upne.com
© 2006 by Andrew S. Crouch
Printed in the United States of America
5 4 3 2 1

Library of Congress Cataloging-in-Publication Data
Crouch, Andy (Andrew S.)
The good beer guide to New England / Andy Crouch.
    p. cm.
Includes index.
ISBN–13: 978–1–58465–469–8 (pbk.: alk. paper)
ISBN–10: 1–58465–469–4 (pbk.: alk. paper)
1. Beer—New England—Guidebooks. 2. Beer—New England—Directories.
I. Title.
TP577.C76 2006
647.9574—dc22   2005036112

For Jim, Marsha, and Michael

★ Contents ★

Massachusetts

New Hampshire

Rhode Island

Vermont

★ Acknowledgments ★

I researched and wrote this book, the first comprehensive guide to craft beer in New England, at a blistering pace over eight short months. What started as an idea for a small book on Massachusetts breweries quickly turned into something much larger. A project of this scope and size never comes together without the help of many supportive, patient, and dedicated people. While you might think it's the world's easiest thing to recruit people to help research a book on beer, the deal seems far less sweet when the prospective helpers realize they're to serve as designated drivers, holders of my pens, locators of various maps, and meeting timekeepers. Only a few brave people rose to the challenge and accompanied me on these journeys, including non–New Englanders Jeff Fecke and Erika Goedrich, and I thank them for their company.

I am grateful to the brewers and owners who participated in the research process, gave their time freely, shared beers and knowledge, and put up with pesky phone calls and unexpected visits. Others helped provide technical or historical information along the way that rounded out the edges of this guide. And of course, the countless, nameless people who advised me about good local bars and even provided hand-drawn directions on frayed napkins. I thank each of them for their ideas, assistance, and interest.

For sharing my passion for the subject and helping me pull together loose ends, I am lucky to have my brother Myk, who moved to the region in the middle of the book-writing process. My parents, Jim and Marsha, raised me in the occasional Chicago barroom, where I developed an early passion for napping on bar tops and pool tables, and thus initiated my interest in the present subject. All three have indulged my interest in beer at every turn, including asking the guide on our tour of Australian wineries to direct the van to the nearest brewery, which he promptly did.

Jon "Benny" Hill and his lovely girlfriend, Mary Barter, introduced me to their friends in the Maine beer community and opened their home to me on numerous occasions. I greatly enjoyed sitting around their dinner table, watching the sun set, drinking beers from Maine and much further afield, and generally discussing beer. I thank them for their hospitality and the blueberry muffins.

Fellow beer writer Lew Bryson, who has written several similar guides that I highly recommend for New York and the mid-Atlantic states, provided some welcomed early advice on the project, including that I was crazy for taking it on.

With her inside knowledge and love of good beer, Carmen Mitchell also generously offered her counsel regarding the publishing industry and the project itself.

The founders and participants at BeerAdvocate.com provided support, news of intriguing openings, and gossip about possible closures, and made the completion of this book in such a short period of time a lot easier. I spent a great deal of time on the Web site researching items for this guide and interacting with its colorful inhabitants. I highly recommend BeerAdvocate for anyone who wants to learn more about beer or for detailed reviews of the beers listed in these pages.

The staff at the University Press of New England, especially my editor, John Landrigan, exhibited extraordinary professional and personal enthusiasm about the project from the earliest stages. I thank them for their interest, assistance in making this guide more readable, and patience during this whirlwind process.

Finally, I raise a special toast to my dear friend Jennifer Cox, without whose help I could never have accomplished this project on any remotely acceptable timetable. Lots of writers lightly throw around such praise. I do not. Her unfailing support and optimism, endless patience, willingness to travel anywhere at anytime, and selfless contributions made the words and images on these pages possible. My deepest and sincerest thanks go to her.

And to you, the readers. This book was born out of the love that we share for New England beer. Please help support the industry by drinking locally and traveling widely throughout this great beer region. I hope you enjoy reading this guide as much as I enjoyed writing it.

★ Introduction ★

There has been no better time in the history of mankind to be a lover of good beer and no better place to experience it. American brewers can compete with the best craftsmen Germany, the Czech Republic, Ireland, and Britain have to offer. Never before has the selection been so diverse, the domestic beers so flavorful and refined, and the brewers so knowledgeable, skilled, and passionate. Craft beer—that made with malted barley and without cheapening adjuncts— is widely available in an incredible variety of styles. No longer do Americans have to travel abroad in search of good craft beer; instead, beer lovers from around the world dream of coming to our shores to roam our breweries and frequent our brewpubs. Among American brewers, New England's craftsmen stand with the best, producing some of the most widely respected beers in the world and generating a lot of excitement for beer lovers.

Bleak Days for American Beer

Things were not always so good for American beer drinkers. Since the end of Prohibition, beer had been on a long, slow decline in terms of character and flavor. To be sure, the science of beer had never been so advanced. Large breweries, often referred to as macrobreweries or simply as macros, continually refined the microbiology and biochemistry behind the brewing process. Employees at Anheuser-Busch, Coors, Miller, and Stroh's analyzed beer down to its core molecules in order to meet exacting standards for production consistency. But treating beer as a chemical puzzle rather than as a source of nourishment and cheer yielded a pitiful, uninspired pint at the bar.

More than simply losing its flavor, beer lost its soul. While quality control became the new brewery buzzword for the scientists, advertising and marketing gurus stripped beer of its heritage. The traditions and styles brought to America by immigrant brewers from such places as Germany and Czechoslovakia quickly disappeared. The ingredients, brewing process, and character of the beer no longer mattered. Beer became a prosaic widget, nearly interchangeable with the next widget. By the end of the 1970s, less than fifty breweries operated in America and industry observers predicted that the number could drop to a mere handful after further consolidations.

In response, many beer lovers simply bowed their heads and awaited an eternity of indistinguishable brews. Instead, something radically different happened. In a step that would revolutionize the American brewing industry, President Jimmy Carter quietly signed a law amending the excise tax on trucks, buses, and tractors. Buried deep within House Resolution 1337 was an amendment allowing people to brew one hundred gallons of beer per year for their own personal use. Combined with the importation of full-flavored beers from abroad, a small, enterprising group of beer lovers slowly realized that they didn't simply have to accept what the big brewers told them to drink.

The Rebirth of American Beer

The 1980s was the decade of the craft brewing pioneer. A handful of beer enthusiasts conspired, raised capital, and started their own breweries. They lobbied their legislatures to pass laws allowing them to open brewpubs, scoured ancient texts for brewing ideas, and tested and retested recipes. With reckless abandon, these pioneers discarded safe career options for the entirely uncertain world of craft brewing.

These groundbreaking spirits included Fritz Maytag of the Anchor Brewing Company, Jack McAuliffe of the long-defunct New Albion Brewery, and Ken Grossman of the Sierra Nevada Brewing Company. Not to be outdone by its West Coast rivals, New England produced its own set of pioneers, including Richard Wrigley of the now-closed Commonwealth Brewing Company, Jim Koch of the Boston Beer Company, and Peter and Janet Egelston of the Northampton Brewing Company.

New breweries and brewpubs opened, first in the cities and then throughout America. Although the process was slow at first, the popularity of the new, strangely colored beers grew and word of their full flavor spread; indeed, growth started climbing at a rate that both surprised and alarmed those involved. If the 1980s were the pioneer years, the 1990s were the years of unrealistic enthusiasm. The level of exuberance was matched only by that of the dot.com age. By 1995, there were 500 breweries operating in the United States, with an average of 3 to 4 new breweries opening every week. By 1996, that number had more than doubled, to 1,102 breweries, and 300 more opened that year.

People with no brewing experience and little business sense jumped at the chance to run their own brewery; existing breweries expanded beyond their means, often rushing into new markets with insufficient support. Breweries packed store shelves with microbrewed beers, resulting in great brand confusion. The products often went stale on the shelves before consumption, leaving consumers with a bad taste in their mouths about craft beer. By 1998, openings and closings nearly equaled one another as a major correction in the industry plunged growth from a high of a 51 percent increase in production volume in 1995 to flat growth in 1998.

Instead of disappearing like some fad, as many in the mainstream media still falsely believe, craft brewers regrouped after the shakeout. Poor performers and the inexperienced resumed their day jobs and left the business to the professionals. The beer you sample today will be stable and flavorful for the most part, quality issues generally being a thing of the past. The brewers who have survived have done so not only because of their passion, but because they also appreciate the importance of consistently producing high quality beers.

The craft brewing business, which accounts for more than 6.5 million barrels of beer per year and $3.5 billion in retail sales, is now as stable as any other industry, with breweries enjoying measured growth and consumers embracing fresh, clean, and well-constructed beers. In the first decade of the twenty-first century, the craft brewing industry is not experiencing stark sobriety, but a pleasant buzz filled with hope and optimism.

Good Beer and This Guide

Welcome to *The Good Beer Guide to New England,* a book designed to be both an escort and a companion to your journeys through the exceptional abundance of craft brewing riches on offer in this region. With the stability of the industry, now is the proper time to offer such a guide. These brewers have survived the test of time, overcome hurdles of size and scale, and secured their roles and niches in a highly competitive marketplace.

In New England, seasoned brewers produce a range of quality ales and lagers. Put together, the 106 craft brewers profiled in this book do not brew as much beer as Anheuser-Busch does at its small Merrimack, New Hampshire, plant. But the breweries and brewpubs profiled in this guide each have distinct identities, shaped by the men and women who have spent long hours gently raising them from infancy to adulthood. In reading about the breweries that bring you beer in New England, you will meet brewers who run the gamut from unbelievably small, one-person operations to farm brewers to industrial mammoths. Common to nearly everyone featured in this book is a true love for brewing, its tradition and heritage, and the experience of enjoying beer.

This is a guide not only to tell you the stories and capture the spirits of individual brewers, but also to encourage you to get out and see New England and experience its distinctive, locally crafted products, with a focus on its beers. The geography of New England is diverse, with miles of rocky coastlines, snow-capped mountains, still lakes, hearty islands, farming flatlands, and beautiful scenery at every turn. In my experience, beers are often best enjoyed in their natural homes, which properly contextualize their individual spirits. The Magic Hat Brewing Company just wouldn't work anywhere outside the People's Republic of Burlington. Boston is a natural location for three Harvard guys who had the crazy idea to start a little brand called Harpoon in 1985. And it's hard to picture Shipyard operating anywhere other than on a hill overlooking its hometown of Portland, Maine.

I developed an interest in good beer while spending a semester in London during college. While at my local pub in southwest London, I tasted my first

Guinness and the world suddenly changed. Though tame compared to many beers available today, that beer possessed a thick body and light roasted flavors that I had never previously experienced. So the next weekend I hopped a plane to Dublin and went on my first brewery tour, at Guinness's historic St. James Gate brewery. With that first sip, I caught the good beer bug and have never looked back. When I started writing about beer professionally a few years later, I had the chance to meet the people behind the brands and learn their fascinating stories. Intensely dedicated to their craft and defiantly enduring long hours, strenuous manual labor, sleepless nights, and little money, these brewers and owners are deserving of great praise and respect for their tireless efforts.

This guide holds at its core two values: first, that beer is a beverage worthy of respect and praise, brewed by artisans who deserve our thanks and patronage; and second, that there is no such thing as a person who doesn't like beer. I firmly believe that there is a beer for every drinker out there, one that will open their eyes and hearts to good beer and cause them to firmly smack their foreheads exclaiming, "What have I been thinking all these years?" To my mind, people who don't like beer are like leprechauns, the Easter Bunny, and World Series ring ceremonies at Wrigley Field: they simply don't exist.

To encourage the exploration of good beer in this great brewing region, I not only seek to provide information, I also aim to be discerning. The profiles have more in common with restaurant reviews than traditional guidebook entries. While I deeply respect the brewers in New England, I strive to be frank and honest. These reviews do not sugarcoat things. The craft beer business is like any other; there are some places that excel, many that perform well, and others that don't get the job done.

I have thoroughly enjoyed writing this guide, meeting brewers throughout New England, and sampling their beers. The state of the beer union here is strong and growing stronger. Traveling to the places profiled here is a great way to spend a day or a week. I hope you enjoy it as much as I have and that this guide helps you raise a pint or two to the hard-working brewers of New England.

This comprehensive guide includes profiles of the breweries and brewpubs of New England, along with articles about beer, brewing, and the art of enjoying beer. The book is organized by state, with a short description of the highlighted region's beer culture and history of brewing.

While existing breweries occasionally close and new brewpubs open, the industry is proving itself to be more secure than at any other time in its history. Many of the breweries listed in this book are enjoying their tenth, fifteenth, or even twentieth anniversaries.

I have to acknowledge certain limits in the scope of this project. In recent years, American brewers have embraced experimentation in a way never before seen in the course of beer brewing. Beyond producing world-class versions of every defined beer style, American brewers also now produce beers that defy categorization. Some of the beers employ highly unusual ingredients, ranging from the traditional, such as fruits, to the unthinkable, such as garlic. While New England brewers have generally shown remarkable restraint in the face of the so-called extreme beer movement, new offerings still appear with great frequency. These special releases often come and go quickly, with some produced only once. Because of the inordinate volatility of such releases, I have not attempted to create an exhaustive list of every beer offered by each brewery. The beers listed in these pages are those that the breweries produce on a regular basis, either as part of their year-round offerings or as recurring seasonal products.

While this guide lists the beers available at each location, I do not provide detailed tasting notes on every beer made in New England. Tasting notes are inherently subjective and I want you to experience the beers for yourselves. I try to provide an overview of the quality of the beers and the approaches taken by each of the brewers, and I recommend that you use popular Web sites listed elsewhere in this guide if you want more information on a particular beer.

The breweries and brewpubs profiled here are described in the following manner. The name of the brewery, its address, phone number, and Web site. Each review then attempts to detail the history of the brewery, profile the owners, and capture the story behind the brewery and its particular approach to brewing.

★ Best beer: For each place, I feature one specific beer, detailing its flavor profile and its history or origin.

Opened: The month and year the brewery opened.

Type: Brewpub or brewery. A brewpub is a pub or restaurant whose beers are primarily for sale on site. A brewery is a producer with its own brick-and-mortar facility that brews beer primarily for sale in bars, restaurants, and liquor stores. Contract breweries, or those that have no physical location and brew on another brewery's system, are not listed in this guide.

Owner: The name of the individuals or company.

Brewer: This remains a very fluid area; the name of the head brewer of each establishment at the time of publication is listed here.

Brewing system: The size and type of the equipement used to brew the beer.

Amount produced: The total amount of beer brewed, in barrel units.

First beer: The name of the brewery's first product.

Flagship beer: The name of the lead product, often the top seller.

Year-round beers: The beers an entrant produces regularly throughout the year.

Seasonal beers: The beers an entrant produces on a limited basis.

Tours: Whether tours are available, either by a regular schedule or by appointment.

Beer to go: Whether beer is available for purchase and take away.

Food: For brewpubs that serve food, a basic overview of the menu is provided.

Amenities: A catch-all category detailing the parking situation, whether a pub has a full liquor license or live music, and other related details.

Other attractions: An occasional entry suggesting other places of note in the area, either beer-related or tourist in nature.

Directions: A few brief words about how to get to the profiled destination.

Pub hours: The hours of operation. Please call ahead to confirm before you visit, as hours may change.

THE *Good Beer* GUIDE TO NEW ENGLAND

★

Connecticut

Caught in the middle between New York and the rest of New England, half Yankees fans and half Red Sox Nation, Connecticut is a state with a bit of an identity problem. This identity problem extends to its local beer scene. As one Connecticut brewer put it, people are either from somewhere else, headed somewhere else, or identify with somewhere else. For craft brewers, Connecticut can be a very tough place to sell beer. While it boasts several excellent producers, the state really has no regionally identifiable brand or beer it can call its own.

Formed from the Mohegan word *Quinnehtukqut,* meaning "beside the long tidal river," Connecticut was first settled in 1635 and it didn't take long for beer

to come to the area. New Haven has the richest brewing history in the state, with evidence of a brewery existing as early as 1638. Commercial brewing in the state did not really take off until the later part of the 1800s.

Connecticut boasts perhaps the most compressed placement of breweries and brewpubs, geographically speaking. Instead of enjoying wide dispersal to all points across the state, most of Connecticut's brewing action is centered near Hartford and along the coast near I-95. There are absolutely no breweries in the western part and very few in the eastern part of the state.

While the geographic tug-of-war has made it difficult for Connecticut's breweries to cultivate their own local identity, there is plenty of good news to raise spirits. Several enterprising breweries, from the Troutbrook Brewing Company (which confidently refers to itself as "Connecticut's Beer") to the New England Brewing Company, are poised to make a run at becoming the state's brand of choice. On the brewpub front, locals continue to support their hometown pubs. In 2004 and 2005, pubgoers teamed with the state's brewers to help pass a law allowing brewpubs to sell beer in growlers for off-site consumption.

Eschewing quantity as a meaningless reward, Connecticut offers some real treats for beer lovers. For breweries, Troutbrook produces a welcome variety of hearty lagers to supplement its already impressive portfolio of full-flavored, American-influenced ales, while New England Brewing proves that craft beer packaged in an easily portable aluminum can is just as good as that in a clunky old bottle. For brewpubs, you would be hard pressed to find a more enthusiastic supporter of craft brewing than Dave Wollner at Willimantic Brewing, while stalwart brewer Ron Page at City Steam proves that Hartford, the sole capital of the state since its founding, offers more than just insurance adjusters and risk managers.

Southport Brewing Company

2600 Post Road
Southport, Connecticut 06490
Tel. (203) 256-BEER
www.southportbrewing.com

> ★ **Best Beer:** Mashing Pumpkin Ale. DaSilva enjoys brewing different fruit beers as a way to tempt people into trying craft beers. This very drinkable beer is a subtle mix of spices and is not overwhelmed with pumpkin flavor as are some other fruit-flavored attempts.

Opened: April 1997.

Type: Brewpub.

Owners: Mark DaSilva and William DaSilva.

Brewer: Mark DaSilva.

Brewing System: 7-barrel Pub Brewing System (Branford), 7-barrel DME System (Stamford), and 5-barrel DME System (Southport).

Amount produced: 1,500 barrels.

First beer: Bones Light.

Flagship beer: Fairfield Red Ale.

Year-round beers: Thimble Island Light, Big Head Blonde, Big Head Brunette, Fairfield Red Ale, Pequot IPA, and South Porter.

Seasonal beers: Black Rock Stout, Mashing Pumpkin Ale, Mill Hill Pilsener, and Southtoberfest. Each brewpub also has several different fruit ales on tap throughout the year.

Tours: By appointment or upon request if brewing is in process.

Beer to go: None.

Food: As with the décor, the food is slightly more upscale than your average brewpub. Asian influences dot the menu, with chicken satay and Szechwan dumplings, along with brick-oven pizza and plentiful amounts of seafood.

Amenities: Southport has two additional locations in southern Connecticut. SBC Restaurant and Brewery, 850 West Main Street, Branford, Connecticut 06405, tel. (203) 481-BREW, and SBC Downtown, 131 Summer Street, Stamford, Connecticut 06901, tel. (203) 327-BEER.

Pub hours: Open Monday through Thursday, 11:30 A.M. to 10 P.M.; Friday and Saturday, 11:30 A.M. to 11 P.M.; and Sunday, 11:30 A.M. to 9 P.M.

Directions: Southport location: From I-95 North, take exit 19 to Route 1 (Post Road). Go right on Route 1 and the restaurant is on the left. Branford location:

From I-95 South, take exit 54 and go left onto Cedar Street and right onto Route 1. Stamford location: From I-95 South, take exit 8 and turn left off ramp onto Atlantic Street. Turn left on Broad Street and left onto Summer Street. SBC Downtown is on the left.

Brewing six days a week on three different systems at three separate locations is no enviable task. For Mark DaSilva, it's his job. As co-owner and head brewer for the Southport Brewing Company, it is DaSilva's responsibility to make sure the tanks are always full at each of the brewpub chain's three southern Connecticut locations.

Mark DaSilva learned the sacred art of fermentation at a very early age from his Portuguese father, who taught his sons to make wine in the family's backyard. It took an acquaintance to turn the DaSilva brothers from winemakers to hopheads. At college, Mark's brother William was a fraternity brother to Steve Slesar, co-owner and executive head brewer of the Beer Works chain of brewpubs. When Slesar reunited with the brothers at a party in New York City, both were impressed with his beer business. Mark traveled to Boston, where he learned more about the brewing trade while living and working with Slesar.

As the co-owner, Mark DaSilva enjoys the ultimate freedom as a brewer. He can brew what he wants, when he wants, and his main outlet for experimentation has been Southport's extensive offering of fruit beers. DaSilva treats these special beers as a chef would specials on the food menu. His regulars expect a routine change in the lineup, and DaSilva believes variety helps spawn greater interest and awareness in the pub's own beers.

Southport's concept is that the locations are "restaurants with breweries in them," according to DaSilva. "We are not just a restaurant that serves Bud or a brewpub that serves hamburgers." The locations are upscale in design and approach compared to most brewpubs. The Branford location has a distinct lounge feel to it, with crescent-shaped booths and stylish lighting fixtures. The fashionable décor attracts a similar clientele; the pub sells a lot of Cosmopolitans and other fashionable mixed drinks of the moment, along with a fair amount of Bud Light for those who don't recognize that the place makes its own beer.

While Southport might serve its share of frou-frou Cran-Apple-Tinis, it doesn't mean that beer is relegated to secondary status. The brewhouse at the Branford location is in the restaurant, available for all patrons to see and almost touch. Four fermenters stand tall on a platform directly over the bar and seating area. The owners, however, clearly understand that their clientele isn't made up of beer geeks. The beers are clean and unpretentious and generally brewed for a more mainstream beer-drinking audience.

Another nice feature is Southport's beer menus, which provide detailed descriptions and a two-tiered approach for sampling platters. Tier One is designed to educate the novice craft beer drinker, with lighter offerings that are easier on the palate. Tier Two supplies a range of Southport's heartier beers for sampling. Beyond the generally well considered fruit beers, the lagers are also of note.

Olde Burnside Brewing Company

776 Tolland Street
East Hartford, Connecticut 06108
Tel. (860) 528–2200
www.oldeburnsidebrewing.com

★ **Best Beer:** Ten Penny Ale. A slightly hazy, Scottish-style ale with light aromas of caramel and even a bit of smoke. It remains very lightly carbonated and possesses a mild, pleasant sweetness balanced slightly by Cascade hops.

Opened: October 2000.

Type: Brewery.

Owner: Bob McClellan.

Brewer: Tim Gordon.

Brewing system: 15-barrel Specific Mechanical Systems brewhouse.

Amount produced: 2,100 barrels. 3,000-barrel total capacity.

First beer: Ten Penny Ale.

Flagship beer: Ten Penny Ale.

Year-round beers: Ten Penny Ale, Dirty Penny Ale, and Highland Chieftain Reserve Ale.

Seasonal beers: Father Christmas Highland Ale, Highland Fling Spring Ale, Highland Piper Tartan Ale (fall), and St. Andrew's Summer Ale.

Tours: Tours by appointment but you are welcome to stop by during business hours, Monday to Friday, 8:30 A.M. to 4:30 P.M.

Beer to go: None.

Amenities: Limited parking is available in front of the ice house.

Other attractions: The turn-of-the-century, family-owned ice plant here is a working antique, producing 300-pound monster blocks of ice. It is the last of its kind in Connecticut and one of only three such institutions remaining in New England. The owners offer tours of the ice plant as well as the brewery.

Directions: Head into East Hartford on the Tolland Turnpike, which becomes Tolland Street. Look for the Burnside Ice Company sign to know you're in the right place.

"It just seemed like a natural move," says Bob McClellan, the third-generation owner of the Burnside Ice Company and first-generation owner of the spin-off Olde Burnside Brewing Company. In 1911, Bob's grandfather, Albert McClellan, opened an icehouse and supplied his product to homes and businesses through-out the greater Hartford area. He passed the business down to his son, Clifford, who eventually turned it over to his son, Bob. While the eldest McClellan origi-nally cut his slabs of ice from a nearby pond, Clifford dug a four-hundred-foot well to provide a more reliable supply of water for the growing ice plant.

After he took over the family business, Bob McClellan, who describes himself as a "marketing guy," decided to offer the fresh well water for sale through a dis-penser on the front of the building. For a quarter, you can still take away a gallon of water. By 1995, McClellan noticed that several customers returned frequently to purchase sizable quantities of his water. After inquiring about the practice, he learned that the group was using the water to brew beer. Intrigued by their story, McClellan had the water tested to determine its mineral levels. With an eye toward entering the burgeoning craft beer market himself, McClellan took the test results and compared the water's composition with that of great brewing regions around the world. He discovered that the water matched the famous hard waters of Edin-burgh, Scotland, which produce excellent malty ales with low bitterness. With this information in hand, McClellan saw an opportunity to expand his business later-ally while tying the new operation into his family's Scottish heritage.

As a kid, McClellan heard his grandfather tell stories about Scotland. Albert used to tell his family about locally brewed beers and their power to refresh after a hard day of work. The price of an average pint of ale was a nickel; special releases cost a little bit more. From his grandfather's opinion that a good beer cost a nickel and a really good beer cost ten pennies, McClellan developed the name of his first beer, the Ten Penny Ale. He befriended a homebrewer named Ray Ballard, who helped him open the brewery and who designed the flagship Scottish-style ale.

The brewery served as a natural extension of the long-standing family ice busi-ness. Both operations require refrigerated warehouses and delivery trucks, the infrastructure and water source exist on-site, and McClellan already provided ice to most of the local liquor stores. The new business also provided a safety net for the historic and somewhat shaky ice business.

Much of Olde Burnside's promotional materials rely heavily on McClellan's Scottish heritage. A small poster on the outside of the brewhouse showcases a Scotsman clad in a traditional kilt, turned up in the front toward a confused farm animal, encouraging people to expose themselves to good beer. The brewery also cosponsors an annual one-day music festival, called "Pipes in the Valley." Located on the banks of the Connecticut River in downtown Hartford, the festival draws musical acts from great distances to play traditional and nontraditional Scottish music. Proceeds from the twelve-hour music festival benefit Riverfront Recap-ture, a private, nonprofit organization leading efforts to restore public access to the Connecticut River in metro Hartford. Along with step dancing and Celtic music, visitors enjoy plenty of Ten Penny Ale as they learn more about the little brewery in an old icehouse on Tolland Street.

Cambridge House Brew Pub

357 Salmon Brook Street
Granby, Connecticut 06035
Tel. (860) 653-BREW
www.cambridgebrewhouse.com

★ **Best Beer:** No selection. Each of the beers I tried were smart and clean, but were all the first versions on a new system. I look forward to visiting in the future when all the recipes are finally tweaked and the system is dialed in.

Opened: March 2005.

Type: Brewpub.

Owners: Steve Boucino and Scott Scanlon.

Brewer: Steve Schmidt.

Brewing system: 7-barrel Pub Brewing Systems brewhouse.

Amount produced: Figures not yet available.

First beer: Holcomb Hefe-weizen.

Flagship beer: Old Mill Pond ESB.

Year-round beers: Old Mill Pond ESB, Copper Hill Kolsch, Newgate Mild, and Holcomb Hefe-weizen.

Seasonal beers: Schmidt intends to offer a variety of seasonal beers not yet determined.

Tours: Tours by appointment.

Beer to go: Growlers are for sale.

Food: The menu is slightly more upscale than typical pub fare, with nice additions of steaks and some Asian-influenced dishes, including tuna steak marinated in sake and ginger. Two fire-grilled pizzas use spent grain from the brewing process in the pizza dough.

Amenities: Ample parking available behind the brewpub. Full liquor license. Family-friendly. "Little Brewster's Menu" offers a smattering of kid-friendly meals for less than $4, including macaroni and cheese and peanut butter and fluff sandwiches.

Pub hours: Closed Mondays. Bar: open Tuesday through Thursday, 3 P.M. to 12 A.M.; Friday through Sunday, 3 P.M. to 1 A.M. Dining: open Tuesday to Sunday, 4 P.M. to 10 P.M.

Directions: This location is at a crossroads of winding streets not far from Bradley International Airport. From Granby Center, go north on Route 202/Salmon

Brook Parkway. The Cambridge House Brewpub is less than a mile up on the left, across the street from the Hayes Carmon Funeral Home.

This long-awaited addition to the New England beer scene spent so much time in the rumor stage that most beer geeks almost gave up on it. Occasional reports of renovations and gossip of (erroneous) start dates, not to mention a Web site with pictures documenting the torturously slow construction project, made the Cambridge House Brew Pub seem destined to live in mere lore. A few weeks before I finished my research, I finally received confirmation that the latest rumors were true: the Cambridge House Brew Pub was brewing and actually had some beers on tap.

The brewpub is built from the ground up on the site of the former Copper Lantern. The owners like to joke that if the previous building were a horse, you'd have to shoot it. Riddled with problems and delays, the project finally opened in March 2005, several years after the idea for it was born.

I visited the pub a few weeks after opening day and it still glowed, as did the proud new owners, Steve Boucino and Scott Scanlon. The notion of two insurance guys—one a salesman and the other a risk management consultant—opening a brewpub in the middle of Connecticut may sound like a harebrained business idea torn straight from the profligate dot-com era. But that's not the case here. Boucino and Scanlon spent a lot of time researching before settling on this roadside location in Granby. They conducted market surveys, reviewed traffic patterns, and parsed demographic information. The pair, who possessed absolutely no restaurant or brewing industry experience before opening Cambridge House, also knew they wanted to open a concept restaurant that mixed elements of good food, company, and drinks.

At first blush, their approach may seem a bit fly-by-night. However, the partners are the first to admit they rely heavily upon two key and underappreciated secrets to restaurant success: borrow what works and surround yourself with smart, knowledgeable people. After visiting brewpubs in fifteen states to sharpen their concept, Boucino and Scanlon found the key missing ingredient when they met soulmate and brewer Steve Schmidt.

The former head of brewery operations for the Empire Brewing Company chain in western New York State, Schmidt is the recipient of numerous awards for his beers, including three gold medals at the Great American Beer Festival. He may also be the hardest working brewer in New England. After meeting Boucino and Scanlon through a beer writer, Schmidt agreed to serve as a consultant for the fledgling operation. Though his role eventually advanced to that of head brewer, the Cambridge House gig is only Schmidt's weekend job. During the week, Schmidt travels to Portsmouth, New Hampshire, where he is a lead brewer for Redhook. He is understandably exhausted but remains in great spirits as this new project comes to life. When I ask how he is able to balance both jobs, Schmidt states that brewing on the 100-barrel, multiple-vessel brewhouse at Redhook offers him very different challenges as a brewer from his work on this comparatively puny 7-barrel system. At Redhook, consistency, efficiency, and the science of brewing are key. On the weekends at Cambridge House, Schmidt unwinds and explores his creative side.

The pub, which resembles a large house, is a little unusual in its design. From the front of the building, the brewery element is immediately apparent, with gleaming new copper kettles and stainless-steel fermenters on display through the large, sliding-glass windows. From the road, however, it looks like the contractors built the structure 180 degrees in the wrong direction. The entrance is located in the back of the building, which causes many potential customers to wander around the front in a desperate search for a means of entry.

Boucino, who bears an eerie resemblance to a young Jim Koch, frequently praises Schmidt as a "god-send" and a "great ambassador of beer." The owner's gratitude and admiration is not just show; Schmidt is clearly the bond that holds the brewing side of the operation together.

Inside, the pub is split into several distinct rooms, with the main dining areas and a pub on the first floor, and a quieter dining room, perfect for families, available on the second floor. The present decoration is fairly nondescript, with wood floors and cream colored walls atop wainscoting panels. The small, U-shaped bar offers views of the brewhouse. For enjoyment in warmer months, a large deck extends off the back of the structure.

City Steam Brewery Café

942 Main Street
Hartford, Connecticut 06103
Tel. (860) 525-1600
www.citysteam.com

★ **Best Beer:** Dexter Gordon Old School Strong Ale. It would be easy to play upon the Naughty Nurse's racy appellation and succumb to her temptations, but I choose this Belgian-influenced beer. Lightly carbonated, this complex ale offers true beer geeks the opportunity to parse its exotic aroma and flavor. Is that a hint of plum, raspberry, or perhaps black licorice? Find out for yourself with the brewer's nod to the legendary bop saxophonist.

Opened: November 1997.

Type: Brewpub.

Owner: Privately held corporation.

Brewer: Ron Page.

Brewing system: 15-barrel Pub Brewing Systems brewhouse.

Amount produced: 1,000 barrels.

First beer: City Steam Ale.

Flagship beer: Naughty Nurse Amber Ale.

Year-round beers: Colt Light Lager, Blonde Export Lager, Naughty Nurse Amber · Ale, and the City Steam Ale.

Seasonal beers: The enormous list of rotating seasonal offerings is enough to both raise your heart rate and sacrifice some serious trees. Suffice it to say, the brewer dabbles in almost all brewing styles to create a wide range of seasonal beers, including Russian imperial stout, American Double IPA, French Biere de Garde, and German Maibock.

Tours: Tours available by appointment on Saturdays.

Beer to go: After a change in Connecticut law, City Steam now offers beer for take-away in 1- and 2-liter swing-top bottles, along with standard 64-ounce jugs. The brewpub also fills empty growlers brought in by customers. 5-liter metal kegs and bottle-conditioned versions of the house ales are also under consideration.

Food: No surprises here, but with some healthier salad and low-carb options. Stone-baked pizzas made with ale yeast are also featured.

Amenities: With its location in the middle of downtown Hartford, there is limited on-street parking available near the brewery, along with a variety of paid lots. Happy hour Monday through Friday, 5 P.M. to 7 P.M. Full liquor license. Wireless internet available. Live music Wednesday to Saturday, with no cover. The Brew Ha Ha comedy club is located in the pub's basement and offers shows Thursday through Saturday evenings.

Other attractions: With the loss of the Whalers hockey team and the rise of competition with the Indian casinos, Hartford's downtown economy suffered. Since 2000, local politicians and business owners have begun an extensive revitalization of both the city's tired downtown area and its rundown image.

Pub hours: Open daily. Bar: Monday through Thursday, 11:30 A.M. to 1 A.M.; Friday and Saturday, 11:30 A.M. to 2 A.M.; and Sunday, 4 P.M. to 10 P.M. Dining: Monday through Thursday, 11:30 A.M. to 10:30 P.M.;, Friday and Saturday, 11:30 A.M. to midnight; and Sunday, 4 P.M. to 10 P.M.

Directions: City Steam is on Main Street right in the heart of downtown Hartford, not far from the Civic Center.

Located in the historic Cheney Building in downtown Hartford, one of the finest examples of Romanesque architecture in the country, the City Steam Brewery deftly balances the competing interests of modernity and antiquity. In 1875, noted architect Henry Hobson Richardson designed this glorious, seven-story building, with its signature wide arches, to serve as the main sales and distribution center for the Cheney Brothers Silk Mills. While the Cheney boys eventually moved their operations to New York City (and Richardson went on to create the monumental Marshall Field Building in Chicago), the building bearing their names remains a fixture in this insurance capital.

Architectural historians praised Richardson for his appreciation of the basic qualities of mass, simplicity, proportion, and concentration—descriptive terms that can also be applied to the work carried on here by brewer Ron Page. Richardson likely would have appreciated the sheer scale of Page's massive beer list, which boasts more than forty-five different styles on offer at various times throughout the year. He also might have raised his pint in celebration of the balanced intensity of flavors achieved in each batch.

A brewer for more than fifteen years, Page spent time working for Elm City and the New England Brewing Company before becoming City Steam's first and only brewer. More than two million pints later, Page's influence can be felt throughout the place, from the breweriana on the walls—most of which come from the brewer's own collection—to the saucy names of the listed beers. City Steam boasts some of the most creative and entertaining beer names around, including the Naughty Nurse; Bewitched, Bothered, & Bewildered maibock; Stepford Weiss; Deidre Does Dublin dry Irish stout; and the Devil and 67 Virgins strong ale. My personal favorite is the English-style milk stout named the Milk of Amnesia.

Beyond the creative names, there are some great pints available here. The variety of offerings is both exciting and fulfilling in their execution. Unlike many other brewpubs that claim to brew lagers, City Steam actually does them right. Each of the lagers, which include light American styles, a Dortmunder, several bocks, and a few Octoberfests and Vienna-styles, is properly conditioned up for at least eight weeks before release. As he enjoys ample tank space, Page must thank the founding architect's appreciation for massive structures.

Another key historical element at play here is evidenced by the brewery's name. The brewhouse is one of the few in the country fueled entirely by steam heat, which runs in massive pipes under the streets of Hartford. Steam heat played an important role in the history of brewing, allowing many brewers to move from direct fires and hot coals to a more constant and controllable energy source. The historic force occasionally manifests itself in ear-piercing screeches that emanate from one of the brewpub's many steam whistles (no longer powered by steam).

The owners clearly appreciate the beauty of the building, which is on the National Register of Historic Places. They have done much to keep its charms alive, including salvaging many of the cast-iron railings and millwork in the space. The pub's sprawling, 350-seat interior sometimes resembles an M. C. Escher drawing with its assortment of sweeping staircases, small dining nooks, and open balconies spread over multiple levels. Be sure to take time to wander around the old structure and enjoy its bountiful architectural pleasures.

Music is also a key component of the City Steam operation. The cornerstone of the schedule is the Irish jam session on Wednesday evenings, when prices on the house stout drop to two dollars. Once a year, the brewpub sponsors a monster Irish jam session that attracts more than forty players, some from as far away as Alaska.

Troutbrook Brewing Company

55 Bartholomew Avenue
Hartford, Connecticut 06106
Tel. (860) 951–2739
www.troutbrookbeer.com

★ **Best Beer:** Liberator Doppelbock. An underappreciated lager style that is rarely brewed in New England. Troutbrook's version blends Munich, Vienna, and Moravian malts with noble German and Czech hops to create a complex, richly malty beer. The beer starts with a slight fruitiness up front, reminiscent of plums and black cherries, and dissolves into a surprisingly aggressive hop bitterness in the finish. The deep, roasted malts come more into play as the beer warms. Perhaps more edgy than most lush and flabby versions of the style. The beer is served in a giant 1-quart, swing-top bottle.

Opened: 1997 by Jack Streichs (under new ownership in June 2001).

Type: Brewery.

Owners: Mike Altott, Chris Cook, Nancy Dornenburg, Ron Michonski, and Randy Gian.

Brewer: Paul Davis.

Brewing system: 20-barrel Pub Brewing System brewhouse.

Amount produced: 1,200 barrels, with 600 contracted out of house.

First beer: American Pale Ale.

Flagship beer: American Pale Ale.

Year-round beers: Thomas Hooker American Pale Ale and Thomas Hooker Blonde Ale.

Seasonal Beers: Thomas Hooker Hop Meadow IPA, Thomas Hooker Imperial Porter, Thomas Hooker Irish Red, Thomas Hooker Liberator Doppelbock, Thomas Hooker Munich Style Golden Lager, Thomas Hooker Octoberfest Lager, and Thomas Hooker Old Marley Barleywine.

Tours: By appointment.

Amenities: Parking available in the brewery's lot.

Directions: Located just off of Route 6 near Park Street. Take the second left onto Bartholomew Street and keep an eye out for the brewery on the right side.

Hidden away in a crowded little warehouse in a sketchier section of Hartford, the people behind the Troutbrook Brewing Company are dedicated to making "great beer every time." From the outside, nothing hints that stellar ales and lagers are made behind the less-than-welcoming barred windows and steel door. When asked about the location, brewer Paul Davis jokes in his usual way that they can't leave anything outside, be it kegs or equipment, because of the neighborhood residents' "aggressive recycling program."

At a mere twelve hundred barrels a year, Troutbrook is a little brewery with a big reputation. Davis enjoyed great success at the now-defunct Castle Springs "brewery in the clouds" in New Hampshire. His beers won many awards, including at the Great American Beer Festival. He has rocked both sides of the brewing dial, mastering lagers with his bold, flavorful Munich-style lager, and producing one of New England's best India pale ales. But after five years at Castle Springs, Davis suddenly found himself out of a job when the brewery closed. Have brewing skill, will travel: Davis finished his job at Castle Springs on a Friday and started work for Troutbrook the following Monday morning.

With his regular beers as well as his special releases, Davis has clearly picked up where he left off. The brewery's owners have complete confidence in Davis. They allow their brewer to focus on the beers, while they each apply their own special skills to the marketing, distribution, and business operation. Davis and affable owner Mike Altott are the most public faces of the brewery; their interaction is emblematic of the freedom Davis enjoys. During my visit to the friendly working confines of Troutbrook, the two openly express opposing views about certain beers and about the beer industry in general. During the amicable discussion, each occasionally reaches over to refill the other's glass with a recent run of Imperial Porter.

From the beers, you quickly discern that Davis is not your typical East Coast brewer. "You can tell I went to school twenty minutes from the Sierra Nevada Brewing Company," he jokes. The aforementioned IPA, which has resurfaced in a slightly tweaked version at Troutbrook, was laden with hop flavor. Far from the standard weak-kneed pale ale with only a kiss of hops, Davis's version set an early standard for New England brewers. Davis has also resurrected several other lost recipes from his days at Castle Springs, including Blonde Ale, Old Marley Barleywine, and Munich Style Golden Lager. "Those beers suffered a death they didn't deserve," Davis concludes.

To see the incredibly tight working space at Troutbrook is truly to appreciate the hard work that goes into crafting the brewery's special releases. When I visited the brewery, Davis was busy hand bottling a recent batch. On the Melvico hand system, Davis bottles a whopping four cases per hour. When I saw the mind-boggling size of the operation, I actually felt guilty about how casually I had consumed my last bottle of Troutbrook's barleywine the week before.

The brewery contracts about half of its production to F. X. Matt in Utica, New York, but produces its popular specialty bottles in-house. This line of beers, which includes higher octane lagers and ales, is a major focal point for Troutbrook. The brewery's bottles also serve as points of focus for consumers. The oak-aged Old Marley, for example, comes in a striking cobalt blue bottle resembling a genie's magic lamp. Although rubbing it accomplishes very little, I'm sure you will be plenty happy with what comes out of the bottle.

Hops Grillhouse & Brewery

110 Buckland Hills Drive
Manchester, Connecticut 06040
Tel. (860) 648–4677
www.hopsonline.com

★ **Best Beer:** IPA. The IPA stands tall above its weaker brothers, with intense grapefruit and pineapple aromas. The flavor is unexpectedly earthy, with some raw malt notes that tend more sweet than hoppy. Overall, a very enjoyable offering and a nice session ale.

Opened: 2000.

Type: Brewpub.

Owner: Avado Brands, Inc.

Brewer: Todd Hammond.

Brewing system: Pub Brewing Systems brewhouse.

Amount produced: Figures not available.

First beer: Clearwater Light.

Flagship beer: Thoroughbred Red.

Year-round beers: Clearwater Light, Lightning Bold Gold, Thoroughbred Red, and Alligator Ale.

Seasonal beers: Single Hop Ale, Powder Horn Pilsner, Royal English Amber, Big 'Skeeter' Pale Ale, Flying Squirrel Nut Brown Ale, Lumberjack Oatmeal Stout, Beat The Heat Summer Wheat, Hoptoberfest, as well as a few of the local brewer's own recipes.

Tours: Tours by appointment.

Beer to go: None.

Food: Think chain, casual dining restaurants in terms of food, with ample servings and offerings familiar to anyone who has spent time in a local T.G.I. Friday's or similar establishments. Menu ranges from steaks and Jamaican chicken to burgers and pizzas.

Amenities: Ample parking in the lot. Full liquor license. Family-friendly operation.

Other attractions: A second Hops location can be found south of Hartford at 3260 Berlin Turnpike, Newington, Connecticut 06111, tel. (860) 594–8808.

Pub hours: Open Sunday through Thursday, 11:30 A.M. to 10:30 P.M.; Friday and Saturday, 11:30 A.M. to 11:30 P.M.

Directions: For the Manchester location, travel on I-84 and then go north on Buckland Street. Hops is next to the Buckland Hills Mall. The Newington location is on the Berlin Turnpike near the Lowes store.

There is no hiding that Hops is a chain brewpub enterprise. To the company's credit, it doesn't try and hide that fact. The chain promotes its outlets as restaurants first and breweries second. Food sales comprise 80 percent of the chain's income; beer accounts for a meager 10 percent of sales.

"We brew beer with training wheels," a company spokesperson admits in an article proudly displayed on a wall in the Manchester location. The acknowledgment is on target. Overall, the beers are clean but lack any notes of particular interest, and some are downright poor representations of their attempted styles. If the local brewer has gone beyond the chain's brewing playbook during your visit, you may be in luck. Ask the bartender which beers the local brewer made, if any, and stick with those. They likely won't provide too much amusement for your taste buds, but they are usually solid offerings.

The Hops concept was born in Florida, where the first location opened in a shopping plaza in Clearwater in 1989. Within three years, the company expanded to three locations, with ten more following by the mid-Nineties. In 1996, Avado Brands, owners of the Don Pablo's chain of Mexican-themed restaurants, purchased the operation. During the boom days of the craft beer movement, new Hops establishments spread quickly; by 1999, the company was the largest brewpub group in America, with seventy-two restaurants in sixteen states.

The good times, however, didn't last long. After the shakeout of the late Nineties in the brewing industry, the Hops chain floundered and was forced to scale back its operations. The company now has twenty-two locations in six states, mainly concentrated in the South and Colorado.

Perched atop a hill with distant mountain views and wonderful sunsets, the Manchester outlet rises high above the nearby Buckland Hills Mall. Most of the Hops locations tend to gravitate toward malls, which gives you an idea of their general ambience. The sporadic pieces of breweriana dotting the walls do little to up the street cred of this brewpub.

The narrow, glassed-in brewhouse separates seating in the bar from the restaurant. The pub possesses the air of a sports bar, with numerous televisions broadcasting everything from the Red Sox to the University of Connecticut Lady Huskies. The mix of an open kitchen turning out abundant portions of comfort food, a waitstaff trained to cater to families and young kids, and pints of beer offering more flavor than most chain restaurants has proven popular here.

Brü Rm at BAR

254 Crown Street
New Haven, Connecticut 06511
Tel. (203) 495–8924
www.niteimage.com/clubs/BAR/bru.html

★ **Best Beer:** Damn Good Stout. Created from a mixture of seven different malts, this stout manages to live up to its bold name. There is an initial burst of light alcohol flavors up front, followed by a wash of mild, roasted notes, and the beer ends with a slight sweetness. The Damn Good Stout possesses slight cocoa and coffee flavors but ends up best expressing some notable maltiness.

Opened: February 1996.

Type: Brewpub.

Owners: Randal Hoder and Stuart Press.

Brewer: Jeff Browning.

Brewing system: 10-barrel Liquid Assets brewhouse.

Amount produced: 800 barrels. Presently at capacity.

First beer: BAR Blonde.

Flagship beer: Toasted Blonde.

Year-round beers: Toasted Blonde, AmBAR Ale, Pale Ale, and Damn Good Stout.

Seasonal Beers: Armadillo IPA, Autumn Ale, Bunghammer Barleywine, Damn Good Espresso Stout, Doctor's Orders Hefe Weizen, Harvest Ale, Kringle's Nightcap (winter warmer), Majestic Brown Ale, Presumptuous Porter, Raven Haired Beauty Mild, and Watermelon Ale.

Tours: Tours by appointment.

Beer to go: None.

Food: The restaurant specializes in wood-fired pizzas with many toppings available, ranging from hot cherry peppers to mashed potatoes.

Amenities: On-street parking is tight in this area, especially at night. Full liquor license.

Other attractions: When you get tired of the attitude at BAR, consider visiting two of New Haven's most casual and historic restaurants. Located directly across the street from the brewpub in a tiny, brick shack, Louis' Lunch grilled up America's first hamburger in 1900. The wait is sometimes long, the burgers delightfully simple: toasted white bread, cheese spread, and hand-packed ground beef. The atmosphere is relaxed and worth the wait. 261–263 Crown Street, New Haven, Connecticut 06510, tel. (203) 562–5507, www.louislunch.com. A short distance away on Wooster Street, Frank Pepe's Pizzeria hosts an enormous and elaborate brick-oven pizza system in an authentic Napoletana environment. Wooster Street is the heart of the competitive New Haven pizza scene. 157 Wooster Street, New Haven, Connecticut 06511, tel. (203) 865–5762.

Pub hours: Open for lunch Wednesday and Thursday, 11:30 A.M. to 2:30 P.M. Dinner nightly, 5 P.M. to close; the bar area opens nightly at 4 P.M.

Directions: Located in downtown New Haven near the Yale University campus. The pub is just a few parallel blocks south of the main strip of downtown stores on Crown Street.

If you're looking for a small, eclectic brewpub in which to have a pint and a conversation, you're in the wrong place, brewer Jeff Browning admits of Brü Rm at BAR. "It's not like going to McNeill's," he says. Truer words were never spoken. Brü Rm is a lot of things, but a place to enjoy good beer in a friendly atmosphere is, frankly, not one of them.

BAR was born from owners Randal Hoder and Stuart Press's general dissatisfaction with the local New Haven club scene. Once an automobile showroom, the space sat vacant for ten years before the owners opened the club with the simple name in fall 1991. They designed BAR in a very eclectic fashion, with each of the distinct spaces appealing to a different group of people. The Front Room, which is to the left as you enter, is a wide-open space with long, communal tables and large, glass, garage doors (which open to the street in warmer months). The feeling is decidedly industrial, with exposed cement walls, elements of brick and steel, and weaving ductwork. The Lounge has a quieter atmosphere, in contrast to the Back Room, a warehouse space that hosts club dancing.

In early 1996, the owners added the Brü Rm, New Haven's first brewpub, which combines English-style ales and traditional New Haven brick-oven pizza. The Brü Rm is to the right as you enter; it includes a bar area and the brewing system. There are smaller, shorter tables and chairs mixing funky elements of metal, leather, and wood. From the grain loft above the space, five fermenters tower over the scene.

At first glance, BAR is quite eye-catching. Its industrial-chic design, filled with contrasting natural elements, clearly shatters the tired, corporate designs employed by many brewpubs and restaurants. The slick, club environment, however, comes with a serious downside. With the smell of stale beer and spilled mixed drinks floating noxiously through the air, the bar area often resembles a frat house the morning after a Friday-night rager. While the bathroom is another design coup: enormous, illuminated racy images loom over the sinks; empty bottles litter the space; and swarms of ants happily march around the floor. And this isn't at closing time; it's the following day, more than twelve hours after the club closed the previous evening.

Mimicking the pub's cold interior, the disposition of the bar staff runs the gamut from petulant to mindlessly disinterested. Bartenders frequently make customers wait without reason, even when the place is empty, and hostesses behave as if patrons are a burdensome annoyance. When I attempt to get a sampler of the brewpub's beers, the server tells me I am in the wrong room and they only provide them in the other room. When I switch rooms, a hostess breezes by and tells me the room isn't open yet. So I retreat back to the completely empty Front Room to find that my table now sports a reserved sign.

Sadly, the place is more about the form-over-function design and maintaining an aloof, club atmosphere than it is about promoting an enjoyable dining and pub experience. And like any overconfident, self-assured entity, BAR is more than willing to cop to the qualities other brewpubs would clearly regard as faults. Browning notes that many people don't understand the concept and that BAR is first and foremost a nightclub, not a brewpub. All of this is entirely disheartening, especially in light of the quality ales Browning and his staff produce here. Brü Rm focuses on brewing English-style ales, and it rarely breaks from this traditional model. While other brewers break new ground, Browning says he prefers to take a few steps backwards. He has worked with author Terry Foster to recreate some ancient beer recipes, including a 180-year-old porter. Once a year, Browning tweaks one of the staple beers to create a special offering, taking the pale ale and jazzing it up to become an India pale ale, or transforming the mild-mannered stout into an Imperial offering.

On a more positive note, BAR graciously plays host to the Connecticut Real Ale Festival, an event whose proceeds go entirely to the Pediatric AIDS Fund at Yale New Haven Hospital. Featuring more than twenty-five different cask ales and free slices of pizza, the event is one of the largest showcases for cask-conditioned ales in the country.

Cottrell Brewing Company

100 Mechanic Street
Pawcatuck, Connecticut 06379
Tel. (860) 599–8213
www.cottrellbrewing.com

★ **Best Beer:** Old Yankee Ale. Cottrell's only beer is a fairly complex ale, with a pleasant, biscuity malt flavor mixed with some earthy, citrusy hop flavors. The beer finishes more malty than hoppy and with greater flavor than most amber-style ales.

Opened: February 1997.

Type: Brewery.

Owners: Charles and Ann Buffum.

Brewer: Woodrow Culpepper.

Brewing system: 40-barrel New England Brewing Systems brewhouse.

Amount produced: 1,500 barrels; 3,000-barrel total capacity.

First beer: Old Yankee Ale.

Year-round beer: Old Yankee Ale.

Seasonal beers: None.

Tours: Tours by appointment.

Beer to go: None.

Amenities: Limited parking next to the brewery.

Other attractions: You can sample some of Cottrell's Old Yankee Ale down the street from the brewery at C. C. O'Brien's Sports Café. The first keg of Cottrell's beer was tapped here on February 28, 1997, and it remains popular. The bar offers a solid selection of twenty-eight taps, inexpensive food, and some fabulously mouthy waitresses and bartenders who give hell equally to locals, tourists, and visiting dignitaries. 8 Mechanic Street, Pawcatuck, Connecticut 06379, tel. (860) 599–2034.

Directions: From downtown Pawcatuck, head south on Mechanic Street, running alongside the Pawcatuck River. The brewery is on the left side.

The Cottrell family helped establish the twin towns of Westerley, Rhode Island, and Pawcatuck, Connecticut, a few miles from where the narrow river that separates the two flows into Little Narragansett Bay and then to Block Island Sound. In the mid-1700s, Nicholas Cottrell and a group of yankees purchased land from the native Narragansett Indians that led to the creation of Westerly. Several generations later, Calvert Byron Cottrell started a manufacturing company that revolutionized printing press operations in America. C. B. Cottrell, as he was known, invented many devices used in modern printing, and his son, Charles P. Cottrell, developed the process allowing rotary presses to print four colors on one side of paper.

After the manufacturer closed, the sprawling 350,000-square-foot factory long sat vacant, a short walk from downtown Pawcatuck. Many years later, C. B. Cottrell's great, great grandson, Charles Cottrell Buffum, Jr., sat unhappily in a Boston office. Working as a management consultant, Buffum was unsatisfied. While living in Britain a few years earlier, he had gained an appreciation for classic English-style ales. Upon his return to the United States, Buffum was constantly disappointed with the available beers, so he took up homebrewing. After getting more serious about brewing, he spent his spare time volunteering at the Ipswich Brewing Company (now called Mercury Brewing) on Cape Ann. One day Buffum decided to "throw in the corporate towel" and open his own place.

All for fortifying family traditions, Buffum decided to open his brewery in the area his family has called home for many generations. The Cottrell Brewing Company now leases nine thousand square feet of the very space that used to house his ancestor's manufacturing plant. From the beginning, Buffum knew he wanted to focus on producing fresh craft beer for the local market. He could never understand why other new breweries, with absolutely no history or following, chose to release four or five beers from the start. Buffum decided to brew a single beer that his customers could quickly relate to and enjoy.

With the help of head brewer Woody Culpepper, Buffum designed an approachable American amber and called it the Old Yankee Ale. On February 28, 1997, the pair literally rolled the first keg down the street to a local pub, C. C. O'Brien's, much to the enjoyment of its patrons. With its simple red, white, and blue label depicting an old man in a wooden rowboat, the Old Yankee Ale screams New England. Building upon his family's historical ties to both states, Buffum hopes his Old Yankee Ale will become the local beer of Rhode Island and Connecticut.

The Brew Pub at Mohegan Sun Casino

1 Mohegan Sun Boulevard
Uncasville, Connecticut 06382
Tel. (888) 226–7711
www.mohegansun.com

a world at play

> ★ **Best Beer:** Peeping Frog Ale. The seasonal ales each take their names from the lunar moons of the Mohegan tribe, which are integrated as design elements throughout the casino. The sole exception is the pleasant Peeping Frog Ale, which is simple and clean with a touch of maple syrup sweetness and a light hop bite of Fuggles in the finish.

Opened: September 1998.

Type: Brewpub.

Owners: Mohegan Tribal Gaming Authority, Sun International, and Trading Cove Associates.

Brewer: Joel Johnson.

Brewing system: 8-barrel extract Micropub Brewing Station brewhouse.

Amount produced: 240 barrels.

First beer: Matahga Lager.

Flagship beer: Matahga Lager.

Year-round beers: Sachem's Ale and Matahga Lager.

Seasonal beers: Peeping Frog Ale, Thunder Moon Ale, Hunting Moon Ale, and Cold Moon Ale.

Tours: Tours available by appointment.

Beer to go: None.

Food: A small café/snack bar is located directly across from the brewpub in the sports book area.

Amenities: Valet parking at the casino's entrance. Full liquor license throughout the casino and brewpub.

Other Attractions: Mohegan Sun is its own destination for many people. Beyond watching customers mechanically dump nickel after nickel into the clanging slot machines, there is a range of other entertainment and dining options available. Restaurants with celebrity chefs, poker tables, and boxing matches are some of the attractions.

Pub hours: Open Sunday to Thursday, noon to 1 A.M.; Friday and Saturday, noon to 2 A.M.

Directions: The Mohegan Sun complex in Uncasville has its own exits off of I-95, I-91, and I-90. The brewpub is in the Race Book section of the casino.

Mixing vices is a quintessential American activity. At the Mohegan Sun Casino complex in southeastern Connecticut, you can enjoy craft brewed beer while betting a fiver on the ponies at Pimlico. The pub, formerly named the Race Book Brew Pub, basks in the flickering lights of countless large and mini television screens broadcasting horse racing from dozens of venues, along with smatterings of jai alai.

In visiting this typical casino bar, it's clear that most of the patrons don't even realize it's also a brewpub. Most visitors, looking down to play assorted video games, miss the copper kettles hovering over the bar. A lot of Budweiser and mixed drinks slide across the bar and then disappear into the Race Book area as well. The brewpub's history is equally as unassuming. The space that the small, extract brewing system now occupies was originally slated to be a utility closet. That all changed when a salesman from a brewing systems manufacturer called on one of the new casino's vice presidents. After some discussion, the salesman convinced the executive and the owners of the value of adding a brewing system to the entertainment complex.

A short dice-throw away from the present brewhouse, Joel Johnson was busy managing a different section of the casino. Johnson possessed no brewing experience, but he was keenly familiar with the restaurant industry. A few years back, he had owned an eclectic place with his brother called Don Juan's International Combat Style Cuisine. After that quirky establishment closed, Johnson applied for a position with Connecticut's newest employer. After nearly two years with Mohegan Sun, he learned about the plans for the brewpub and immediately wanted to be a part of it.

Johnson now manages the Race Book section, along with the pub next door. In between fulfilling these duties, he also brews the occasional batch of beer for the casino. Working with a consultant for Micropub systems, he learned how to brew on the straightforward system. By using an extract-only system, which is akin to an enormous homebrewing system, Johnson does not use actual grains in the production of his beers. He brews six different beers throughout the year and strives to have at least two offerings available at all times.

Although the limitations of his set-up only allow him to brew once every three weeks, the friendly Johnson exhibits great enthusiasm for craft brewing. He regularly judges at the annual Great Northeast International Beer Festival in Providence and puts his beers on tap throughout the casino. He proudly notes that chefs in the buffet use his Sachem's Ale—named, along with the Matahga Lager, for former heads of the local tribe—in sauces for their dishes and meats.

New England Brewing Company

7 Selden Street
Woodbridge, Connecticut 06525
Tel. (203) 387–2222
www.newenglandbrewing.com

★ **Best Beer:** Elm City Lager. A spot-on German-style pilsner that proves that "good canned craft beer" is not an oxymoron. Crack open an Elm City Lager and you will be amazed by its crisp, clean, and powerful flavor. To my mind, this brilliant pilsner single-handedly proves the benefits of canned craft beer.

Opened: 1989 (under new ownership August 2002).

Type: Brewery.

Owners: Rob Leonard and Pete Seaman.

Brewers: Rob Leonard and Pete Seaman.

Brewing system: 15-barrel Specific Mechanical Systems.

Amount produced: 1,500 barrels, with 3,500-barrel capacity.

First beer: Atlantic Amber.

Flagship beer: Atlantic Amber.

Year-round beers: Atlantic Amber and Elm City Lager.

Seasonal beers: Gold Stock Ale and 3 Judges Barleywine.

Tours: By appointment.

Amenities: A limited allotment of parking space is available near the brewery.

Directions: From Route 15, go north onto Amity Road. Take the second left onto June Street and then a right onto Selden Street.

Opened in 1989 by Dick and Marsha King, the New England Brewing Company (NEBC) has experienced more than its share of tumultuous times. The brewery was originally located in South Norwalk, Connecticut, and it quickly expanded to new markets. Like so many other craft breweries, the expansion was too fast—and unsuccessful. Eventually, the owners exited the business and sold the brands to their brewer, Rob Leonard, and his partner Pete Seaman, in August 2002. The brewery, which produces nearly fifteen hundred barrels per year, is now located in a nondescript little warehouse in a small shopping complex outside of New Haven.

As the owner of a small brewery, Leonard is a jack-of-all-trades out of necessity. Before coming to NEBC, he consulted as a brewer for several New England breweries. Leonard soon found himself driving all over the Northeast, from Cape Cod to Saratoga Springs, to brew beer for other people. Eventually, he settled down as the brewer at NEBC. Now that he owns the brewery, Leonard has to stay put and cover all the angles; he describes his job as being part brewer, plumber, marketer, and distributor.

The New England Brewing Company first appeared as a brewery in Hartford in 1897, where it lasted for fifty years before closing. When visiting the newest incarnation of NEBC, the first thing you notice about the Woodbridge brewery is the enormous stockpile of aluminum-can pallets lying around the place. While the practice of canning craft beer has blossomed in other countries, including Canada and New Zealand, American brewers have been slow to accept it. For them, cans are directly associated with macrobrewed products.

Despite the prejudices of the industry at large, Leonard was intrigued by the idea of canning when he first read about it in a newspaper article. After doing some research, Leonard was convinced that canning was the way to go for NEBC; it is now at the heart of NEBC's business plan. Leonard touts cans as a cost-effective way to provide a superior product. Aluminum cans are lined to protect the beer's flavor and provide an environment free from beer's arch-enemies, light and air. To try one of New England Brewing Company's beers is to put to rest any doubts about canned craft beer.

Leonard also realized that canned craft beer fills a fairly unoccupied niche for active better-beer drinkers, since cans are portable in ways that bottles are not. Before canned craft beer, people enjoying the outdoors had severely restricted options: carry heavy, awkward, and hard-to-dispose-of bottles or tote along a case of an otherwise bland, macrobrewed product. In addition, bottled beer is simply not allowed in many outdoor venues, including most golf courses.

Willimantic Brewing Company

967 Main Street
Willimantic, Connecticut 06226
Tel. (869) 423–6777
www.willibrew.com

Restaurant & Pub Brewery

★ **Best Beer:** Address Unknown IPA. Wollner is known across New England for his incredibly expressive India pale ales, many of which employ little-used but powerful hop varieties. This perfectly balanced, unfiltered IPA successfully tantalizes the palate with caramel malts, while sucking every last essence out of the powerfully hoppy Columbus and Cascade varieties.

Opened: February 1997.

Type: Brewpub.

Owners: David and Cindy Wollner.

Brewer: David Wollner.

Brewing system: 7-barrel New England Brewing Systems brewhouse.

Amount produced: 400 barrels. Presently near capacity.

First beer: Certified Gold.

Flagship beer: Certified Gold.

Year-round beers: Certified Gold, Pushing the Envelope IPA, and Rail Mail Rye.

Seasonal beers: The list is too long to record and offerings range from numerous IPA's and strong ales, to a variety of stouts and occasional lagers.

Tours: Tours available by appointment.

Beer to go: Growlers are for sale at the brewery.

Food: While it contains many of the same offerings as found in most brewpubs, the menu is more thoughtful than most in its presentation. After concluding your beer sampling, be sure to try the overwhelmingly spicy Oy Vey chicken wings, made with habanero peppers grown by owner Dave Wollner.

Amenities: A small parking lot wraps around the brewpub. Limited on-street parking is also available. Full liquor license.

Other Attractions: If you happen to be near Willimantic on the Fourth of July, stop by to watch, or even participate in, the annual Boom Box Parade. The parade began in 1986 when a local resident learned that officials had canceled the annual parade due to the lack of a high school marching band. After convincing the local radio station, WILI-AM, to broadcast a few hours of marching music, the resident gathered up some friends, gained her own parade permit, and started a march down Main Street with radios tuned to WILI. The parade has blossomed into one of those peculiar small-town events that you occasionally see on the evening news. The parade has no preregistration requirements, so if you want to join in, grab a boom box and meet in the local movie theatre's parking lot.

Pub Hours: Sunday and Monday, 4 P.M. to midnight; Tuesday through Saturday, 11:30 A.M. to 1 A.M.

Directions: The brewpub is an easy-to-locate granite and limestone converted post office on Main Street in the town of Willimantic.

Simply put, I wrote this book to celebrate guys like Dave Wollner. The owner and head brewer of the Willimantic Brewing Company represents the greatness of the craft beer industry and he busts his butt brewing, kegging, and keeping the beers flowing at his pub. On the evening I visit, he is directing traffic in the restaurant. After graciously sitting down with me to discuss the brewery during the pub's busy dinner session, Wollner returns to action, hustling back and forth between tables and the kitchen. Despite all the work and constant bustling, Wollner remains calm, collected, and driven by a love of great beer.

Although its name may not be well-known beyond the local market, Willimantic is legend to many beer geeks. In a sea of flabby, English-style ales, Willimantic's offerings have more in common with the assertively hoppy beers of the Pacific Northwest and Southern California. Even hardcore, West Coast hop heads might startle at Wollner's obsession with hops. Name me another brewpub that produces nearly twenty kinds of India pale ales throughout the year.

The characteristic that differentiates Wollner from your above-average, passionate brewpub owner is his unabashed dedication to the promotion of craft beers. For understandable reasons, other brewpubs staunchly refuse to put guest beers from other breweries on tap; Wollner zealously seeks out such beers to complement his own arsenal of quality offerings. Though Wollner concedes the guest-tap policy stems in part from the capacity limitations of his present brewing operation, his eagerness in offering other beers surprises even his fellow brewers. Paul Davis, head brewer for the Troutbrook Brewing Company, was amazed when Wollner asked him for a keg of Troutbrook's Imperial Porter. Wollner didn't want it to fill an empty tap line but, instead, desired to offer his customers a chance to compare it to his own version of the rarely produced style.

Each of Willimantic's beers is clean, stylish, and expressively flavorful for the style represented. Even the house's light offering, the flagship Certified Gold, impresses ardent beer snobs. The bright, golden-colored ale busts wide open the notion that every brewpub must offer a Budweiser clone. The Certified Gold balances Munich malts with British Goldings and German noble Hallertau hops to create a complex yet drinkable beer that everyone can agree is delicious.

In 1991, before the brewpub was even a gleam in their eyes, Dave and Cindy Wollner opened a small deli in the lobby and concession area of the old Capitol Theatre building on Main Street. After three years, the café was outgrowing its space and Cindy wanted to add a bar component. The couple moved the operation down the street and opened a full-scale restaurant and pub, featuring a variety of American craft beers.

Willimantic's current home, also on Main Street, is in a quirky old post office building constructed in 1909. Abandoned by the federal government in 1967, the granite and limestone structure lay vacant and decaying for almost thirty years before new owners renovated the building in 1996. The pub's airy dining room was the former workroom, the long pub with its sixty-foot mahogany bar was a customer lobby, and a private dining room was the postmaster's office. Elements of the building's postal history and twentieth-century architecture are integrated throughout the pub, from the beer names to the twelve-by-seventeen-foot hand-painted mural depicting a slice of 1920s Main Street living.

In an attempt to drum up additional business and connect with its staff and the local community, the brewpub sponsors a series of quirky events throughout the year. During Movie Night, the brewpub hosts a large screen in the main dining room and turns into a minitheatre. The pub's annual Halloween party is a huge costumed event and the Wollners also host an employee talent show. Of the daily specials, Stein & Postal Workers Night is a clear favorite. You can bring in your own favorite drinking vessel and receive discounted prices, with $3.50 getting you up to 16 ounces and $4 for 20 ounces. Postal workers, of course, receive an additional 10 percent off their bill.

For lovers of craft beer, the mark of a great brewpub is whether you would drive a couple hundred miles solely for a seat at the bar and a chance to sample anything on tap. Willimantic is isolated deep in northeastern Connecticut, surrounded by a lot of nothing—I simply can't wait to visit it again.

About Beer and the Brewing Process

Any novice spectator can sit in the bleachers at Fenway Park and enjoy a Red Sox game, but understanding how the game works adds a new dimension of appreciation and enjoyment to the experience. The same principle applies to beer. Even a little bit of knowledge about how beer is made can enhance the experience of enjoying a pint and help you distinguish between different styles of beer. Making yourself a smarter consumer helps explain the flavors and aromas in your beer and equips you with the ability to distinguish the beers you love from those you simply don't enjoy.

Start at the Beginning

At its core, beer is an alcoholic beverage made from water and malted cereal grain, such as barley or wheat, flavored with hops, and then fermented with yeast. While innovative modern brewers have greatly expanded the list of possible ingredients, these key four ingredients comprise the vast majority of beer made today. Some larger breweries have long used adjuncts, such as rice and corn, to lighten the bodies and flavor profiles of their beers. Beer geeks and purists believe such efforts reduce the overall flavor of the beers and strip the resulting product of the nobler qualities of beer. On the opposite end of the brewing spectrum, experimenting craft brewers have produced some painfully esoteric beers from beets and garlic. Most brewers meet somewhere in the middle and borrow a little from both sides.

How the Ingredients Interact

Understanding how the ingredients in beer work together is crucial to differentiating between the many styles of beer available. Malt is commonly referred to as the soul of beer, its core, workhorse ingredient that leads all other ingredients, while hops are the spice, providing flashes of flavor against the malt backdrop. Comparing beer to wine:

malts replace grapes as the primary fermentables. To create brewer's malt, malt-sters (including Samuel Adams in his time) dampen barley until it germinates, then dry it at controlled temperatures, causing the barley's starches to convert to sugar. Maltsters create different types of malt based upon the length of the kilning process: longer periods create dark-colored malts and deep, roasted flavors.

In designing a beer recipe, the brewer carefully selects between different malt varieties in order to craft the color and flavor of the final product. Brewers use spe-cialty malts, including chocolate and black malts, to create such dark beers as stouts and porters, while less-roasted, pale malts lighten pilsners and pale ales.

Brewers next use pellet or whole leaf hops, close relatives of the cannabis plant, to add a balance of bitterness and earthy aromas. As with the use of spices in mak-ing a sauce, a brewer must artfully decide which hops to use and at what point dur-ing the process to use them. During the boil, early hop additions impart bitterness, middle additions contribute flavor, and those added in the final minutes are pri-marily for aroma. Hops also act as a natural preservative for the beer, allowing it to fight against spoiling.

While malt, yeast, and hops each significantly influences the character of the final product, the particular qualities of the water used in the brewing process also leave indelible marks. As water comprises more than 90 percent of beer, the mineral content of a brewer's water supply has a strong impact on the final flavor. In Burton-on-Trent, the brewing water's high calcium and sulfate content pro-vides the qualities needed for strong-flavored pale ales. In contrast, the soft water of Pilsen in the Czech Republic helped give birth to the region's world-famous crisp lagers.

The Brewing Process

After the brewer develops and tests a recipe and the materials arrive at the brew-house, the brewing process begins. The brewer runs the malted barley through a mill to crush it finely into grist in order to extract the sugars that the yeast will use in fermentation. The brewer then mixes the grist with water in a large brewing vessel, called the mash tun. The mix is gradually heated to a set temperature, which converts the malted barley's starches into sugars. This process is crucial to the beer's head retention and final body.

The brewer next transfers the mix to another large brewing vessel, called the lauter tun. The brewer adds hot water to the vessel to wash the sugars from the malt, resulting in a thick, sweet liquid called wort. A false bottom in the lauter tun strains the spent grain from the water and allows the wort to transfer to the brew kettle. In a spirit of environmental friendliness, many breweries give their spent grain to local farmers to use as livestock feed.

In the brew kettle, the wort is brought to a rolling boil and the brewer adds hops at different intervals to achieve different flavor profiles. After the boil is finished, the wort is transferred to the fermentation tanks, where the brewer adds, or pitches, yeast to start fermentation. During the fermentation process, the yeast feeds on the sugars in the wort and creates alcohol as a by-product. Through the magic of fermentation, wort becomes beer.

For thousands of years, brewers had no idea what added that little extra kick to their beverages. Early brewers relied upon airborne yeast strains to innoculate their brews. This several-thousand-year-old tradition continued until a well-known French scientist started tinkering around with beer cells under a microscope. In his 1876 *Etudes sur la Biere* (Studies concerning Beer), Louis Pasteur discovered that yeast microorganisms were responsible for the secret of fermentation. By establishing the existence of yeast cells, Pasteur allowed brewers to exercise greater control over the fermentation process and the resulting product.

Yeast also plays a defining role in the life of beer. Depending on the yeast strain used by the brewer, a beer will either become an ale or a lager. Ales are beers whose yeasts gather at the top of the vessel and that undergo fermentation at warmer temperatures. Like trying to classify a bold, ranging style of art in a word or two, no short description could possibly hope to capture the essence of such a broad category. Generally speaking, ale yeasts produce fruitier, estery beers. Lagers are beers whose yeasts gather at the bottom of the vessel and undergo fermentation at cooler temperatures. The cool lagering process produces smoother beers with less aggressive aromas and flavors. The type of yeast used and the fermentation temperature also influence the length of the aging process.

Ales generally age for one to three weeks, while lagers age for six to eight weeks. Certain high-powered ale and lager styles can age for a year or longer in order to mellow or fully develop their flavor profiles.

Maine

Maine is one of America's great brewing states, with a beer culture as distinctive as its craggy coastline, unspoilt lake expanses, and rugged, rocky lands. By far the biggest state in New England, Maine supports a number of successful microbreweries and brewpubs. While many are concentrated in Portland and Bar Harbor, there are plenty of breweries and pubs situated on the connecting highways and on wonderful, out-of-the-way roads. Despite its enormous size, Maine remains a relatively easy and pleasant place to travel for a beer vacation. From Prohibition to David Geary, the story of Maine's relationship with beer is richly complex and worthy of its own telling.

Maine is an unlikely pioneer in the annals of craft brewing. The state long flirted with prohibition and brewing never gained a stronghold here as a result.

In the early part of the nineteenth century, voices of temperance started testing their range. In 1808, members of a congregational church near Saratoga, New York, formed America's first temperance group. The idea quickly spread to New England, with the formation of the Total Abstinence Society in Portland in 1815 and the Boston-based American Society for the Promotion of Temperance in 1826. By 1829, the latter group claimed over 100,000 members. By 1833, temperance groups swelled to more than 5,000, with total membership numbering greater than 1.5 million.

A similar temperance group formed in Maine in 1834. Twelve years later, the group scored a political victory with the passage of the nation's first prohibition law. Promoted by Colonel Neal Dow of Portland, widely acknowledged as the Father of Prohibition, the act prohibited the sale of alcoholic spirits except for medicinal and mechanical purposes. The Maine law became a frequent topic of debate among people in New England. In 1852, three more New England states, Massachusetts, Vermont, and Rhode Island, fell to prohibition. Connecticut followed suit in 1854 and New Hampshire joined in 1855. The idea began to gain national prominence and several other states followed the Maine model. With the ratification of the Eighteenth Amendment, in 1919, America became a dry nation on January 16, 1920.

While many other states celebrated the repeal of the national dry spell by clanking glasses of beer made in recently unshuttered breweries, there was little to no revelry among Mainers. There is scant evidence of a brewery existing in Maine from this point until the time David Geary came along with the revolutionary idea of opening his own place. Since that fateful decision in 1986, Mainers have thrown off the old chains with great flourish. Hardy, generally reserved, and hardworking, the brewers of Maine operate twenty-three breweries and brewpubs throughout the state. Unlike any other state in New England, and few anywhere in the country, many of these dedicated souls brew only a few hundred barrels a year (or in one case, less than one hundred), in an astonishing rebirth of the ancient cottage brewery tradition. These small, blessed producers serve their communities by brewing for their local areas. While a few brewers here dream about achieving wider distribution, many, like Andy Hazen, don't have the time to even consider it. They're too busy working seven days a week in the name of providing their neighbors with good, flavorful beer. As Hazen says, "You have to make your own way up here."

Maine is also home to some of the most influential brewing outfits in New England. Before founding Maine's largest brewery, the Shipyard Brewing Company, Alan Pugsley ran a consulting business that helped dozens of breweries open in the state and beyond. When he arrived from his native England, Pugsley brought with him a hardworking yeast strain that he shared with his new clients. Pugsley's brewing systems and Ringwood yeast strain have greatly shaped the flavor and direction of Maine beer. In Bar Harbor, pioneers Tod and Suzi Foster opened a little brewery in their basement that would serve as an inspiring model for many would-be brewers. Many of the people profiled in this guide point to these trailblazers as guiding lights in their decisions to become professional brewers.

Gritty McDuff's

396 Fore Street
Portland, Maine 04101
Tel. (207) 772-BREW
www.grittys.com

★ **Best Beer:** Best Bitter on cask. The Portland location specializes in cask-conditioned ales and regularly changes the lineup. The flagship bitter pours smooth with light beads of carbonation and possesses a slight grassy aroma imparted by East Kent Goldings hops. The flavor is quite understated, achieving a delicate balance between paler English malts, hop bitterness and yeast bite, and the occasional light, fruity flavors of cider or apples.

Opened: December 1988.

Type: Brewpub.

Owners: Richard Pfeffer and Ed Stebbins.

Brewers: Andy Hainer (Portland) and Greg Sansone (Freeport).

Brewing system: 7-barrel Peter Austin brewhouse (Portland) and 14-barrel custom-designed brewhouse based on Peter Austin model (Freeport).

Amount produced: 5,500 barrels (1,200 barrels at Portland, 1,000 at Freeport, and 3,300 contracted out to the Shipyard Brewing Company).

First beer: Pale Ale or Best Bitter.

Flagship beer: Best Bitter.

Year-round beers: McDuff's Best Bitter, McDuff's Best Brown Ale, Blackfly Stout, Sebago Light Ale, and Original Pub Style (pale ale).

Seasonal beers: Scottish Ale, IPA, Vacationland Summer Ale, Halloween Ale, and Christmas Ale.

Tours: By appointment.

Beer to go: None.

Food: Standard pub fare is available until late.

Amenities: Parking spaces are limited in the old port, so try municipal lots. Full liquor license. In 1995, Gritty's opened a second location in Freeport, Maine. With its larger capacity, Gritty's brews many of its seasonal ales in Freeport and bottles them in 22-ounce packages. Lower Main Street, Freeport, Maine 04032, tel. (207) 865–4321. Gritty's newest location is 68 Main Street, Auburn, Maine 04210, tel. (207) 376-BREW.

Pub hours: Portland: daily, 11:30 A.M. to 1 A.M. Freeport: daily, 11:30 A.M. to midnight. Auburn: daily, 11:30 A.M. to 1 A.M.

Directions: For the Portland location, take the Franklin Arterial, turn right onto Fore Street in the historic Old Port district. For the Freeport location, head into Freeport on Route 1, and find Gritty's about a quarter mile up the road. For the Auburn location, take Exit 75 off I-95 and head north on Route 4 (Washington Street) into downtown Auburn. The pub is on Main Street on the banks of the river.

From its popular Fore Street location, just steps from the cobblestones of Wharf Street, Gritty McDuff's brewpub is both a mainstay on the Maine brewing scene and an anchor in Portland's historic Old Port district. When it opened in 1988, Gritty's became Maine's first brewpub since Prohibition and was an early pioneer in the state's craft-brewing movement.

The idea for Gritty's was born during a trip to Hawaii by co-owner Richard Pfeffer. While basking in the glow of Waikiki Beach with a traveler from Australia, Pfeffer began discussing his dream of opening a pub. The Australian, whose name has long since been forgotten, suggested that Pfeffer open a brewpub. The concept was entirely foreign to the twenty-two-year old soon-to-be stockbroker. After a brief stint working in finance, Pfeffer turned his attention back to the brewpub idea, scouting possible locations from Bangor to Boston. After visiting the Commonwealth Brewing Company, one of the first craft brewpubs to open in New England, Pfeffer summoned the courage to visit David Geary at his new brewery in Portland. After considering the young man, Geary sent him on his way with a single piece of advice: get some money.

With the help of three friends, two of whom would depart the operation shortly after it opened, Pfeffer took the first steps toward securing capital. One of Pfeffer's partners, his college friend Ed Stebbins, talked his grandmother into lending them the money to open Gritty's. The novice entrepreneurs leased a prime downtown location and purchased a Peter Austin brewing system from Alan Pugsley. So at twenty-three and twenty-five years of age, respectively, Pfeffer and Stebbins embarked on an exciting new project that put them out in front of a sweeping movement soon to follow.

The simple, inviting exterior of the main Portland pub includes a sign with the image of an amiable young bartender raising a freshly pulled pint of ale. The figure isn't "Gritty"—a fictitious name selected by Pfeffer because it had a British ring to it. The proud worker is actually a rendering of a young Stebbins.

Spread over two levels, Gritty's is warm and welcoming. The main entrance leads to the tavern, a sizable room with loads of exposed brick and a copper-topped bar surrounded by rows of ceramic tankards from the pub's mug club. Be sure to note Gritty's unofficial slogan, based upon an old Czech proverb, located on a sign hanging in the pub: "Blessed be the mother who gives birth to a brewer." Cast as a long, narrow expanse surrounded by brick and flanked on the front side by wide, plate-glass windows looking out onto the street, the main dining room provides an engaging environment complete with communal tables and benches. A large mural depicting the founders as adult cherubs buzzing around the brewing system anchors the room. A few modern touches, including industrial lighting and exposed ductwork, remind you that this is not actually England.

The atmosphere at Gritty's mimics the mixed ambience of the Old Port. Although Gritty's owners strive to create an Old World pub atmosphere, the pub starts to stray from the mark as soon as the sun sets. At its best, Gritty's is a quintessential New England beer experience. At its worst, Gritty's is the last place you'd want to go for a pint and conversation. Late at night, the pub takes on a frat party feeling, complete with rowdy pubgoers and loud, live rock music. However, when the upstairs bar becomes overwhelming, comfort and repose can usually be found downstairs in the Brewery Bar. The basement pub, with views of the small brewhouse, is the true heart of Gritty's. On a cold winter's day, there are few better places to pull a warming pint or two of ale.

For being so young, Pfeffer and his partners certainly chose a very traditional path with their beers. Following the Pugsley model, the brewers use established English ingredients and the Ringwood yeast to make classic, English-style ales. The beer menu chalked on a sign next to the front bar is as no-frills as they come, usually listing the beers by a single word: brown, IPA, bitter, or stout. The pub once produced a smoked porter, but that didn't last long. In fact, the pub's seasonal products are slightly ramped-up versions of the traditional English Special Bitter style. Even the Halloween Ale, which some mistake as a pumpkin or spiced beer, is a straightforward ESB.

The owners plan to expand the Gritty's concept into several other locations in Maine and perhaps into New Hampshire. As the first step, Gritty's opened its third location (in Auburn, Maine) in August 2005. The pub feels more like the original Portland pub, except with the addition of a seven-hundred-square-foot deck overlooking the nearby Androscoggin River.

Atlantic Brewing Company

15 Knox Road
Bar Harbor, Maine 04609
Tel. (207) 288-BEER
www.atlanticbrewing.com

★ **Best Beer::** Brother Adam's Bragget Ale. While I am a big fan of the Coal Porter, Atlantic's Bragget Ale is beer with few peers. The brewers produce this special ale only once a year, using a simple malt and hop schedule but with the key addition of 2,000 pounds of wildflower honey added to the boil. Atlantic then cellars the beer for a year before bottling it. The resulting product is a complex mix of flavors, ranging from coconut and oak to passion fruit. Similar to a barleywine in presentation, the beer is lightly carbonated and at nearly 12-percent alcohol by volume, it remains best enjoyed as a sipping drink.

Opened: 1991.

Type: Brewery.

Owner: Doug Mafucci.

Brewer: James Taylor.

Brewing system: 15-barrel DME brewhouse.

Amount produced: 4,000 barrels.

First beer: Bar Harbor Real Ale.

Flagship beer: Bar Harbor Real Ale.

Year-round beers: Coal Porter, Bar Harbor Real Ale, Bar Harbor Blueberry Ale, and Mount Desert Island Ginger.

Seasonal beers: Special Old Bitter Ale (SOB) and Brother Adam's Bragget Ale.

Tours: A well-stocked gift shop is open daily from 10 A.M. to 5 P.M. Tastings are available from 10:30 A.M. to 4:30 P.M. From May 15 through October 15, hourly tours are available from 2 P.M. P.M. to 4 P.M. During the slow season, tours are available by appointment.

Beer to go: A variety of beers are available for sale in the brewery's shop.

Food: During the high season, a small pub with outdoor seating operates next to the brewhouse. In its present incarnation as the Knox Road Grille, the pub offers delectable barbeque selections smoked on-site from Mainely Meat Barbeques. The combination of Atlantic's line of ales, tasty barbeque, and outdoor seating makes the brewery a necessary stop if you're anywhere near Bar Harbor.

Amenities: Ample parking is available on-site.

Directions: Approach Mount Desert Island on Route 3 going toward Bar Harbor. Turn right onto Knox Road, and then turn left into the driveway of Atlantic Brewing Company about a mile and a half down the road, across from the Town Hill Market.

Opened by Tom Mafucci in 1991, the Atlantic Brewing Company began life as the Lompoc Café in an incredibly crowded two-story saltbox house in downtown Bar Harbor, Maine. Mafucci became acquainted with a local homebrewer whose beer was a welcome respite from most other beers. When the homebrewer—none other than Maine beer legend Tod Foster—decided to take his craft to the next level, the Lompoc Café became his first account. Eventually, Mafucci decided to get into the brewing business himself and added a brewpub to his cramped restaurant.

Mafucci left the downtown location in 1998 for an old, abandoned farmhouse on the outskirts of town. With well-sculpted grounds that blend well with the surrounding natural scenery, Mafucci had a vision of making the brewery a tourist destination; he positions the place as an "estate brewery." With nearly twenty thousand visitors per year, he has clearly succeeded. Each of the elements—regular tours, outdoor seating in the granite courtyard, barbeque—complements the brewery. Mafucci designed the property to have the brewery, the small bar and café, and the gift shop all in view from one central location. To maximize the visiting experience, he coordinates the production schedule to coincide with the times most tourists stop by the brewery.

Visiting Atlantic offers tourists the opportunity to view a functioning brewery and to interact with its friendly and quirky staffers. On the day I visit late in the season, the brewing staff and some locals were busy preparing an elaborately configured track for the brewery's annual belt sander races. Surveying the unfolding frivolity, Mafucci explains that in Maine, far from the glow of cities and with its host of weather-related challenges, you sometimes have to make your own fun. One by one, people line up to race belt sanders down two long, parallel wooden tracks. The race usually occurs during the brewery's annual Town Hill Garlic Festival, a family event featuring garlic-packed dishes prepared by area chefs and restaurants in a wood-fired oven. The event benefits local charities and also includes a keg race and the coronation of a garlic king and queen.

Atlantic's beers include your mainstay Maine ales, but with better structure and more distinctive flavor than others. The brewery also produces two particularly noteworthy beers, one that stands out for its origin and the other for its unique place among Maine beers. In Mafucci's second year, a guy with a pickup truck loaded with blueberries stopped by the brewery and offered to sell him his stock. Not sure what he would do with them but intrigued by the peddler's cheap price, Mafucci purchased the stock. His brewer made the fateful mistake of suggesting that they juice the berries for their sugars and add the liquid to a batch of beer. After juicing four hundred pounds of blueberries in a little Cuisinart, they had a terrible mess on their hands and a wildly popular beer. Fearing a return to hand juicing the berries, Mafucci found a supplier who provides juice directly to the brewery and the Bar Harbor Blueberry remains one of the brewery's most popular offerings.

The second beer, Brother Adam's Bragget Ale, is one of the best beers regularly produced in all of New England. At nearly 12 percent alcohol, this sublime honey-influenced beer is full of character and ages beautifully. The beer is based on a recipe for a honey beer found by Mafucci in an old book and modified by his brewers. The Bragget attenuates extremely slowly and requires the care and attention of the brewers until it is bottled as an unfinished product. The earliest releases continue to hold up many years later.

Bar Harbor Brewing Company

135 Otter Creek Drive
Bar Harbor, Maine 04609
Tel. (207) 288–4592
www.barharborbrewing.com

★ **Best Beer:** Cadillac Mountain Stout. Easily one of New England's best-regarded beers, the Cadillac Mountain Stout is a beer I could drink any day of the week, in any season. Born from an old homebrewing recipe formulated by Charlie Papazian, Tod Foster uses an unusual mix of one-third extract and two-thirds mash to create this stout's distinctive, creamy flavor. The beer is very layered and possesses great complexity, mixing a mild sweetness, light caramel and chocolate flavors, and hints of roasted malt.

Opened: 1990.

Type: Brewery.

Owner: Tod and Suzi Foster.

Brewer: Tod Foster.

Brewing system: 4-barrel Pierre Rajotte brewhouse.

Amount produced: 325 barrels. 400-barrel capacity.

First beer: Thunder Hole Ale.

Flagship beer: Thunder Hole Ale.

Year-round beers: Thunder Hole Ale, Cadillac Mountain Stout, Ginger Mild Brew, Peach Ale, and Harbor Lighthouse Ale.

Seasonal beers: None.

Tours: Tours available seasonally, usually Tuesday through Friday at 3:30 P.M. and 5 P.M. from the third week in June to the end of August. As the brewery is run solely by the Fosters, times are subject to change; please call ahead to confirm.

Beer to go: 22-ounce bottles are for sale at the brewery.

Amenities: Limited parking is available on the street in front of the brewery.

Directions: Follow Route 3 east into Bar Harbor for a few miles until it changes names and becomes Otter Creek Road, then look for house number 135 on the left. If you hit the Blackwoods Campground, you've gone too far.

From the basement of their Bar Harbor home, Tod and Suzi Foster started a little brewery that influenced the next generation of Maine brewers. While living in California, the couple sat front row center for the early days of microbrewing. Tod took up homebrewing while a student at the University of California–Santa Barbara and the Fosters traveled throughout the state visiting new breweries as they opened. After moving to Suzi's hometown of Bar Harbor, Tod took some odd jobs, including house painting. During the evenings, he would talk about his idea for opening his own brewery. He knew Bar Harbor had a huge tourist industry and that anything with the town's name stenciled on it sold quickly as souvenirs. He discussed the idea with his wife so often that one day Suzi just looked at him and asked him whether he was actually going to do anything about it.

Tod knew that he wanted to run a very small operation, called a cottage brewery, where he would handle the brewing and Suzi would run the business. On a return trip to California, the Fosters met with several brewery and pub owners to get a sense of what they'd need to accomplish their goal. The Fosters repeatedly heard that such an operation would require four hundred thousand dollars of start-up capital to succeed. They returned to Bar Harbor thoroughly discouraged.

The idea stayed on hold until Tod came across an advertisement run by Pierre Rajotte of Montreal in *Zymurgy Magazine,* a homebrewing journal. Rajotte specialized in building very small breweries, including 2- and 4-barrel systems that other manufacturers considered too tiny to bother making. Before finalizing the deal to purchase a 2-barrel extract brewhouse, Tod first decided to test the market. With an oversized, 15-gallon brewpot and twenty-five 5-gallon plastic buckets, Tod created the first batches of his flagship Thunder Hole Ale. When the beer proved popular, the Fosters confirmed the order with Rajotte and started making arrangements to turn their cramped, 150-square-foot basement into a functioning brewery.

Bar Harbor Brewing quickly outgrew the small space and after scouting some downtown locations, the Fosters eventually settled on a new house on 2.5 pretty acres a few miles outside of town near tree-lined Otter Creek. The brewery is again located in the Foster's basement, but now boasts 850 square feet, which still feels incredibly cramped. The owners upgraded to a four-barrel, all-grain system in 1994 and they now exclusively bottle their beers. As the brewery's reputation grew, strangers started showing up on the doorstep of the Foster homestead, asking about the beers and tours. The Fosters welcome visitors during the season, though they now hang signs in the off-season to discourage people from stopping by. The scheduled tours start in an attractive wooden shed that the Fosters converted it to a small, tasteful gift shop and tasting bar.

Despite the fact that Bar Harbor has grown in reputation, its distribution and production remain highly constricted. Tod and Suzi watched as many other small brewers extended beyond their means, purchasing expensive, oversized systems and expanding distribution to untenable lengths, only to fail and close. Because of the seasonality of Bar Harbor's tourist industry, the couple reduce their brewing operation in the winter. In early May, they ramp up production, blending a two- and four-barrel batch in a fermenter for twelve days, then continuing to brew until early October. After priming with a little sugar for carbonation, the couple uses a six-head Italian wine-bottling machine to fill their signature twenty-two-ounce bottles. A former bartender, Suzi ably fills forty-five cases an hour while husband Tod can knock off around thirty. Stacks of finished bottles fill much of the crowded brewhouse.

While tourists and beer lovers comprise most of the visitors to Bar Harbor Brewing, several would-be brewers have made the pilgrimage here to learn more about cottage brewing. Andy Hazen, owner of Andrew's Brewing Company, admits that it took him several months to summon the courage to make the drive from Lincolnville. He had been thinking about opening his own brewery and greatly respected the Fosters, though he remained nervous about meeting them. Steve Gorrill of the Sheepscot Brewing Company had similar feelings before he visited. Tod views their early willingness to help other would-be Maine brewers as an extension of the courtesy shown to them by New England brewing pioneers, including Greg Noonan of the Vermont Pub and Brewery and Ed Stebbins of Gritty McDuff's. Professionals and novices alike continue to marvel at the undersized operation at Bar Harbor Brewing and its fantastic results.

Maine Coast Brewing Company / Jack Russell's BrewPub

102 Eden Street
Bar Harbor, Maine 04609
Tel. (207) 288–5214
www.bhmaine.com

★ **Best Beer:** Maine Coast specializes in stouts and brews six different styles throughout the year, ranging from mild Irish styles to a quirky espresso offering.

Opened: 1994.

Type: Brewpub.

Owners: Tom St. Germain and Nina Barufaldi.

Brewer: Tom St. Germain.

Brewing system: 6-barrel Peter Austin brewhouse.

Amount produced: 300 barrels. 650-barrel total capacity.

First beer: Bar Harbor Gold.

Flagship beer: Bar Harbor Gold.

Year-round beers: Jack Russell's Best Brown, Wild Blueberry Ale, Black Irish Stout, Eden Porter, Great Head Ale, and Precipice Pale Ale.

Seasonal beers: Bar Harbor Gold, Bar Harbor Gold Mettle Ale, Frenchman Bay IPA, Summer Wheat Ale, Bar Harbor's Best Bitter, Tap Room Red, Oktoberfest, Winter Warmer, Eden Special Bitter, Sweet Waters Stout, Sweet Waters Imperial Stout, Oatmeal Stout, Bar Harbor Espresso Stout, Dry Stout, Strong Ale, ESB, and Imperial Stout.

Tours: Daily in the summer from 2 P.M. to 5 P.M. By appointment in the winter. Call to confirm hours.

Beer to go: Bottling accounts for 55 percent of Maine Coast's business and it bottles seven of its beers, which are for sale in the gift shop along with kegs and growlers.

Food: A stable, upscale menu with five steaks and seafood. Lunch menu offers gourmet burgers.

Pub hours: Closed Monday and Tuesday. Open Wednesday through Sunday, at 4 P.M. until close.

Amenities: Parking available in the pub's lot. Full liquor license. As the name would suggest, Jack Russell's is very dog friendly, allowing your canine friend to dine with you in the garden. In the winter, dogs with "impeccable manners" are allowed to accompany their owners into the dining room as long as no one else in the room objects.

Directions: Follow Route 3 into Bar Harbor and find the brewery across the street from the College of the Atlantic once the road name changes to Eden Street.

The Maine Coast Brewing Company has come a long way from its original, cramped perch in downtown Bar Harbor. Despite some aggravating setbacks, including the seventeen hours it took to brew the first quarter-batch of beer on the new system, owner Tom St. Germain remained confident that his business would succeed. When he opened the brewery's fifteen-seat, eight-hundred-square-foot tap room in May 1995, the resulting consumer silence tested St. Germain's confidence. For six weeks he anxiously waited for some of the town's four million annual visitors to stop in for a pint. When business finally started picking up, St. Germain realized that Maine Coast had already outgrown its downtown space.

In 1997, Maine Coast found a new home a little more than a mile out from downtown in a space formerly occupied by a fine-dining restaurant. St. Germain rechristened the restaurant as "Jack Russell's BrewPub." The pub is named after a meanspirited terrier named Tucker, who reportedly did not like men, women, children, boots, rain, snow, heat, noise, or fun. With its distinctive eyebrow dormers, the building once served as a caretaker's cottage for an estate located across the street on the shores of Frenchman Bay. In 1939, its new owner moved the cottage across the street to its present location; the estate itself was razed in the 1950s.

A pleasant outdoor seating area, resembling an English garden, provides an intimate, alfresco dining experience. The pub houses several little rooms and nooks, including the "intimate room," a small bedroom with a door. Jack Russell's also wins the award for the smallest bathroom in Bar Harbor.

The site has experienced a cascade of changes since St. Germain took over, including the renovation of an old garage on the property into which the brewery moved in 2001. A short while later, a new structure was built to house the brewery, the bottling line, a small gift shop, and a malt storage room. Crammed into the basement is perhaps the most awkward brewing set-up in New England. The kettles nearly touch the extremely low ceiling, forcing the brewer to stand on a ladder to stir the mash.

When Jack Russell's upgraded its amenities, the pub also matured. Where the taproom once focused on selling the world's greatest cheeseburgers, the brewpub now specializes in upscale fare. The owners added lounge areas and a new deck in 2003, and are planning to open a chichi drink and dessert bar upstairs from the main dining room. Here they intend to serve special batches of higher-alcohol, nightcap beers to serve on six taps. They also plan to cultivate business among the martini scenesters.

While it remains to be seen whether the brash St. Germain can successfully "make beer upscale," there are some nice touches planned for this space. He salvaged the original bar from the taproom and plans to reinstall it here. The upstairs pub serves a practical purpose as well, allowing the staff to turn over their dining tables more quickly without shooing the diners out the door.

St. Germain brews three to four days a week in season, and three to four times a month out of season. Though the brewery self-distributes its products along the Maine coast from Bar Harbor to Portland, St. Germain estimates that 95 percent of his beer is sold within one mile of the brewery.

Sunday River Brewing Company

U.S. Route 2
Bethel, Maine 04217
Tel. (207) 824–3541
www.stonecoast.com

★ **Best Beer:** Black Bear Porter. One of Stew's only regular brews to hit the taps here is this complex, roasted delight. The porter boasts robust, roasted aromas from a fantastic mix of dark malts. The interaction between the different malts results in a satisfying mix of sweetness and bitterness, ending in a cacophony of bitter, roasted flavors. Despite its strength of 6 percent alcohol by volume, the beer remains a good session brew.

Opened: 1992.

Type: Brewpub.

Owner: Grant Wilson.

Brewer: Stewart Mason.

Brewing system: 7-barrel JV Northwest brewhouse.

Amount produced: 126 barrels per year.

First beer: 420 IPA.

Flagship beer: Black Bear Porter.

Year-round beers: Black Bear Porter and an assortment of beers from the pub's parent company, Stone Coast Brewing Company, including 420 IPA, Sunday River Lager, Sunday River Alt, and Sunsplash Golden Ale.

Seasonal beers: Deep Powder Stout, Jack's Winter Ale, and Stone Coast's Knuckleball Bock.

Tours: Very infrequently and only by appointment.

Beer to go: Not available.

Food: Average pub fare with a few notable additions of barbequed items and some creative takes on the usual, tired burger.

Amenities: Ample parking next to restaurant. Full liquor license. Guest taps available.

Other attractions: With 128 trails spread across eight interconnected mountain peaks, the Sunday River ski area is the main attraction here. With the ski environment comes a small après-ski scene as well. The free Mountain Explorer shuttle connects the town of Bethel and the resort: www.sundayriver.com.

Pub Hours: Daily, 11 A.M. to close.

Directions: Follow the signs on Route 2 in Bethel for the Sunday River ski resort. The brewery is located at the beginning of the Sunday River access road.

With his scraggly blond beard, baggy clothes, and skier's gait, Stew Mason looks a little like a young Trey Anastatio. The head brewer at Sunday River Brewing Company, Mason is also clearly a little off-kilter in an entirely lovable way. The brewer's introduction to beer started early when he began homebrewing at age eight and slept on Budweiser bedsheets as a child.

Like many other brewers in New England, Mason spent time working at the Commonwealth Brewing Company before landing at the Back Bay Brewing Company. After some undisclosed allegation—and unsupported, according to Mason— the brewer found himself out of a job. Instead of simply picking up his paycheck and brewer's boots and hitting the road, the inimitable Mason locked himself in the brewhouse and declared it "The People's Republic of Stoo." After judging that his newly founded nation was likely to fall to elements angered by its rise, namely Back Bay's owners and the police, Mason happened upon the name and telephone number for the owner of the Stone Coast Brewing Company in Portland, Maine. The unemployed brewer dialed him up and asked for a job. As luck had it, the company was looking for a replacement brewer. In what was his final act as governor, Mason sent out his résumé, was hired straightaway, and promptly went into exile in Maine, where he remains to this day.

Whether the story is fact or simply lore, what we do know for sure is that the Back Bay Brewing Company eventually suffered the same fate as Mason's republic, closing in 2000. The story remains characteristic of this curious creature who so defines the Sunday River Brewing Company. Mason is clearly comfortable at this comely ski-bum pub, and the locals and carpetbaggers alike adore him. His name adorns the menu (he proclaims the beer menu "Stoo's Brews") and is heard frequently throughout the pub as patrons call out to chat with him.

As both general manager and brewer at Sunday River, Mason is required to be a do-it-yourself employee, tending bar, managing the staff, and brewing on occasion. Even with its sizable 7-barrel system, by the numbers Sunday River is one of the smallest breweries in New England. Due to the importation of beers from Stone Coast, the pub's sister production brewery in Portland, Sunday River produces only a scant 126 barrels per year. Stone Coast sends much of its lineup here to complement Mason's quirkier offerings. Sunday River brewed much of its own beer until economies of scale at the larger brewery unfortunately made much of Mason's work here redundant.

With the shift in production, the brewhouse, at a prime location in the middle of the restaurant, lost much of its space to a recent expansion of the pub's bar. In the process, Stone Coast requisitioned several of Sunday River's fermenters. The pub is obviously in constant flux and its future as a brewery remains in question. The excess tank space and light brewing schedule allow Mason to be creative, even giving him time to produce a properly lagered doppelbock. It is doubtful, however, that Sunday River can sustain such diminished production and waste of valuable restaurant space.

What is not in question is the future of Sunday River as a successful ski-side pub. Perched at the beginning of the access road to the ski resort of the same name, the brewpub is a true ski-lodge pub in design and atmosphere. Turn right into the parking lot at the misplaced Moose's Tale Food and Ale sign and you are greeted with the massive, sloped peaks of the snow-white structure. After recent construction, the pub now has an enormous and inviting wooden deck, pleasant for both warm summer nights and frosty afternoons. Inside, the pub's atmosphere befits its surroundings. A laid-back, casual vibe hovers around the big, horseshoe-shaped bar as skiers and locals bask in the late-afternoon sunlight pouring in from a half-moon window. Instead of grilling Mason on the original gravity for his delightful porter, I quickly became lost in the casual camaraderie of those simply enjoying the beer.

The clientele here appreciates good beer and knows Sunday River is a brewpub without having to ask. Mason's talents are occasionally employed to an enjoyable end. Hopefully someone at Stone Coast will recognize the value of Mason's talents before he fades from the brewing scene.

Freeport Brewing Company

46 Durham Road
Freeport, Maine 04032
Tel. (207) 650–9255

★ **Best Beer:** Amber Wheat. A slightly tangy offering that closely resembles an English brown ale, the Amber Wheat starts slightly sweet with toasted malt flavors and ends with a surprisingly zesty finish.

Opened: 1999.

Type: Brewery.

Owner: Ken Collings.

Brewer: Ken Collings.

Brewing system: 2-barrel self-fabricated brewhouse.

Amount produced: 50 barrels; 100-barrel capacity.

First beer: Brown Hound Brown Ale.

Flagship beer: Brown Hound Brown Ale.

Year-round beers: Brown Hound Brown Ale and Ex-Wife Bitter Blonde Ale.

Seasonal beers: Amber Wheat and Oktoberfest.

Tours: Tours available by appointment.

Beer to go: None.

Amenities: Very limited parking is available in front of the brewery. Please note that the parking here is actually for a private residence, so inquire at the brewery.

Other attractions: Due to the small scale of its production, Freeport's beers are incredibly difficult to find outside of the town. You can certainly find them at the pleasant Broad Arrow Tavern at the Harraseeket Inn, where Collings works for his day job. The tavern's staff is friendly and the atmosphere is generally low-key. 162 Main Street, Freeport, Maine 04032, tel. (207) 865–9377.

Directions: From I-295, take Exit 22 and head west on Route 125/136 toward Durham. Turn right onto Durham Road. The hard-to-find brewery is located in a barn behind the house at number 46. There is a small sign noting the brewery's existence.

I know homebrewers who brew nearly as much beer as Ken Collings does on his little two-barrel system at the Freeport Brewing Company. Housed in a simple brown barn in back of his former partner's house on the outskirts of town, the brewery strikes you as more hobby than vocation, and Collings agrees. The brewer also works full time as a chef at the nearby tony Harraseeket Inn and runs Freeport Brewing in his spare time.

Easily the smallest brewery in New England, if not America, Freeport Brewing was founded by Collings and his business partner Mike Olinsky. To keep costs down, the pair renovated Olinsky's shell of a barn for the brewery, adding septic and water systems. They bought the brewinghouse, along with the brands, from a small brewer in Mystic, Connecticut, who gave up the craft. Olinsky eventually left the partnership and Collings carried on, delivering a few kegs to three accounts and providing twenty-two-ounce bottles to a handful of package stores.

Collings grew up in the South and had never even heard of homebrewing until he moved to Maine as an adult. He and Olinsky homebrewed in the barn and Collings was immediately intrigued with the hobby, experimenting with great vigor. The present digs aren't too far removed from the old homebrewing set-up. The small-scale brewer fires up the ridiculously small system, partially adorned with a few pieces of wood bound to the kettle, and then knocks off into a 55-gallon, bright blue plastic fermenter that closely resembles an industrial-sized garbage can with a lid. The fermenters are housed in a makeshift space—marked off by two-by-fours and plastic sheeting—that is smaller than most walk-in closets. To keep the fermentation temperature of the bucket within the proper range, Collings simply switches on a small, 3,000 BTU home air-conditioning unit affixed to the wall, attaches a small door to cover the opening to the closet, and lets the new batch bubble away.

The remarkable operation continues with Collings's keg storage and conditioning space. When his beer finishes fermenting, Collings transfers it to the small cold room, also cooled by a room air-conditioner (whose temperature gauge sticks out into the other room so that the unit constantly runs). When space is tight, Collings sometimes transfers ready kegs to a decommissioned Coca-Cola convenience-store display case to cool his products before delivery.

It boggles the mind that someone would run such a small operation, but Collings happily brews each batch. As I head back to my car, my head is swimming over the miniscule size of the brewery. At Collings's suggestion, I head down to the Harraseeket Inn and pull up a chair at the bar in the Broad Arrow Tavern. While I was enjoying my first pint of Freeport's beer, a tourist strides in and asks about the local beer. The bartender's face lights up; she turns and pours a pint of Freeport. After placing the beer in front of the grateful patron, the bartender nods to him and says, "That's Kenny's beer. Enjoy it." In that moment, it's easy to see what drives Freeport's local brewer.

Kennebec Brewing Company

625 Water Street
Gardiner, Maine 04345
Tel. (207) 582–2707

★ **Best Beer:** ESB. A nicely balanced English-style bitter, with well-placed touches of malt sweetness and bittering hops. The hazy ESB starts with an elevated malt level that gives way to a long, slow fade into bitterness from an unconventional use of Cascade hops. Very drinkable at 5.2 percent alcohol by volume.

Opened: August 1998.

Type: Brewpub.

Owner: Frank Lever.

Brewer: Frank Lever.

Brewing system: 4-barrel self-fabricated brewhouse.

Amount produced: 100 barrels; 750 barrels total capacity.

First beer: Bootleg IPA.

Flagship beer: ESB.

Year-round beers: Cream Ale, ESB, Granite City Pale Ale, and Gurglin' Sturgeon Stout.

Seasonal beers: Irish Red Ale and Kennebrau (helles).

Tours: By appointment or ask at the bar.

Beer to go: 22-ounce bottles available for purchase.

Food: A small kitchen serves slightly upscale pub food, including crab cakes and reasonably priced seafood.

Amenities: Parking is available in the brewpub's lot. Full liquor license. Outdoor seating in warmer months.

Other attractions: Though I haven't done this anywhere else in this guide, I recommend you head to the nearby Liberal Cup brewpub if you arrive to find the Kennebec Brewing Company unexpectedly closed. Turn left out of the parking lot and head up the road following the signs to Hallowell. Also, a small selection of Kennebec Brewing Company's 22-ounce offerings can be found at the New Mills Market. 17 Cobbossee Avenue, Gardiner, Maine 04345, tel. (207) 582–4400.

Pub hours: Call ahead! While the pub claims to be open daily from 11 A.M., it sometimes opens after 3 P.M. and sometimes not at all.

Directions: Head into the town of Gardiner on Route 201. Turn south onto Water Street and follow it along the Cobbossee Stream until you see the brewery on the right, marked by the Gurglin' Sturgeon sign.

Of all brewery shapes and sizes, by far the most interesting is the single-person operation. These quirky breweries and pubs often confound all logical business models and usually take on the personalities of their owners. Some brewers treat their outfits solely as businesses and diligently go about their routines, while others infuse their breweries with their own enthusiasm and friendly spirit. At Kennebec Brewing Company, a small brewpub on the side of the road near Gardiner, Maine, owner Frank Lever is the quirky type. Often unpredictable, Lever quickly jumps topics, always talking a mile a minute about future plans. His brewpub follows suit, existing in a constant state of flux, with opening hours that merely serve as suggested guidelines and beers that stray greatly in terms of flavor and consistency.

As a teenager in junior high school, Lever started homebrewing under the tutelage of a friend's dad. After working a series of regular jobs, he attended the Siebel Institute and took a position with the Shipyard Brewing Company. On the side, he helped set up the now-defunct Brew House at Danvers, where he eventually worked as a brewer. Never one to sit still, Lever helped run the Whale Tail Brewpub in Old Orchard Beach while also working as a brewing consultant for a handful of brewpubs. He originally opened Kennebec Brewing Company as a place where he could train other brewers and help them produce test batches, in the model of Alan Pugsley.

Originally designed as a package brewery, Kennebec Brewing Company has seen some significant changes in its tumultuous existence. Shortly after opening his brewery, Lever immediately faced a trademark lawsuit from fellow Maine brewery, the Kennebec River Brewing Company. Located in The Forks, Kennebec River Brewing opened in January 1997, a year and a half before Lever's brewery; its owners sued Lever, citing brand-name confusion. While the basis for the lawsuit is obvious, the details are sketchy. According to Lever, he won the legal fight and retained the right to use his brewery's name. Several years later, Lever focused his efforts on recasting Kennebec Brewing as a brewpub. In early 2004, he scaled back his brewing operations, renovated the industrial structure, and achieved his goal of opening the small pub.

As you reach the edge of town, turn into the pub's big gravel parking lot marked by a sign displaying a large sturgeon stewing in a mug of beer. On a hot summer day, taking a seat at the shaded picnic tables is a pleasant way to enjoy a beer. A hundred feet away, the Cobbossee Stream roars behind the trees. You couldn't pick a better location in terms of licensing: already zoned for brewing, the building once housed a wine and alcohol bottling plant.

The first challenge for any visitor to the Firkin' Sturgeon Pub at the Kennebec Brewing Company comes when you reach for the door. While the brewery regularly advertises in local and beer-related newspapers that it opens daily at 11 A.M., many visitors end up dumbfounded when the pub isn't actually open, even in the middle of the afternoon. While I skulked around the premises, trying to find a secret way into the pub, a local patron drove up. After exiting his car and trying the door himself, he asked what time the place was scheduled to open. I said, "An hour ago." He nodded his head, turned toward his truck, and with a wave replied, "It must have been a really good night."

The no-frills pub is sparsely decorated, with the occasional Picasso print and a large-screen television anchoring one wall. A few tables are scattered around the concrete floor and a long wooden bar faces opposite the entrance. The brewhouse is located down the hallway and behind the small giftshop. A small back room is decorated in a vague tiki theme, with colorful yet dim lighting and figurines right out of the Hawaiian Brady Bunch episode.

When I finally catch up with Lever on an unplanned return visit, he describes his operation as an Irish-style brewery. Several of Kennebec's beers strike that tone, especially his Gurglin' Sturgeon Stout. Of the ten beers on tap, five are brewed on-site, with a macro offering and a few craft beer offerings rounding out the selection. The Kennebec beers vary widely in terms of their flavor profiles and the consistency of their results. While the ESB is quite enjoyable, the pale ale and Irish red ale don't perform to their potential. The brewing operations are now starting to regain Lever's focus, after a year of trying to open and stabilize the pub. I look forward to charting his progress and plans in the near future.

Sebago Brewing Company

48 Sanford Drive
Gorham, Maine 04083
(207) 856-ALES
www.sebagobrewing.com

> ★ **Best Beer:** Frye's Leap IPA. A well-balanced IPA that is not afraid to puff out its chest once in a while. The beer starts with a sustained, frothy head and follows with citrusy Cascade hop aromas. There is a nice equilibrium struck between the juicy hop flavor, mild yeast bitterness, and sweeter pale malt flavors, culminating in a substantial hop bite in the finish. Assertive without being uncontrolled, Frye's Leap is a wonderfully balanced IPA.

Opened: June 1998.

Type: Brewery.

Owners: Kai Adams, Brad Monarch, and Timothy Haines.

Brewer: Tom Abercrombie.

Brewing system: 20-barrel DME brewhouse.

Amount produced: 1,400 barrels. 7,000-barrel total capacity.

First beer: Frye's Leap IPA.

Flagship beer: Frye's Leap IPA.

Year-round beers: Northern Light Ale, Boathouse Brown, Frye's Leap IPA, and Lake Trout Stout.

Seasonal beers: Presidential Pale, Runabout Red, Sha Wheat, Bass Ackwards Berryblue, Hu Ke Brau Octoberfest, Retro Porter, and Slick Nick Winter Ale.

Tours: By appointment. Tours are planned at the new package facility.

Beer to go: None.

Food: Sebago's pubs are as much a destination for the quality beer as they are for the artfully prepared food. The menu offers upscale pub fare, with a heavy focus on seafood. Salads and other vegetarian options available.

Amenities: Limited on-street parking is available in the Old Port, though it is very difficult to find a spot in the evenings. Municipal lots are also available. Full liquor license. Guest taps also available, providing locals access to offerings such as Sierra Nevada Bigfoot Barleywine.

Other attractions: Sebago has three restaurant locations to go along with its new package facility. Old Port pub is located at 164 Middle Street, Portland, Maine 04101, tel. (207) 775-BEER, open daily, 11 A.M. to 1 A.M. Sebago's original location is near the Maine Mall in South Portland, 150 Philbrook Avenue, South Portland, Maine 04106, tel. (207) 879-ALES. Open daily, 11 A.M. to 1 A.M. Also in Gorham in the village, 29 Elm Street, Gorham, Maine 04083, tel. (207) 839-BEER. Open Wednesday to Saturday, 11 A.M. to midnight; Sunday to Tuesday, 11 A.M. to 9 P.M. Sunday brunch available from 9 A.M. to 2 P.M.

Directions: For the production facility, enter Gorham on Route 25 and turn left onto Bartlett Road. Take the next right onto Hutcherson Drive into the Gorham Industrial Park. Take a left onto Sanford Drive and look for the building with the grain silo out front. For the South Portland location, take Exit 45 from I-95 toward the Maine Mall. For Portland, head into downtown Portland from I-295 via Exit 7. Follow Franklin Street and then turn left onto Middle Street. The pub is on the corner at the start of the Old Port. For the Gorham pub, enter Gorham on Route 25 and turn onto Elm Street just outside of the center of town.

Despite its location in the raucous Old Port section of Portland's downtown, Sebago's prime outlet has a decidedly upscale and low-key feel to it. Even during the crush of Saturday-evening revelry in the port, Sebago remains a quiet, reflective place to enjoy a pint and conversation. Compared to the folly unfolding nightly at Gritty's down the street, Sebago's serene environs make it seem like the pub is miles away from the noise.

This location, which opened in May 2000, has a definite bistro feel to it; it is washed in warm browns and burgundies, with darker woods, industrial lighting, and lots of seats at its slick bar or tall tables nearby. The pub also offers a thoughtful selection of wines and a lot of it goes over the bar here. The upstairs dining space is tightly compacted under a low ceiling, while the bar area opens up with a vaulted roof. A cozier second dining room is located downstairs, with views of the brewing set-up.

The service is usually superior, with knowledgeable, friendly bartenders who know their beers well enough to offer comparisons to other commercial examples. They're the kind of people who don't strike you as beer geeks but who readily know the alcohol levels of Geary's Hampshire Special Ale. As the evening progresses, the bartenders also perform impressive tasks, such as offering glasses of water and taxi rides instead of pints to cavorters who wander into the bar having partaken of too much merriment elsewhere in the Old Port.

Sebago is the invention of three enterprising young friends who pooled their resources, along with a matching SBA loan, to open their first location in South Portland in June 1998. Co-owner Kai Adams directs the beer side of the business, which until recently had taken a back seat to the food operations at the company's signature pubs. While attending the University of Colorado–Boulder, Adams started working for a local brewery, putting labels on the bottles; slowly the head brewer relied on him to perform more than menial tasks. When Adams decided to move back to Maine, he applied for and won the head brewer job at the Sea Dog Brewing Company in Camden. After competing against three hundred other applicants for the job, Adams soon realized that he was the only person who actually had commercial brewing experience. After leaving Sea Dog, Adams worked odd jobs, including every position he could find at a local chain restaurant. While there, the enterprising Adams constantly bugged the managers to see the sales figures to learn more about the restaurant's business side, and they freely shared the information. Adams used the numbers to give himself an understanding of how to write Sebago's business plan. By the time he and his partners opened their first location in summer 1998, Adams knew down to the penny what it should cost to run their operation.

With his Colorado brewing experience, Adams consciously chose to deviate from the standard English-style ale formula commonly found in Maine. Sebago's beers each possess a decidedly American influence and use only American ingredients. The company quickly grew to three locations. In February 2005, the team opened a new package facility, complete with a shiny, automated twenty-barrel DME brewhouse.

When I arrive for our meeting, Adams directs me out of the building and races up the brewery's new grain silo, yelling back to me, "You've never been on a brewery tour until you've seen the top of the grain silo." A few harrowing minutes later, with feet firmly planted back on the concrete, Adams proudly covers each of the flourishes of his new system, rousted from the Rocky River Brewing Company in Sevierville, Tennessee.

With the new brewhouse, Sebago now brews all beers for its pubs at the production facility. The brewers produce and finish batches up until the point of carbonation, then pump the beer into a small Grundy tank mounted in the back of a delivery truck and ship the uncarbonated product to tanks at their pubs. Due to a quirk in Maine law allowing for interbrewery transfers, workers are allowed to carbonate the beer and serve it on-site. Despite some ribbing from fellow Maine brewers over Sebago's decision to discontinue brewing at its pubs, Adams didn't see the value in blessing such inefficiency for mere PR reasons.

The brewery is presently bottling its two flagship products, the Boathouse Brown and Frye's Leap IPA, with plans to expand the line soon. Always the forward thinker, Adams also talks about opening perhaps ten more pubs across several states. Sebago is growing quickly, but it's at a well-considered and steady pace.

Liberal Cup Public House and Brewery

115 Water Street
Hallowell, Maine 04347
Tel. (207) MAD-BREW

★ **Best Beer:** Backhouse Bitter. A clearly defined representative of the classic English-style ale that Houghton so enjoyed while in Britain. On cask, the beer pours with a thin, frothy head and offers wonderful hoppy aromas. This straightforward bitter, a great session ale, strikes a fine balance between hops and malt.

Opened: November 2000.

Type: Brewpub.

Owner: Geoff Houghton.

Brewer: Geoff Houghton.

Brewing system: 7-barrel brewhouse of miscellaneous origin.

Amount produced: 400 barrels. 650-barrel total capacity.

First beer: Alewife Ale.

Flagship beer: Alewife Ale.

Year-round beers: Alewife Ale, Bug Lager, Backhouse Bitter, Old Hallowell Ale IPA, and Dummers Lane Brown Ale.

Seasonal beers: Mudflap Springbock, We All (S)cream Ale, Dog Days Summer Wheat, Summer Bitter Summer Not, Achtung Oktoberfest, Late Harvest Bier, Smelt Camp Strong Ale, State Budget Red Ale, Sow Your Oats Stout, Dunkel John's Band, and Ex-Wife Extra Bitter.

Tours: By appointment.

Beer to go: None.

Food: The menu offers some hearty dishes, including classic English specialties, and is thankfully light on fried foods. A variety of salads are served with homemade dressings. The food is moderately priced, with few items exceeding $10.

Amenities: On-street parking is available. Full liquor license. The pub sponsors live music on Thursday and Sunday evenings and a popular trivia night on Tuesday evening.

Pub Hours: Daily, 11:30 A.M. to 1 A.M.

Directions: The Liberal Cup is situated on the west side of Route 201 between Dummers Lane and Central Street.

Step up to the bar, order a pint of cask-conditioned ale, and prepare to listen to the tale of a dream long deferred. The owner of The Liberal Cup knew since he was a young man that he would one day own his own pub. At the age of seventeen, Geoff Houghton spent a year in Britain soaking in the country's unique pub culture, after which he returned to America with the idea of opening a tied-house (a pub directly affiliated with a brewery). While such institutions are found widely across the United Kingdom, such vertical monopolies are prohibited under American law.

While in Oxford in 1985, Houghton met a man who suggested he consider opening his own brewery as well. The idea intrigued Houghton and nicely dove-tailed with his pub dream. After coming home to the United States in a fruitless search for a brewery job, Houghton returned to England for inspiration. The aspiring brewer landed a job working with the newly opened Nethergate Brewery in the small agricultural town of Clare, Suffolk, where he learned the brewing trade in a converted garage that housed the brewery. While there, he met the legendary Peter Austin, mentor to Shipyard's Alan Pugsley, who helped shape the character of New England beers. Austin told him of the happenings on the New England beer scene and Houghton listened.

By the time of Houghton's return in 1989, Maine's brewing scene was showing definite signs of life. Houghton spent time working at both Gritty McDuff's and the Geary Brewing Company. He left Geary's in 1992 with big plans to open his own brewpub in Brunswick. Even with his strong enthusiasm for the project, Houghton wouldn't manage to get the pub running for eight more years, and in a different town. After getting married, settling down, buying a home, and having kids, Houghton finally made good on his idea, almost twenty years after it was first conceived. He selected this space in Hallowell because it was thirty miles from the nearest brewpub and it drew people from the local town as well as nearby Augusta.

It was so obvious that Houghton would one day own a pub that when he was a teenager, his sister used to brainstorm ideas for the perfect name. While in Scotland in the early 1980s, she sent him a postcard with six new names. The Liberal Cup stood out among all he had previously seen.

With natural woods covering nearly every part of the pub, from the floors and ceilings to the inviting booths in the front windows, there is no cozier brewpub in New England. The atmosphere here is serene and the music is kept intentionally low, on Houghton's orders, so that pubgoers can engage in quiet bar conversation. A single television sits off in a corner by itself, collecting dust. Over the attractive brick bar, the staff is friendly. The bartender remembers me from my last visit, a time when I quietly stopped in for a single pint while passing through the area.

Houghton's modest brewhouse stands behind glass at the far back end of the pub. The pub runs five beers along with a few cask offerings. All beers are of course served in 20-ounce pints, to which Houghton became accustomed while frequenting pubs in England. The owner also notes he probably couldn't get away with smaller sizes, what with "having to live up to the pub's name."

The Liberal Cup's mug club grew from a story Houghton's English father once told him about British pubs that would hold onto the mugs of their locals until their next visit. When he opened his pub, Houghton was inspired to create his own version. To join the club, you must demonstrate your loyalty to the Cup by drinking 250 beers in one calendar year. The numbers work out to less than one beer per day and Houghton jokes that he hopes eventually to receive an endorsement from the American Medical Association for his contributions to the public health of the people of Hallowell. Once an aspiring member gets about three quarters of the way finished, their name goes up on the pub's chalkboard announcing them as a Mug Club Wannabe. When the goal is finally reached, the new member receives a very liberal 25-ounce ceramic mug crafted by Houghton's wife, who is a potter. Membership has grown to a little over 40 since the club's inception.

Looking around the Liberal Cup, Houghton says, "It's a marketer's dream: instant feedback." The brewer-owner also enjoys building long-lasting, personal relationships with his customers. "These are the people I'll be with for the next thirty years," he says.

Federal Jack's / Kennebunkport Brewing Company

8 Western Avenue
Kennebunk, Maine 04043
Tel. (207) 967–4322
www.federaljacks.com

★ **Best Beer:** Longfellow Winter. This was one of my early loves in the New England beer scene. With its deep, dark ruby hues and slightly sweet, malty aromas, this winter seasonal ale hits the spot. This medium-bodied offering affords a great creaminess with several layers of flavors, from vanilla to coffee. The typical Ringwood flavor gives way to softer cocoa and chocolate notes and an ever-so-slightly tangy and hoppy finish.

Opened: June 1992.

Type: Brewpub.

Owners: Fred Forsley and Alan Pugsley.

Brewer: Mike Haley.

Brewing system: 7-barrel Peter Austin brewhouse.

Amount produced: Figures not available.

First beer: Export Ale.

Flagship beer: Export Ale.

Year-round beers: Goat Island Light, 'Taint Town' Pale Ale, Brown Ale, Old Thumper, Fuggles IPA, and Blue Fin Stout.

Seasonal beers: Raspberry Wheat, Pumpkinhead, Holiday Prelude Ale, Sirius Wheat, Longfellow Winter, and Summer Solstice.

Tours: Daily, 3 P.M. to 5 P.M. in the winter and noon to 5 P.M. in the summer. Call to confirm times.

Beer to go: The sizable downstairs shop sells a variety of Federal Jack's and Shipyard offerings in bottles, growlers, and kegs.

Food: Federal Jack's serves a variety of well-presented meals, with an unsurprising focus on fresh seafood dishes, including an excellent grilled crab and havarti sandwich served on sourdough. The pub is family friendly and a separate kid's menu is available.

Amenities: Parking is available in the brewpub's lot. Full liquor license. Live music year-round. Outdoor seating in warmer weather.

Pub Hours: Open daily, 11:30 A.M. to 1 A.M. The pub offers a late-night menu after 9 P.M. Sunday brunch, 10:30 A.M. to 2 P.M.

Directions: Federal Jack's is located over the brewery on Western Avenue on the west side of the Kennebunk River bridge.

After setting up breweries up and down the East Coast and Canada, Alan Pugsley was ready to settle down in Portland. His successful consulting business, Pugsley Brewing Systems International, had set up dozens of Peter Austin brewhouses for new businesses. In January 1991, Pugsley received a call from Richard Pfeffer, co-owner of Gritty McDuff's brewpub and a satisfied customer of Pugsley's company. Pfeffer told him that a friend of his was interested in opening a brewpub in Kennebunk and Pugsley should talk to him. A month later, Pugsley and Fred Forsley signed a contract and Federal Jack's was born.

Pugsley was receiving so many inquiries about his brewing systems, which he developed along with his mentor Peter Austin, that he needed a showroom. When he asked Forsley if he could use the Federal Jack's facility as a model operation, Forsley agreed, on one condition: Pugsley would have to run Federal Jack's. With a simple handshake, a regional powerhouse opened for business.

Federal Jack's is located right outside of downtown Kennebunk ('taint Kennebunk, 'taint Kennebunkport) in one of the loveliest settings imaginable for an American brewpub. The scene screams New England, from its faded clapboard siding to its gentle perch above the scenic Kennebunk River. As the sun sets, you can look out one of the pub's large bay windows across the rugged river shore at this picturesque New England town.

The pub's interior splits into several rooms, including the main dining room with a vaulted rotunda design. A rendering of the pub's namesake—a man of dual personality, one the jovial figure with a pint in his hand, the other a rugged, tough-looking character with a hand on his sword—looms over the whole restaurant like a poster of Big Brother. While a seat at the bar is pleasant, a table by the window is ideal.

All of the beers are relatively low in alcohol and make for excellent session offerings. The pub's menu does a nice job of describing the beers and explaining the brewing process. Federal Jack's also boasts a state-of-the-art, glycol-cooled draft system that allows the brewer to set the line temperature for each beer.

Before heading upstairs to the restaurant, take an informal tour of the glassed-in brewhouse. Signs explain the process and you can get some pretty good views of the operation from the sidewalk. The first floor of the structure, opposite the brewhouse, contains a surprisingly large shop with a range of Shipyard's branded materials and other assorted dry goods from around the state.

Andrew's Brewing Company

RFD #1, Box 4975
Lincolnville, Maine 04849
Tel: (201) 763-3305

★ **Best Beer:** English Pale Ale. A wonderfully balanced version of this traditional style but with the intriguing addition of the citrusy, juicy Amarillo hop variety. Hazen's English Pale Ale is a delightfully balanced product that neither over- nor underwhelms the palate. A real joy of a session ale.

Opened: 1992.

Type: Brewery.

Owner: Andy Hazen.

Brewer: Andy Hazen.

Brewing system: 12-barrel self-fabricated brewhouse.

Amount produced: 500 barrels per year. Presently at capacity.

First beer: Pale Ale.

Flagship beer: Pale Ale.

Year-round beers: St. Nick Porter, Northern Brown Ale, and English Pale Ale.

Seasonal beers: Ruby's Golden Ale.

Tours: No sign out front but if you find Andy Hazen at work and he has some time, he'll show you around. Call ahead.

Amenities: The brewery is located in the middle of nowhere. Beautiful nowhere, but don't expect much parking.

Directions: Your best bet is to either call the brewery in advance or stop in one of the shops on Route 1 near Lincolnville. The roads here are small and addresses and street names aren't often provided.

Andy Hazen is a workhouse of a brewer. The former cabinetmaker is also a self-reliant Mainer through and through. He designed the twelve-barrel brewing system himself and enlisted a local welder to help put it together. Hazen notes that when you live in Maine, you have to find some service to provide in order to survive. For him, brewing is the service he provides.

Atop the rolling hills of Lincolnville, Maine, Andrew's is housed in a renovated farmhouse next to Hazen's home. Finding the brewery is more than half the battle. You may have to stop and ask neighbors and some businesses on the way, as I did on my recent visit. Have no fears, however, as everyone knows about Andrew's. Also be aware that due to some thieving souls, the brewery no longer has any sign to announce its existence to the visiting public. Occasional keg deliveries in Hazen's yard are the only indications that a brewery operates here. Hazen hasn't been quick to replace the sign either. While he welcomes visitors, you have to remember to clear a path for the busy brewer. Like many other unsung, small brewers, operating his brewery is a daily operation for Hazen.

Watching Hazen run the brewery is a little like watching Willy Wonka run the Chocolate Factory. When I visit him during a bottling day, Hazen runs between the bottling line and the packaging supplies in a hurried yet methodical manner. He stands up bottles on the line, starts the machine, slides his way across the brewhouse to the packaging materials, and hand assembles the six-packs that will hold the soon-to-be-bottled beer. The small bottling line is a fairly new addition to the brewery; Hazen hand-labeled his beers for more than ten years. The entire operation is crammed into the small former carriage shed, with an addition built by Hazen for his fermenters.

After reading about homebrewing, Hazen tried out the hobby and quickly advanced to all-grain brewing when his friends approved of the samples he provided them. With the kind words and interest expressed by his friends, Hazen anxiously traveled to Bar Harbor to meet with Tod and Suzi Foster of the Bar Harbor Brewing Company. He admits it took him a while to get up the nerve to visit and share his idea for opening his own brewery. After the trip, Hazen returned home emboldened and ready to begin a project that would consume all of his available time.

After furiously working at brewing and managing slow growth over more than a decade, Andy Hazen is happy to announce that his son Ben has finally joined him in the family business. As a member of the National Guard, Ben Hazen recently returned from a tour of duty in Iraq that greatly worried his father. Hazen the elder couldn't be happier to have his son safe at home, though Ben better watch out for his fast-moving father on bottling days.

The hard-working and friendly Hazen is one of the great but little-recognized figures on the New England scene. There is little flash here but lots of heart—his beer is straightforward, unassuming, and entirely enjoyable.

Bray's Brewpub and Eatery

Routes 302 and 35
Naples, Maine 04055
Tel. (207) 693–6806
www.braysbrewpub.com

NAPLES, MAINE

★ **Best Beer:** Yammityville Horror. A self-professed "firm believer in the art of brewing," Bray and his brewer developed the concept for this unusual ale after reading Charlie Papazian's homebrewing bible, the *Home Brewer's Companion*. In his book, Papazian wrote that potatoes can be used as adjuncts in beer without adding any flavor to the final product. With this in mind, the creative minds at Bray's decided to see what kind of flavors could be extracted from using sweet potatoes instead. The tap handle for this beer, a figure with a tall mohawk hair cut, is based upon a style occasionally sported by brewer Rob Prindell.

Opened: August 1995.

Type: Brewpub.

Owner: Michael and Michele Bray.

Brewer: Rob Prindell.

Brewing system: 3.5-barrel McCann and locally fabricated brewhouse.

Amount Produced: 280 barrels.

First beer: Old Church Pale Ale.

Flagship beer: Old Church Pale Ale.

Year-round beers: Brandy Pond Blonde, Old Church Pale Ale, Orien Oatmeal Pale Ale, Pleasant Mountain Porter, and Mt. Olympus Special Ale.

Seasonal beers: Epicurean IPA, Stanley Steamer UnCommon Ale, Yammityville Horror Sweet Potato Ale, Graveyardshift Coffee Stout, Vivacious Vanilla Porter, Quaker Ridge Oatmeal Stout, Ice Palace IPA, Winter Solstice Special Ale, Spring Equinox Special Ale, Summer Solstice Special Ale, Fall Equinox Special Ale, Hessian Wheat Ale, Bay Village Bitter, Songo Loch Scotch Ale, Cristof & Gusthof's Oktoberfest, and Muddy River Bog Brown Ale.

Tours: Tours by appointment

Beer to go: None.

Food: Traditional pub fare with a focus on seafood, pasta, and vegetarian options.

Amenities: Parking is available in the brewpub's lot. Full liquor license.

Pub hours: Open Sunday to Thursday, 11:30 A.M. to 10 P.M.; Friday and Saturday, 11:30 A.M. to midnight.

Directions: Make your way to Naples and you can find Bray's at the intersection of Routes 302 and 25.

When you get to the stoplight, turn and park. That's the extent of the directions given to me by the owner of Bray's Brewpub, and heading up from Portland on US-302, no further guidance is really necessary. This cozy establishment on the side of the road in Naples is located in a 125-year-old Victorian farmhouse. In the late 1700s, the farmhouse hosted a tavern and inn that served travelers moving between Portland and Bridgton. The original tavern burned down in the 1820s. After it was rebuilt, the building was sold to teetotaler John Chute, who turned it into a temperance inn called the Elm House. Abstinence from alcohol ruled here until 1876, when the inn again burned down.

The Brays met during college in Maine, before moving to Washington State. After tiring of corporate politics, Michael, an environmental chemist and avid homebrewer, decided he wanted to open his own brewpub. Though he and his wife, Michelle, lacked any restaurant experience, they started scoping out locations across the country before deciding to return to Maine.

Separated into several different rooms on two floors, Bray's brims with character. The owner's love of Irish pubs inspired the decoration scheme, but the place retains its original New England post-and-beam design and original wood floors. The formal front dining room, which feels like it belongs to someone's grandmother, is one eating area, and there are additional, quirky dining spaces on the second floor. The main pub is split-level, with a raised area providing ample space for the long, wraparound bar weaving throughout the room. The result of the design is that unlike forward-facing structures, Bray's bar actually forces you to look at (and hopefully interact with) the people sitting across from you.

Bray's is popular year-round, with snowmobilers driving right up to the front door during the winter. The pub sponsors music nearly every weekend, the acts setting up on the raised part of the pub area. In the warmer months, the crowds spill out onto the extended, comfortable deck. As the pub evolved from its opening, Bray added new elements to better service his customers. For example, the outdoor beer garden contains a horseshoe pit and is an inviting place to enjoy a house-brewed beer.

Nowadays, Bray spends most of his time trying to keep the building in working condition, constantly tinkering with its design and form. Bray's customers also take an active interest in keeping their favorite pub in business. When neighbors complained about outdoor noise from the pub's beer garden, mug club members helped build a fence, along with extensions of the deck, to shelter the bands.

Bray pieced together this small brewhouse through a lot of bartering, including trading his coveted homebrew for part of his brewing kettle and some valves. The little system heavily relies upon gravity to move the beer around the brewhouse and resembles nothing more than a large homebrewing set-up. The resulting beers are all unfiltered and remain alive with yeast.

Bray's sponsors a series of events throughout the year, including an Oktoberfest with keg tossing and a Spam-carving contest, a Halloween costume party, and a five-course beer dinner with exotic foods, including bison, elk, and emu. Bray's also participates in the town's annual winter carnival in February, hosting a snow sculpture contest and offering a few pints to warm up the crowd.

Bear Brew Pub
36 Main Street
Orono, Maine 04473
Tel. (207) 866–2739

★ **Best Beer:** Chocolate Porter. Pushed through a nitrogen tap, this beer possesses a mild cocoalike flavor, a slight creaminess in the middle, and finishes with a distinct bitterness. The best of the lot here.

Opened: 1995 (under new ownership in 2002).

Type: Brewpub.

Owner: Matt Haskell.

Brewer: Tim Gallon.

Brewing system: Not available.

Amount produced: Figures not available.

First beer: Honey Bear Brown.

Flagship beer: Honey Bear Brown.

Year-round beers: Bear Brew IPA, I'll Be Darned Amber Ale, Honey Bear Brown, Midnight Stout, Tuff End Porter, and Crow Valley Blonde.

Seasonal beers: Hefe-weizen, Chocolate Porter, Pumpkin Ale, Quad Berry, and Peach Ale.

Tours: Tours available by appointment.

Beer to go: Growlers available for purchase.

Food: Standard pub fare, specializing in soups, wraps, and desserts made on-site.

Pub hours: Daily, 11:30 A.M. to 1 A.M.

Amenities: Parking is available on the street and in the lot behind the brewpub. Full liquor license.

Directions: Right in the heart of Orono on Main Street near the intersection with Forest Avenue. The entrance is around the back of the building.

Standing in front of the Bear Brew Pub's sign on Main Street, you get the sneaking suspicion someone nearby is filming you for a candid-camera show. Though there is a sign for the pub outside the building at the corresponding address, you see no door into the place. You look on the sides as well and find nothing. As my friend Jon noted, a predicament of this nature is only supposed to happen when you leave a pub, not when you're going in.

The brewpub's entrance is around back, but there is little to direct you there. When you walk around to the back of the freestanding building, an entrance presents itself, as does the pub's pleasant deck. On the inside, there is a small pizza bar on your left, followed by a cozy, dark pub possessed by an underground vibe. Attractive wooden booths run the length of the small room, including two inviting, semicircular booths anchoring two sides. There are lots of dark woods and a modest bar overlooks some brewing implements partitioned by glass.

Milos Blagojevic, an immigrant from Belgrade, Yugoslavia, originally opened the place in 1995, and Matt Haskell bought it in 2002. Under the new ownership, the future of beer at the Bear Brew Pub is presently in question. The pub, near the University of Maine's lead campus, is undergoing major renovations and an image change. Haskell has announced plans to modernize the upstairs space into a nightclub, called SOMA 36. He also recently opened a bar and billiards room of the third floor, complete with a cover charge, to attract a more upscale crowd.

While I can't attest to the quality of the beers under the Bear Brew Pub's previous ownership, their present state is less than impressive. Each of the beers possesses a common off-flavor in the form of a slight, off-putting bitterness. While the Chocolate Porter had enough going on to cover the unfortunate flavors, the IPA and the Brown were sadly unsalvageable.

Allagash Brewing Company

100 Industrial Way
Portland, Maine 04103
Tel. (800) 330–5385
www.allagash.com

> ★ **Best Beer:** Allagash White. One of the best witbiers produced today, and one of New England's great beers. The Allagash White scored a gold medal in the Belgian-style White (or Wit) Ale category at the 2005 Great American Beer Festival. Pours with a hazy blonde color and a substantial, foamy, white head. The aroma is a pleasurable mix of spices, from orange to coriander and lemon, and a slight, biting note of yeast. At times effervescent, the flavors are softly spicy with a balance of malt and not too much of any one ingredient. The perfect beer for summer.

Opened: 1995.

Type: Brewery.

Owner: Rob Tod.

Brewer: Rob Tod.

Brewing system: 30-barrel self-fabricated brewhouse with DME kettle.

Amount produced: 4,000 barrels. 5,000-barrel total capacity.

First beer: Allagash White.

Flagship beer: Allagash White.

Year-round beers: Allagash White, Double Ale, Tripel Reserve, and Dubbel Reserve.

Seasonal beers: Summer Ale, Grand Cru, and Allagash Four.

Tours: Tours given Monday through Friday at 3 P.M. Company store open Monday through Friday, 10 A.M. to 4 P.M.

Beer to go: 6-packs and 750-milliliter bottles are for sale at the brewery.

Amenities: Parking is available in the brewery's lot.

Directions: From the Maine Turnpike, head west on Forest Avenue. Turn right onto Riverside Street, and then turn right again onto Industrial Way. Look for the brewery on the left.

When Rob Tod moved back to his old college town of Middlebury, Vermont, after a few years kicking around in Colorado, he took the first job he could get. A geology major with absolutely no brewing experience nor any particular interest in the subject, Tod started washing kegs at the Otter Creek Brewing Company as a way to make money. As the company grew, Tod's job responsibilities shifted to cleaning tanks, working the bottling line, and eventually to brewing and working in the lab. Before long, he had inadvertently completed an informal education in how to run a microbrewery.

The more Tod learned about beer, the more he realized American brewers, including those in New England, generally focused on either English-style ales or German-style beers. While these two rich brewing traditions certainly deserve respect, Tod noted that another worthy brewing style went virtually untouched on our shores: that of Belgium.

When Tod opened the Allagash Brewing Company in Portland, Maine, in the summer of 1995, he had made two important decisions. First, he had chosen Portland because he saw several other area breweries succeeding and he believed the locals possessed a strong base of beer knowledge combined with a willingness to experiment. Second, Tod had boldly decided to focus solely on producing Belgian-style ales, offering no pale ales, brown ales, or pilsner beers.

Despite the Portland area's track record supporting better beers, success was not immediate for Allagash. In fact, the initial reaction was quite cool to his flagship Allagash White beer. If differentiation was what Tod sought, he certainly found it. Even beer-smart locals didn't understand Tod's quirky, Belgian-style ale. They expressed concern over its emphatically hazy appearance and were confused by its unusual taste. Tod immediately realized he would have to hand-sell the product, teaching his customers along the way, and that he would have to seek wide distribution of his beers if he was going to sustain any real volume. While a brewery like Casco Bay (located almost directly across the street from Allagash) produces a comparable amount of beer and achieves similar volumes without having to travel too far from home, Allagash has to distribute its beers to many states, including California, Texas, and Florida.

Long before the dawn of the extreme beer movement in craft brewing circles, Tod brewed his flagship Allagash White with orange peels and coriander. All of the brewery's releases are bottle conditioned, with the addition of yeast and a small amount of candi sugar to each bottle. Imported from Belgium and refined from sugar beets, candi sugar is 100 percent fermentable and imparts no additional color to the beer. The mixture of live yeast and candi sugar causes the beer to undergo a secondary process of fermentation, which serves to naturally carbonate the beer and create a unique, Belgian-style flavor.

Allagash is located in the same place it started, a simple building in a Portland industrial park. It also remains the only brewery exclusively focusing on Belgian-style beers in New England, and one of few in the country to do so. Allagash's line of beers breaks into three main groups: the core products served in 6-packs, a reserve line of products packaged in cork-finished 750-milliliter bottles, and a line of ever-changing specialty releases. Allagash's core product line, including its flagship, is found throughout the East Coast, while the distribution of its reserve portfolio expands to the Midwest and western states. Unlike many other breweries that send beer far from home, only to have it sit and become stale on store shelves, Allagash's reserve beers continue to develop because of a combination of bottle conditioning and higher alcohol levels.

Allagash's recent and measured forays into the so-called extreme-beer movement have produced some solid results. While competitors somewhat desperately continue to release unbalanced and ill-conceived new products to curry favor with the beer geek market, Allagash has charted a more sober path. Starting with the release of Allagash Four, a beer brewed with four malts, four hops, four sugars, and four Belgian yeast strains, Allagash started shaking up the classic Belgian styles. The brewery is presently experimenting with aging beers in a range of vessels, including Jim Beam and oak barrels. Stop by the brewery store to check out the barrels stacked off to the side, housing beer slowly fermenting away for your future delight.

Casco Bay Brewing Company

57 Industrial Way
Portland, Maine 04103
Tel. (207) 797–2020
www.cascobaybrewing.com

★ **Best Beer:** Casco Bay Old Port Winter Ale. You get the best of both worlds with this strong and hoppy seasonal ale. The brewers create the snappy, citrusy hop aroma by running the beer through whole-leaf hops in a hop percolator. The Old Port is remarkably smooth for 7.2 percent alcohol and the hops impart a slightly zesty bitterness that is balanced by a substantial amount of sweet malt. It's a great India pale ale, without the name.

Opened: Spring 1994.

Type: Brewery.

Owner: Brian Smith, Alex Fisher, and Stewart Maloney.

Brewer: Nate Duston.

Brewing system: 20-barrel DME brewhouse.

Amount produced: 6,000 barrels. 20,000-barrels total capacity.

First beer: Katahdin Red.

Flagship beer: Casco Bay Riptide Red.

Year-round beers: Riptide Red, Casco Bay Pale Ale, and Carrabassett Pale Ale.

Seasonal beers: Oktoberfest, Summer Ale, Old Port Winter Ale, Carrabassett Summer Ale, Carrabassett Harvest Ale, and Carrabassett Winter Ale.

Tours: Tours available by appointment.

Beer to go: None.

Amenities: Parking is available in the brewery's lot.

Other attractions: Stemming from owner Bryan Smith's love of the sport, Casco Bay serves as a sponsor of the local AHL hockey team, the Portland Pirates. The Pirates play in the Civic Center in downtown Portland and provide a fast-paced game in an entertaining environment at a fair price. Though the crowd is always spirited, the games remain a great place for a family outing. Casco Bay even contract brews a beer for sale at the arena, a solid pale ale named Salty Pete's Peg Leg Ale. The Pirates play from October to April and ticket information is available at (207) 828–4665, www.portlandpirates.com.

Directions: From the Maine Turnpike, head west on Forest Avenue. Turn right onto Riverside Street, and then turn right again onto Industrial Way. Casco Bay is on the right.

Bryan Smith returned to Portland simply to pack his bags and leave. Instead, he ended up buying a brewery. Smith started working part time at Casco Bay Brewing on the bottling line in 1995. A few years later, he moved up the production chain by attending the American Brewers Guild brewing school at University of California–Davis. In that program, Smith learned the crucial minutiae of brewing that many nonbrewers overlook, including biochemistry and microbiology. While learning about recipe formulation and brewery management, Smith fell in love with the aggressive beers found on the West Coast, where he planned to live after he finished the program. However, while on a return trip to Portland, Smith visited his former employer and found the company in serious distress.

Casco Bay opened in 1994 as a project of Bob Wade and homebrewer Mike Lacharite. The pair initially offered two releases under the Katahdin brand, named after Maine's highest peak. The first few years progressed smoothly, with barrelage slowly growing along with capacity. By the time Smith returned, however, the passion had drained from the original owners. In January 1998, Smith and his partners bought out Lacharite; the recent graduate and former employee took over Casco Bay's brewing operations. One of the changes Smith implemented was the addition of contract brewing operations. In June of that year he contracted with the Sugarloaf Brewing Company to produce its Carrabassett Pale Ale. The decision proved consequential, as contract brewing continues to represent an important part of the brewery's business plan.

As part of a plan to differentiate Casco Bay from the ale-producing Maine market, Smith decided to add two new lager products. The new products also sported a fresh brand name, under the newly minted Casco Bay line. The company slowly started dropping old products before finally discarding the Katahdin label in 1999. After Smith tweaked the original recipe for the Katahdin Red and rechristened it as the Casco Bay Riptide Red, the beer scored success at the 2000 World Beer Cup, winning a gold medal in the Irish-style Red Ale category and again at the 2004 Great American Beer Festival, where it won a bronze medal in same style category.

On the contract side of things, the Carrabassett brand continues to exhibit real potential. In 2000, when the brand's owner went out of business, Casco Bay took the bold step of purchasing the rights to Carrabassett. The brewery is attempting the delicate exercise of keeping the two rival flagships from competing with one another. Smith intentionally markets the brands in different ways and in distinct markets, with Casco Bay mainly competing in Portland and Carrabassett fighting for the northern territories.

For a long time, Casco Bay resisted offering a pale ale or IPA, as many other breweries offer. The company recently gave in and released its Casco Bay Pale Ale, which it contends is the first and only year-round, American-style pale ale brewed in Maine. The influence for such products inevitably lies to some degree in the addition of new head brewer, Nate Duston. A longtime employee at Oregon's Bridge-Port Brewing Company, Duston comes from the heart of America's hoppiest beer culture. He brings to Casco Bay a great deal of technical knowledge and experience from BridgePort, one of America's largest and oldest craft breweries.

The outside of Casco Bay's longtime home in a Portland-area industrial park lacks much soul, but the staff has done a commendable job of bringing life to the brewery's tasting room. A sizable collection of craft beer bottles lines one wall and the little pub, with its wood beams and tiny bar, takes on the feel of a small lodge.

D. L. Geary Brewing Company

38 Evergreen Drive
Portland, Maine 04103
Tel. 207–878–2337
www.gearybrewing.com

★ **Best Beer:** Hampshire Special Ale. Once limited to being brewed "when the weather sucks," Geary's now offers the superb Hampshire Special Ale on a year-round basis. Made with classic English pale, crystal, and chocolate malts and a touch of American Cascade and Mt. Hood hops, along with traditional East Kent Golding hops, Hampshire is perhaps the best-balanced Ringwood beer produced by any brewery in New England. Packed with toasted malt flavors and warming alcohol notes, the ale balances between a light fruitiness and slightly grainy malt notes. Drinkers throughout New England no longer have to wait for turbid winter weather to enjoy this offering.

Opened: December 1986.

Type: Brewery.

Owner: David Geary.

Brewer: David Geary.

Brewing system: Not available.

Amount produced: 16,300 barrels.

First beer: Pale Ale.

Flagship beer: Pale Ale.

Year-round beers: Pale Ale, Hampshire Special Ale, and London Porter.

Seasonal beers: Summer Ale, Autumn Ale, and Winter Ale.

Tours: Tours by appointment, Monday through Friday at 2:30 P.M.

Beer to go: None.

Amenities: Parking is available in front of the brewery.

Other attractions: For more than 25 years, Three Dollar Dewey's has been a champion of good beer in downtown Portland. Opened in February 1981 by publican and author Alan Eames, Dewey's has always supported local brewers looking to crack the beer market. While running "Portland's Original Ale House," Eames offered advice, encouragement, and valuable tap space for local brewers. While Eames no longer owns the bar, a love of craft-brewed beer still exists at this location. With its wide-planked, wood floors, exposed beams, long, communal wooden tables and benches, and sparse décor, Dewey's feels very much like an old barroom. While the Great Lost Bear garners most of the attention in Portland, and with good reason, you can still feel the history of the early days of craft brewing while hoisting a pint here. Check out the t-shirts for sale to learn the true, lewd story behind the pub's name. 241 Commercial Street, Portland, Maine 04101, tel. (207) 772–3310, www.3dollardeweys.com.

Directions: From the Maine Turnpike, head west on Forest Avenue. Turn right onto Riverside Street, then turn right at the second street, Evergreen Drive. The brewery is directly on the left.

David Geary is often referred to as the dean of the Maine brewing scene. So clear is his role as a brewing pioneer in this region that the title should probably be extended to all of New England. When Geary decided to open a microbrewery in Portland in the early 1980s, only a handful of other daring entrepreneurs across the entire country had undertaken similar plans. There was no craft beer scene, built-in customer base, or even regional breweries to serve as beacons for a life beyond Budweiser, Miller, and Coors.

The idea to start a brewery was planted in Geary's head by Alan Eames, proprietor of Three Dollar Dewey's, the legendary Portland beer bar. One day Eames introduced his friend to an Englishman named Peter Maxwell Stuart. Better known as the twentieth laird of Traquair and owner of the historic Traquair House Brewery, Stuart was in the United States promoting his imported-beer brands. When Geary expressed an interest in learning more about Traquair's brewing operations, the laird invited him to visit. Geary took him up on the offer and spent time learning the brewing operations in one of the most historic breweries in the world. Now run by Catherine Maxwell Stuart, daughter of the late laird, Traquair House produces some very well-regarded beers, including the House Ale, in Scotland's oldest inhabited castle.

After learning the ropes on the ancient and rudimentary Traquair system, Geary visited other breweries in Britain. During one visit, he met a man with whom he would change the face of brewing in New England. While visiting the relatively new Ringwood Brewery in Hampshire, run by brewer Peter Austin, Geary was introduced to a young brewer named Alan Pugsley. The pair hit it off, and Geary discussed the idea of having Pugsley come to Maine to help him develop his brewery. With input from Geary and using the Ringwood yeast strain, Pugsley designed a beer called Geary's Pale Ale, the brewery's flagship beer.

When it rolled its first keg out the door a few days after Christmas in 1986, Geary's was one of only thirteen breweries in the entire country and the first brewery to operate in Maine in a century; it narrowly missed becoming the first brewery in New England. That honor was won only a few months earlier by the now-defunct Commonwealth Brewing Company in Boston.

The brewery has certainly grown since it opened, but with little noticeable change on-site. The original red sign proclaiming the existence of the D. L. Geary Brewing Company still hangs over the door at the simple, stone building and the brewery continues to produce a well-considered line of English-style ales. Until recently, Geary's produced only two beers on a year-round basis, the flagship Pale Ale and the unparalleled London Porter. The brewery's seasonal offerings remain resolutely restrained in their flavor profiles; they impress as much for their solid construction as for their dedication to tradition and general aversion to swagger and braggadocio.

Shipyard Brewing Company

86 Newbury Street
Portland, Maine 04101
Tel. (800) BREW-ALE
www.shipyard.com

★ **Best Beer:** Old Thumper Extra Special Ale. Brewed under license, this beer was created by Alan Pugsley's mentor, Peter Austin of the Ringwood Brewery in Hampshire, England. Touting itself as a nontraditional English bitter, this beer has scored several awards at home in Britain. Old Thumper is best enjoyed on cask, where it shows a striking balance between toasty, dry malt flavors, a light, hop bitterness and flavor, and the slightly buttery character imparted by the Ringwood house yeast.

Opened: April 1994.

Type: Brewery.

Owners: Fred Forsley and Alan Pugsley.

Brewer: Alan Pugsley.

Brewing system: 100-barrel Peter Austin brewhouse.

Amount produced: 50,000 barrels. 140,000-barrel total capacity.

First beer: Export Ale.

Flagship beer: Export Ale.

Year-round beers: Export Ale, Shipyard Light, Shipyard IPA, Brown Ale, Old Thumper Extra Special Ale, and Bluefin Stout.

Seasonal beers: Summer Ale, Pumpkinhead, Prelude Special Ale, Winter Ale, Battleground Ale, Chamberlain Pale Ale, and Longfellow Winter.

Tours: Daily, 3 P.M. through 5 P.M. in winter and noon to 5 P.M. in summer.

Beer to go: 6-packs, cases, and kegs are available.

Amenities: Parking is available in the brewery's lot.

Other Attractions: With its turn-of-the century, main street–general store look, complete with wood beams and exposed brick, Downeast Beverage is one of Maine's great beer stores. There is a huge selection of offerings from the state, including a wide selection of the 22-ounce bottles Maine breweries are so fond of using. The beer selection is almost exclusively limited to Maine breweries, with several harder-to-find offerings, among which is the delectable Cadillac Mountain Stout from the Bar Harbor Brewing Company. Downeast also offers mix-and-match 6-packs so you can sample a variety of breweries. 79 Commercial Street, Portland, Maine 04112, tel. (207) 828–2337.

Directions: Take I-295 to Exit 7 toward downtown Portland. Follow Franklin Street and make the second left onto Middle Street. Then go left onto India Street and turn right onto Newbury Street.

When he started working for the Ringwood Brewery in Hampshire, England, a young Alan Pugsley had no idea it was the first step on a long journey that would end across the Atlantic Ocean. As a new employee, Pugsley befriended the owner, a master brewer named Peter Austin. In the late 1970s, when Britain's larger breweries started to abandon cask-conditioned ales, Austin decided to help change this. As his brewery grew, other brewers started contacting Austin for help in setting up their own real-ale breweries. Austin relied heavily on his young protégé, Pugsley, whom he sent across the country to set up new locations for his eager customers.

In 1986, a brash American named David Geary came calling at the Ringwood Brewery. Pugsley and Geary immediately got along and soon struck a deal for the English brewer to come to the United States to help Geary start his own brewery. At a time when slightly more than a dozen craft breweries operated in America, Pugsley worked with Geary under a two-year agreement. Pugsley set up a Peter Austin brewhouse and designed Geary's first beer. More importantly, Pugsley brought with him the yeast strain that would make him famous—or infamous, depending on who you ask in New England brewing circles.

After he left Geary's employ, Pugsley set up Austin systems in various countries, among them China, Nigeria, Belgium, and Russia. He also spent a lot of time designing and installing dozens of systems in New England, including at Magic Hat, the Woodstock Inn, and the Shed Restaurant and Brewery. When Pugsley decided to base his consulting operation in Portland, he met Fred Forsley through a former customer (see Federal Jack's profile). Pugsley agreed to set up a brewpub on a strip of commercial land Forsley owned near the town of Kennebunk.

Shipyard began in 1992 at Federal Jack's Restaurant and Brew Pub in Kennebunk, which is one of Maine's original brewpubs and working breweries. The Kennebunkport Brewing Company, located downstairs from Federal Jack's, is where Shipyard ales were first brewed.

Since Pugsley needed a showcase brewery for potential customers and Forsley needed a head brewer to run the system, the pair formed an alliance. As the little brewpub grew in size, the partners started delivering kegs to off-sale accounts in the area. The brewpub hit a critical point in 1994 when demand for its products outstripped Pugsley's ability to make the beer on the small system. Forsley made the momentous decision to build a package brewery in Portland. Instead of breaking ground in one of the area's many industrial parks, the partners instead decided to purchase and rehabilitate a dilapidated foundry building on the edge of downtown. Spread over three floors, the mammoth 125,000-square-foot facility is home to the Shipyard line of English-style ales.

The Peter Austin systems are iconic and easy to spot, with their signature red-brick exteriors and open fermenters. While these systems are attractive and functional, the widely known secret to Pugsley's success is his workhorse yeast strain, named after Austin's English brewery. Only Pugsley and the brewers at the Ringwood Brewery in England have access to the original strain of yeast, which ferments, flocculates, and attenuates very quickly. It tends to eat every sugar in its path; the whole cycle of brewing generally concludes in a brisk, eight-day cycle. "It's beautiful to work with," says Pugsley. "It's aggressive, it's vigorous, it looks after itself. Unless you are very unlucky or have a dirty, dirty brewery, it's going to keep trucking away. And those are the things in a yeast that any brewery would want."

Unlike other yeast strains, which brewers use a limited number of times before discarding, the current Ringwood strains are derived from an original strain dating back more than 150 years. Each brewery takes great pains to keep its strain healthy and active, simply collecting and repitching the yeast, batch after batch. This process is as close as the brewing industry gets to having the influence of *terroir*, the French viticultural notion for the effect of soil on wine, on its products. As each brewery's personal yeast strain ages, depending on how it is treated or even manipulated, the beers produced can develop a certain house character. For some breweries, that house character can either be subtle or overwhelmingly obvious.

Pugsley's influence on the New England beer scene is undeniable; however, his success is not without controversy. Critics often charge that Ringwood beers are one-dimensional products loaded with buttery, diacetyl notes that overpower the contributions of other ingredients. When asked about these comments, Pugsley merely shrugs them off. To him, the Ringwood yeast strain is a thing of beauty. To hear him talk about it is to hear a professional stock-car mechanic sing the praises of his finely tuned, high-performance V-8 engine. Pugsley's work as a brewer and biochemist is an ode to Ringwood and the beers it produces.

"I always talk about a nice, pleasant, easy drinking, well-balanced beer where you take the malt and hops down the aisle and they get married and live happily ever after and have a nice life," he says. "In this case, they make a nice beer." He also points to the popularity of the brand as the final word on the debate. Shipyard continues to grow at significant rates every year, having grown to become one of the largest craft brewers in New England.

Stone Coast Brewing Company

23 Rice Street
Portland, Maine 04103
Tel. (207) 773–2337
www.stonecoast.com

★ **Best Beer:** Knuckleball Bock. A well-rounded lager offering, more in the pale bock style than its heavier, more traditional sibling. The Knuckleball pours bright gold and smells of sweet German malt, with a very clean flavor. A pleasing lager offering in the heart of ale country.

Opened: 1996.

Type: Brewery.

Owner: Grant Wilson.

Brewer: Tom Kostovick.

Brewing system: 15-barrel JV Northwest brewhouse.

Amount produced: 1,500 barrels. 3,500-barrel total capacity.

First beer: 420 IPA.

Flagship beer: 420 IPA.

Year-round beers: 420 IPA, Knuckleball Bock, Sunday River Alt, and Sunday River Lager.

Seasonal beers: Sunsplash Golden Ale (summer) and Black Bear Porter (winter).

Tours: Tours given at 4:20 P.M. on Fridays.

Beer to go: None.

Amenities: Parking is available next to the brewery.

Other attractions: If you miss the tours, stop by the brewery's pizza shop, called the Piehole, which is a short drive away. Specializing in wood-fired pizza with numerous toppings, the taproom also offers the range of Stone Coast's beers in a sports pub environment. 865 Forest Avenue, Portland, Maine 04103, tel. (207) 774-7437.

Directions: From I-95, take Exit 48 and turn right onto Riverside Street. Make a right onto Forest Avenue and then a left onto Riverside Industrial Parkway. Rice Street is on the right.

After ten years in business, the guys at Stone Coast still think the weed joke is funny. The brewery's flagship 420 IPA, a stylish, English-influenced India pale ale that balances toasted malts with light, citrusy hop bitterness, has a cult following in the beer industry. The origin of the number 420—a relatively well known euphemism for cannabis—is hotly debated among the original hopheads (hops are a member of the same family as cannabis). After an extensive investigation, one inevitably fueled by brownies and potato chips, *High Times Magazine* concluded that the term originated in the early 1970s in San Rafael, where a wayward group of teenagers would meet after school at 4:20 P.M. to smoke marijuana. While other researchers and conspiracy theorists see 420 everywhere (it was the time LSD creator Albert Hoffman first ingested the substance; the Beatles' song "Come Together" is 4:20 in length), Stone Coast reaps some benefits from its mildly clever double entendre. To appease federal licensing authorities, the label on each bottle offers that the beer is actually Batch 420 and small lettering notes that Stone Coast tried 419 batches before settling on this recipe. The first label, which included a blurry background of a green, leafy substance, was less subtle.

In trying to find its place in the brewing industry, Stone Coast has taken several directional turns, first opening a brewpub in downtown Portland, then another pub near Lake Winnipesaukee in New Hampshire. The company eventually closed both operations and moved to an industrial park outside Maine's largest city. Stone Coast stopped brewing for a startling nine-month period while it set up the new facility. Armed with four sales representatives, the new Stone Coast hawks both bottled and canned beer in New England, with hopes of expanding to California. The brewers use a five-head filler to can the zesty Sunsplash Golden Ale. No one is quite sure why the machine fills five cans instead of six, much to the operator's consternation.

The present, expansive commercial site—boasting twelve thousand square feet of open warehouse space—hardly looks like an operating business from the outside. No signs denote Stone Coast's tenancy; only a few errant fermenters and kegs outside the loading dock indicate this place is a brewery. On the inside, two dueling brewing systems, one a striking copper-clad DME and the other a dull, stainless-steel JV Northwest, occupy one side of the operation next to a correspondingly unusual assortment of fermenters. The equipment is a mix of leftovers from the New Hampshire pub and the production system that the brewery is quickly outgrowing.

Brewer Tom Kostovick stumbled into a job with Stone Coast while working as a guide in the White Mountains, originally plowing the driveway at the company's sister brewpub, at Sunday River, before working in the restaurant and bar.

Kostovick became friendly with the brewmaster and soon started helping out before assuming head brewer duties and attending the Siebel Institute. His 840 IPA, a doubling of the flagship brand, is a model for extreme beers. With ample dry-hopping, the beer possesses abundant German and American hop notes and a whopping amount of malt.

Kostovick hopes to expand the brewhouse to keep up with growing demand now that Stone Coast has righted its course. The new Knuckleball Bock release, which is served at the bar attached to Fenway Park and is fast becoming the new flagship, couldn't have been timed any better.

Slopes Northern Maine Restaurant and Brewing Company

150 Maysville Street
Presque Isle, Maine 04769
Tel. (207) 769–2739
www.slopesrestaurant.com

★ **Best Beer:** None established yet.

Opened: 2005.

Type: Brewpub.

Owner: Hank Ford and Imbesat Daudi.

Brewer: None.

Brewing system: 8-barrel extract Micropub Brewing Station brewhouse.

Amount Produced: Figures not available.

First beer: Aroostook Amber.

Flagship beer: Aroostook Amber.

Beers: West Chapman Red, Aroostook Amber, Slopes Oktoberfest, Wheat, Moose Lager, County Light, Winter Ale, Presque Isle Pilsner, Big Rock Brown Ale, Marzen, Crown Pilsner, American Light, and Rudolph's Red Nose Ale.

Tours: By appointment.

Food: Upscale menu, including seafood, steak, and create-your-own pasta dishes.

Beer to go: Pricey growlers are for sale at the brewpub.

Amenities: Parking is available at the brewpub. Full liquor license.

Pub Hours: Open Monday, 11 A.M. to 10 P.M.; Tuesday through Thursday, 11 A.M. to 11 P.M.; Friday and Saturday, 11 A.M. to midnight; and Sunday, 11 A.M. to 10 P.M.

Directions: Drive north through Maine and stop just shy of the Canadian border to find the town of Presque Isle. Slopes is located across from the Aroostook Centre Mall near where Maysville Street meets Route 163.

A late-comer to the New England brewing scene, the Slopes Northern Maine Restaurant and Brewing Company has the distinction of being the region's northernmost brewery. Located in Presque Isle, population 9,511, Slopes is also one of New England's largest brewpubs. In 2004, two businessmen secured a substantial, $2.4-million guaranteed loan from the federal government in order to build the enormous 32,000-square-foot restaurant. Slopes seats seven hundred people (or more than 7 percent of the town) and employs one hundred people (another 1 percent of the town) on a part- or full-time basis.

Located across the street from the Aroostook Centre Mall, Slopes is the brainchild of two physicians, urologist Imbe Daudi and oral surgeon Hank Ford. It is designed to be a source of economic development for the community, a fact that led Maine's United States senators, Olympia Snowe and Susan Collins, to support the initiative. After researching the project, the doctors determined that Presque Isle needed an outlet for upscale dining. The owners also recently opened the Northern Maine Bottling Company, which bottles spring water. The company provides the water used by the brewery at Slopes.

The owners purchased a brewing system from Micropub, which allows them to brew a range of extract beers. Known for its ease of use, Micropub's systems do not require the services of a trained brewer; Slopes's owners do the brewing themselves. Micropub provides them with the beers' recipes and ingredients. Whether this brewpub can survive in a county of 73,000 people spread over 6,829 square miles remains to be seen. Because of the brewpub's very recent opening and, frankly, its remote location, I was unable to visit Slopes and try the beers. But I look forward to visiting when the snow melts in July.

Rocky Bay Public House and Brewing Company

7 Lindsey Street
Rockland, Maine 04841
Tel. (207) 596–0300
www.rockybaybrewing.com

> ★ **Best Beer:** Whitecap IPA. A tender balance of American-style hops and slight, buttery malt flavors. The hops, which include Cascade in the hop back, impart a slightly earthy flavor. A real mix of East and West Coast sensibilities.

Opened: 1997.

Type: Brewpub.

Owner: John Swan.

Brewer: Rich Ruggiero.

Brewing system: 3.5 barrel system.

Amount produced: 600 barrels.

First beer: Schooner Point Lager.

Flagship beer: Schooner Point Lager.

Year-round beers: Schooner Point Lager, Whitecap IPA, Katie's Celtic Red, Foghorn Brown Ale, Blackcastle 80 Shilling Scottish Ale, and Nor'easter Stout.

Seasonal beers: Headless Horseman's Red Ale, Mussel Ridge Summer Ale, Seasider Oktoberfest, and Viking Plunder Winter Ale.

Tours: Tours by appointment.

Beer to go: Growlers, party pigs, and mini-kegs are for sale at the brewpub.

Food: Simple tavern fare with an English bent, including bangers and mash.

Amenities: Limited on-street parking is available near the pub. Full liquor license. Pub offers live music Thursday through Sunday. For Firkin Fridays, the pub releases a new cask-conditioned ale and sells pints for $2. The pub continues to specialize in cask ales and plans to offer multiple offerings pushed through beer engines.

Other attractions: Rockland is home to many events during the year, but none matches the pure spectacle of its long-running Maine Lobster Festival. For five days in early August, the town celebrates the crustacean with a series of concerts, a parade down Main Street, and a road race. Some lucky young lady gets crowned the next Maine Lobster Festival Sea Goddess, while amateur cooks from around Maine compete in the lobster-cooking contest.

Pub hours: Daily, 11:30 A.M. to close.

Directions: The pub is located in downtown Rockland on Lindsey Street, which intersects with Main Street. A few steps from Rockland Harbor.

While other breweries fight to expand their markets, Rocky Bay is taking the unusual step of downsizing its operation. For many years, Rocky Bay operated a full-fledged package operation on Park Street in Rockland and distributed its beers to midcoast Maine. In January 1999, John Swan purchased Rocky Bay after his daughter Carrie, a brewer and graduate of Heriot-Watt University with a degree in brewing and distilling, introduced him to her art.

At the time Swan purchased the brewery, one of Rocky Bay's top accounts was Waterworks, an attractive, English-style pub attached to the Captain Lindsey House Inn in downtown Rockland. When the pub came up for sale, Swan purchased it and changed the direction of the brewery. Rocky Bay plans to turn a section of the pub's dining space into a small, functional brewery and return its focus to the local market.

With its warm, inviting atmosphere, the pub itself hardly needs any changing. The structure, which once served as the first water company for the city of Rockland, is a living museum, with original wood pipes used in the early days of water maintenance on display. The lodgelike main bar area boasts a big fireplace, long, communal tables and benches, and a sizable bar extending the length of the room.

At the heart of Rocky Bay is experienced brewer Rich Ruggiero. A former electrical engineer, Ruggiero caught the homebrewing bug and it led him to open his own store for the hobby and start a small brewery consulting business. From there, he decided to build upon his degree in electronic and mechanical technology by attending the Siebel Institute. He moved around between several breweries in Long Island for six years before settling in Maine in 1997. Once there, Ruggiero helped design and construct the brewing system for Rocky Bay, then stayed on as head brewer once his consulting job was finished.

The pub's beer menu covers a number of styles, including crisp lagers; a semisweet stout with torrified wheat, made to replace Guinness; and a few Belgian-style offerings. Ruggiero's popular, strong seasonal, the Viking Plunder Winter Ale, is a remarkably smooth sipping beer at 10 percent alcohol, with hints of dried fruit and light oak on top of a substantial, malt base. The return to small-batch brewing will allow Ruggiero greater opportunities to experiment.

Rocky Bay sponsors a series of events throughout the year, including a keg-tapping party in celebration of Octoberfest, a summer solstice event, and a halfway-to–St. Patrick's Day party. The event that hits the highest note, however, is one sponsored by the city. For two days in July, the North Atlantic Blues Festival takes place in picturesque Harbor Park overlooking Rockland Harbor. Ruggiero highly recommends the event, especially as he also plays left-handed guitar in the Rockland blues circuit.

Oak Pond Brewing Company

101 Oak Pond Road
Skowhegan, Maine 04976
Tel. (207) 474–5952

★ **Best Beer:** Storyteller Doppelbock. A sharp-eyed beer lover will note the one lone 30-barrel, horizontal lagering tank standing off to the side of the fermentation area. Along with its line of straightforward ales, Oak Pond regularly produces several lager beers, including a doppelbock, an Oktoberfest, and a bock beer. The brewery doesn't cut corners, properly lagering the doppelbock for 10 weeks.

Opened: 1996 (under new ownership in 2003).

Type: Brewery.

Owners: Don and Nancy Chandler.

Brewer: Don Chandler. Nancy Chandler, assistant brewer.

Brewing system: 14-barrel DME brewhouse.

Amount produced: 150 barrels. 2,000-barrel total capacity.

First beer: Nut Brown Ale.

Flagship beer: Nut Brown Ale.

Year-round beers: Nut Brown Ale, Dooryard Ale, Oktoberfest, and White Fox Ale.

Seasonal beers: Storyteller Doppelbock and Laughing Loon Lager (bock).

Tours: Tours available by appointment or when the brewhouse door is open.

Beer to go: 22-ounce bottles and ridiculously affordable, freshly filled growlers.

Amenities: Parking is available in front of the brewery and on the street.

Other attractions: No longer a brewpub, the former Narrow Gauge Brewing Company is now the Granary Pub. A pleasant 30-mile drive from Skowhegan, the Granary offers five beers from Oak Pond on draft at all times. 23 Pleasant Street, Farmington, Maine 04938, tel. (207) 779–0710, www.thegranarybrewpub.com.

Directions: From the center of Skowhegan, take Route 2 west toward Canaan. Pass Lake George to the left, then turn right onto Oak Pond Road.

A thirty-second conversation changed the direction of Don Chandler's life. Seated at a local Skowhegan bar, nursing a drink over a holiday weekend, he passively listened as a fellow patron asked his friend if he knew that the local brewery, Oak Pond, was closing its doors. While Chandler's friend was saddened by the news, the discussion quickly turned to another subject. The next day, the friend called Chandler and asked if he had any interest in going to visit the brewery. The pair visited Oak Pond on the brewery's planned last day of existence.

After visiting the brewery, Chandler and his friend began discussing the possibility of buying it. For economic reasons, the friend eventually had to bow out, leaving Chandler as the sole suitor. With a background in manufacturing, the would-be brewer saw the opportunity as a chance to reenter his former field in an entirely new way. When Nancy Chandler first heard about her husband's idea of buying a brewery, she didn't miss a beat. "I told him, 'Whatever makes you happy.'"

The Oak Pond Brewing Company began not in the town of Skowhegan, but nearly one hundred miles to the south in Portland, as the Hedgehog Brewpub. That project never developed to the point of brewing, so the original owners set up the brewery in a family member's converted chicken barn. With a little homebrewing experience behind him, Chandler apprenticed on the brewing system before taking over the brewery. The experience has been educational as well as fun for the Chandlers. Surrounded by towering 20-barrel fermenters, the oversized brewhouse turns out only a small percentage of its potential; the business side of the operation occupies much of Don Chandler's time.

When I visit, Nancy Chandler greets me with an apology for having dirt on her shirt. In addition to her full-time job teaching physical therapy at a local community college, Nancy Chandler also serves as Oak Pond's assistant brewer, a position that requires her to clean the brewing kettles and lay out the ingredients for each batch. While I discuss beer with her husband, she continues to serve customers and friends who stop by for freshly filled Oak Pond growlers. Nancy also directs the tours and enjoys tossing out random beer trivia (ask her about the origins of "99 Bottles of Beer on the Wall").

When I ask Don Chandler about how he developed an interest in good beer, he looks as if I've inquired about the name of that hot, fiery orange object in the sky. After a few moments of wordless silence, he stammers, "Well, because it just tastes so much damned better. Beer is a food product, so why would you want to have something synthetic? It's not much more complex than that."

Kennebec River Brewery

Route 201, P.O. Box 100
The Forks, Maine 04985
Tel. (800) 765–7238
www.northernoutdoors.com

> ★ **Best Beer:** Penobscot Porter. A strong porter blessed with a potent, roasted-malt nose. Penobscot's clean flavor is decidedly assertive, mixing rich, chocolaty malts, a touch of creaminess, and long-lasting, roasted bitterness. A very drinkable, English-style porter from brewer Mike McConnell.

Opened: January 1997.

Type: Brewpub.

Owners: Wayne and Suzie Hockmeyer.

Brewer: Mike McConnell.

Brewing system: 4.5-barrel Pierre Rajotte brewhouse.

Amount produced: 480 barrels (180 barrels on site, 300 contracted by Casco Bay Brewing Company). 600-barrel total capacity.

First beer: Blonde Ale.

Flagship beer: Magic Hole IPA.

Year-round beers: Penobscot Porter, 4 Stroke Lager, Big Mama Blueberry Ale, Arthur's Hazelnut Brown, and Kennebec Summer Ale / Northern Lights.

Seasonal beers: Class 5 Extra Stout.

Tours: Tours available by appointment or ask at the front desk.

Beer to go: 6-packs available for sale.

Food: A clean, simple menu offering traditional pub food, with dinner entrées trending slightly upscale with seafood dishes.

Amenities: Parking is available in front of the lodge. Full liquor license.

Other attractions: Northern Outdoors is a destination unto itself. Most visitors come here to raft, hike, or snowmobile, generally enjoying the outdoors in all seasons. While the brewing component is a nice, value-added experience, plan to stay overnight in one of the cabins or bring your tent and get a campsite.

Pub hours: Restaurant opens at 6:30 A.M. and closes at 9 P.M. on Sunday through Thursday and at 10 P.M. on Saturday and Sunday. Pub opens daily at noon and closes at 1 A.M. on Friday and Saturday evenings, and 11 P.M. all other days. Call to confirm hours.

Directions: The brewery is located at the Northern Outdoors resort center at The Forks on Route 201.

Near the banks of Martin Pond and the rushing waters of the mighty river for which it is named, the Kennebec River Brewery is part of the Northern Outdoors outfitting and adventure company. As a city kid from Lowell, Massachusetts, owner Wayne Hockmeyer frequently visited the area around The Forks on family vacations. As an adult, he would retreat to the remote outdoors region and work as a guide for hunting and fishing trips.

While scouting new fishing locations one day, Hockmeyer inadvertently discovered the quiet secret of the raging Kennebec River. As the whitewater flowed past, Hockmeyer developed an idea that would allow him to move permanently to the area. No other place in New England offered serious whitewater rafting, so Hockmeyer contacted a friend in Maryland to ask about the river's potential. After reviewing flow data collected from the local dam operator, the friend advised Hockmeyer that the river would either kill people or provide them with the greatest ride of their lives. Undeterred by the potential danger, Hockmeyer purchased a used military assault raft, some used paddles, and life vests, gathered a group of hearty hunters (mostly clad in jeans) and headed for the rushing waters. After a harrowing assault on the rapids, half the group jumped from the ridiculous vessel and thanked higher powers for their lives. Energized by the experience, the other half wanted a ride back to the drop zone.

The charming, wood-beamed main lodge at Northern Outdoors, which was entirely rebuilt after a devastating fire on New Year's Eve, 1983, houses the brewery and restaurant. Spread over more than 150 hilly, wooded acres, the Northern Outdoors set-up provides indoor housing for up to 350 people. It includes 28 attractive log cabins and a spacious deck, with a pool and hot tub a mere 15 feet from the pub.

Long-time employee Jim Yearwood suggested that Hockmeyer add a brewpub to the facility as part of a major capital-improvement plan. Yearwood promoted the project as a country brewery dedicated to making quality beers with all natural ingredients. After coming across an ad in *Zymurgy*, Yearwood selected a small system hand-crafted by Pierre Rajotte of Canada (it bears an eerie resemblance to the robot from *Lost in Space*) and replaced the weight and exercise room with the brewery. Yearwood served as the first brewer, crafting a small line of English-style ales. Much of the system is the result of tinkering and homemade innovations, including a heat exchanger comprised of spirals of rubber tubing connected to the lodge's well water.

The brewing approach here is remarkably simple, with unexpected results. Because of space restrictions, Kennebec River has only one serving tank and no conditioning tanks. The fermenters are not jacketed with fancy glycol systems, but simply use the well water to maintain proper temperature controls. The beer is brewed, fermented with London Yeast, and then sent directly to kegs and bunged to condition further in a warm room. The finished product is naturally carbonated and unfiltered but remains surprisingly clear and bright due to the substantial flocculation of the yeast. Though the beer is kegged and served cold, the process bears some surprising similarities to the real-ale approach. (Before CAMRA disciples get too bothered, I concede the brewing operation here lacks some of the required parts, but each of the finished products bears a certain liveliness absent from most brewpub beer.)

Mike McConnell now runs the brewing operations, and brews a delicious porter based on his own recipe. The Kennebec Summer Ale and the 4 Stroke Lager require some discussion. The Summer Ale, which is also known as the Northern Lights ale in the winter—the recipe stays the same year-round—stands out from the other beers for its American flair. While almost all of the beers are brewed with expensive Maris Otter floor-malted barley, the Summer Ale is made with North American malted barley and Cascade hops from the Pacific Northwest. It possesses an impressive crispness, with mild, fruity flavors; a light, yeast tang; and the cleanest of profiles. The 4 Stroke Lager really piqued my interest at the first sniff. Possessing an unusually fruity aroma, the beer is made with dry lager yeast, European pilsner malt, Saaz and Tettnang hops, and is fermented at slightly warmer temperatures. The fruity and zesty result is very drinkable and is similar to the California Common style, best represented by Anchor Steam.

On your visit, take a quick peek at the brewery's logo, which is etched into the wooden covering for the tap box in the pub. A jubilant sun points to his frothy mug as a raftload of happy thrill-seekers paddle into the arms of an enormous wave poised to tear them in half. While the daring folks up here think that barely avoiding a watery death is a welcome daily experience, wearier visitors prefer to pull up a stool and join the sun for a pleasant pint in the bar.

Sheepscot Valley Brewing Company

74 Hollywood Boulevard
Whitefield, Maine 04353
Tel. (207) 549–5530

★ **Best Beer:** Damariscotta Double Brown Ale. Offered as the brewery's winter beer, this hazy brown ale, brewed with 6 malts and oatmeal, is slightly tangy and full of roasted flavors.

Opened: June 1995.

Type: Brewery.

Owners: Steve and Louisa Gorrill.

Brewer: Steve Gorrill.

Brewing system: 7-barrel locally fabricated system.

Amount produced: 350 barrels.

First beer: Mad Goose Belgian Ale.

Flagship beer: Pemaquid Ale.

Year-round beers: Pemaquid Ale and Sheepscot River Pale Ale.

Seasonal beers: Damariscotta Double Brown Ale, New Harbor Lager, and Sheepscot Wee Heavy Ale.

Tours: By appointment only, with a greater likelihood of success in the summer.

Amenities: This rural, residential area has limited parking in front of the brewery.

Directions: Finding the brewery is a challenge, even more so than with other small breweries in Maine. Gorrill's self-described "small cottage brewery" is located deep in the heart of rural Maine, far from the coastal tourist meccas. Take Route 194 (Head Tide Road) from central Whitefield and then turn left onto South Fowles Lane. After about a quarter mile, turn at the telephone pole spray-painted "Hollywood Boulevard." The brewery is in a barn on the left side shortly after the road hooks off to the right.

Even among Maine's lot of unconventional brewers, Steve Gorrill stands out. At one beer festival, Gorrill arrived with his beer, brewery signage, and a duct-tape monkey riding on his shoulder. While I was talking with the self-described "Count of Whitefield" at an outdoor event in Bar Harbor, a guy wanders out of the woods and ambles toward us. Seeing Gorrill, his face lights up. "Aren't you Sheep Scotty Too Hotty?" Gorrill brushes him off with a slight smile and a wave and then finishes his answer to my brewing-related question. When I look utterly confused, Gorrill admits that a while back, he adopted a wrestling persona. Mind you, Gorrill never actually wrestled—he just took on a wrestling nickname known even to random strangers.

Gorrill grew up in Quincy, Massachusetts, and moved to Maine to get a degree in animal science. He originally planned to embark on a career in poultry science but fell prey to the joys of homebrewing. As a homebrewer, Gorrill developed a great respect for Belgian brewers who serve their local communities. When he opened Sheepscot, he adopted the same approach. The brewery's limited production is mainly distributed to the mid-coast region of Maine.

Gorrill began his brewing career fiddling with less traditional styles. His initial Belgian offerings were difficult to sell outside of the Portland market, and his drive to remain local required him to focus on more traditional English-style ales in Sheepscot's portfolio.

Designed in collaboration with a local restaurateur, Sheepscot's flagship Pemaquid Ale is unfiltered, unpasteurized, and employs a Scottish yeast strain. The beer is very popular in this region and fulfills Gorrill's dream of brewing a beer for local Mainers. Shortly after Pemaquid Ale became the brewery's flagship offering, Gorrill created a cartoon-character mascot to match it. In true eccentric, Gorrill style, the brewer developed a cigar-chomping, beer-drinking, cartoon lobster buoy that urged potential customers to "Haul in a Pint."

Understanding Beer Styles

Many people fail to try new beers in part because they simply don't realize the wide range of flavors available for sampling. With the boundless creativity of American brewers, there are now beers to match nearly any flavor you desire. There are stouts that taste like coffee or chocolate, India pale ales that remind you of oranges and citrus, and Belgian-style tripels that smack of bananas and Wrigley's Juicy Fruit gum. One of the easiest ways to learn more about beer is to educate yourself about beer styles.

Brewmasters have been developing new styles of beer from time immemorial, many of which were born out of necessity and even accident. In the early days of brewing, brewers dried malt by the warmth of the sun and the air took care of fermentation. With the development of kilning, maltsters dried their wares over open fires, resulting in beers with a distinctly smoky flavor. After the dawn of the Industrial Revolution, maltsters developed the ability to kiln malt through other means, thus relieving beer of its smoky flavors and allowing brewers to experiment further with malts roasted to different levels. Brewers also learned the importance of yeast in flavor development and the fermentation process. With the introduction of hops as a flavor component and natural preservative, the glorious quadruple combination was complete.

Some modern styles have also developed out of necessity and accident, while others have been created through tightly scripted, scientific production. It's well-known that necessity gave birth to the India pale ale style. British troops sailing to the faraway Indian subcontinent required a strongly hopped brew that would not spoil during the long traveling period. Creative brewers also birthed wild new categories, ranging from simple honey ales to rye beers and lagers made with chili peppers. Chocolate- and cocoa-flavored beers are the creation of some brewers decidedly addicted to confections. In a twist of historical irony, a few enterprising brewers started smoking their own malt in order to recreate the acrid flavors our ancestral maltsters worked so hard to avoid.

As this guide has previously described, the fruits of the art of brewing fall into two main groups: ales and lagers. Among many other styles, ales include porters, stouts, barleywines, and wheat beers, while lagers include bocks, pilsners, dunkels, and Dortmunders. In each of the two families, there are dozens of individual, fussy yeast strains that require very specific circumstances in order to produce desired results. Brewers mix and match these yeast strains, along with select malts, hops, and types of water (hard or soft with certain mineral contents) to create specific styles of beer.

Critics and historians have long contemplated the differences between styles and have made many attempts to define them. This exhaustive process is unlike the mapping of the human genome or cartography of distant lands—far easier endeavors, to be sure. The most widely accepted source elucidating beer styles is the guide produced by the Brewers Association (BA), available on-line at www.beertown.org. This guide is the work of the BA's upstart group of founders, including Charlie Papazian, the so-called father of the modern homebrewing movement. Since 1979, the BA has distributed a list of beer style descriptions as a reference for brewers and beer judges; the list draws heavily upon historical research and examples produced by world-class brewers.

The BA's guidelines attempt to bring order to an otherwise chaotic scheme of eclectic brewing methods and styles. The current list details more than fifty distinct styles of beer, each providing a short description of the expected criteria for a properly styled beer. For each style, the guidelines suggest the proper color, body type, aroma and palate flavors, bitterness level, quality of perceptible hop aroma, types of esters or diacetyl, and the acceptable levels of chill haze.

For example, the guideline for a proper Vienna-style lager reads, "Beers in this category are reddish brown or copper colored. They are medium in body. The beer is characterized by malty aroma and slight malt sweetness. The malt aroma and flavor may have a dominant toasted character. Hop bitterness is clean and crisp. Noble-type hop aromas and flavors should be low or mild. Fruity esters, diacetyl, and chill haze should not be perceived." The Original Gravity (OG) should be between 1.046 and 1.056 (11.5 to 14 degrees Plato), the Final Gravity (FG) between 1.012 and 1.018 (3 to 4.5 degrees Plato), the Alcohol by Weight (ABW) at 3.8 to 4.3 percent (ABV 4.8 to 5.4 percent), with International Bitterness Units (IBUs) between 22 and 28, and a Standard Reference Method (SRM) of 8 to 12 (European Brewing Convention 16 to 24).

It may seem like this last paragraph has sucked all of the fun out of beer. Be reassured that while beer is greatly related to mathematics on a production level, on a drinking level, much of this information is useless. The guidelines and their technical mumbo-jumbo are mainly intended to give brewers guidance and historical perspective for the creation of their recipes and judges a set of somewhat objective criteria for the comparison of beers. For consumers, the guidelines explain the nuances of beer styles and help you choose the proper beer for the right occasion. While you certainly don't need to keep the original gravity of Altbiers in your wallet (unless you're the biggest of beer geeks), learning about beer styles can be an interesting process.

Outside of undertaking some homework on the subject, simply reviewing the tap selections at a good bar is perfectly good on-the-job training. Beers come in different colors and flavors and their names often bear the styles they represent. Ask your bartender for samples and compare a stout, India pale ale, and a wheat beer. The flavors in each of these widely available styles are quite contrasting. When you become conversant in the broader differences, try comparing several beers within a single style to hone in on the subtler differences.

Beyond beer styles, the methods of presenting beers also influence their taste. Almost every drinker is familiar with the gently cascading beer known as Guinness. Created by the infusion of nitrogen into the typical carbon dioxide delivery system, the resulting beer is frothy and creamy and unlike regular keg beer. The delivery method increases the body of the beer, while also mellowing its flavors.

Real ale, on the other hand, is defined by the Campaign for Real Ale (CAMRA) as beer that is conditioned in the container from which it is to be served. With the addition of live yeast, each cask undergoes a process of secondary fermentation, which produces natural carbonation. Far from flat, warm beer, real ale is alive and flavorful. After the cask is tapped, the beer quickly evolves and must be consumed within days. With lower levels of carbonation and carbon dioxide, real ales remain among the most expressive ways of presenting beer.

Massachusetts

Because of its central geographic location and plentiful good-beer opportunities, Boston serves as a logical center for any beer traveling around New England. While many debate whether Boston is truly the "Hub of the Solar System," as Oliver Wendell Holmes once jokingly referred to the folks on golden domed Beacon Hill, it is quickly becoming a focal point for American brewing. Anchoring the commonwealth's eastern shores, the Boston area features several top-notch brewpubs, the largest craft brewery in New England, and some of the best beer bars you will find in the country. Boston's reputation as a regional capital for good beer continues to grow, with many out-of-state and foreign breweries increasing their focus on the city's educated and experimental beer-lovers.

While a beer vacation to Boston is an excellent idea, it only tells a small part of the rich brewing story here in Massachusetts; every corner of the commonwealth is part of the good-beer community. Western and Central Massachusetts offer great breweries, pubs, and beer bars. While the South Shore remains unusually quiet, the North Shore, Cape Cod, and the Islands are also active and showing great potential for growth. The People's Pint, the Opa Opa Steakhouse and Brewery, Offshore Ale Company, and the Northampton Brewery remain among my favorite brewpubs in the commonwealth, each offering a distinctive atmosphere that would be impossible to imitate in the Boston area. Breweries like Berkshire, Wachusett, and Hyland quietly produce some of the most underappreciated beers in New England.

With all of its political history, Massachusetts also boasts a great deal of beer history. The first licensed tavern in Boston dates to 1634; Captain Sedgwick opened one the first credited breweries in New England three years later. From the earliest days of pioneering souls on the Mayflower to the founders of the Massachusetts Bay Colony, beer played an important role in early American life. That tradition continues to this very day, as Massachusetts has the most breweries, brewpubs, and great beer bars of any state profiled in this guide. Word has it that several new, beer-focused establishments are planned for the future, including new brewpubs and beer bars in the Boston area.

Amherst Brewing Company

36 North Pleasant Street
Amherst, Massachusetts 01002
Tel. (413) 253–4400
www.amherstbrewing.com

★ **Best Beer:** Cascade IPA on cask. This mildly hoppy India pale ale is perfectly suited for the mellowing influences of service by cask. A great balance of malt with a wonderful expression of the often-used Cascade hop. The IPA downplays the somewhat grainy, husky malt flavors found in the carbonated version.

Opened: August 1997.

Type: Brewpub.

Owner: Private corporation; John Korpita, president.

Brewer: Mike Yates.

Brewing system: 10-barrel self-fabricated brewhouse.

Amount produced: 750 barrels. 1,500-barrel total capacity.

First beer: Honey Pilsner.

Flagship beer: Cascade IPA.

Year-round beers: Massatucky Brown, Cascade IPA, North Pleasant Pale Ale, Two Sisters Imperial Stout, ESB, Puffers Smoked Porter, Salamander Crossing, and Steam Lager.

Seasonal beers: Heather Ale, Black Magic Dark Lager, Raspberry Brown Ale, Lewmeister Oktoberfest, Half in the Bagpipe Scottish Ale, Patch Porter, Banker's Gold, Workingman's Wheat, Honey Pilsner, Boltwood Bock, Graduation Ale, and Anniversary Ale.

Tours: By appointment.

Beer to go: A cooler stocked with counterpressure-filled growlers sits across from the bar.

Food: Typical pub grub complemented by a solid list of vegetarian-friendly plates.

Amenities: On-street parking. Full liquor license. Live entertainment Thursday, Saturday, and Monday evenings. On the first and third Mondays of each month, the pub hosts an 18-piece local jazz orchestra playing big-band music.

Other attractions: Downtown Amherst sports several interesting stores and a slew of less interesting pubs. Head down the street to the Moan and Dove (460 West Street, Amherst, Massachusetts 01002, tel. (413) 256–1710) for the best selection of beer available in the state west of Boston (see "Eleven Great Beer Bars" in this guide). With a giant barrel as its door frame, the nearby Spirit Haus offers a wide selection of good beers for purchase (338 College Street, Amherst, Massachusetts 01002, tel. (413) 253–5384, www.spirithaus.com).

Pub hours: Open daily, 11:30 A.M. to 1 A.M. Lunch, 11:30 A.M. to 5 P.M.; dinner, 5 P.M. to 10 P.M.; late-night menu, 10 P.M. to midnight.

Directions: The brewpub is in the heart of downtown Amherst on North Pleasant Street, directly adjacent to Amherst College.

Surrounded on all sides by colleges in the Pioneer Valley, the Amherst Brewing Company is a welcome respite from frat bars serving three-dollar pitchers. Opened in 1997, Amherst is primarily run by John Korpita, an award-winning homebrewer. The place is also owned in part by Vermont Pub and Brewery owner Greg Noonan. Though he has long given up the boots, many of the recipes date back to when Korpita ran the kettles here and offered his personal touch. His heavy-handed Two Sisters Russian Imperial Stout, a staple on the beer menu, derives its name from two Russian sisters Korpita and his family adopted.

The house staff does a nice job of making the available beers known to the public. A chalkboard next to the bar lists the beers, along with occasional trivia facts about a tapped offering. The pub's beer menu provides further description and detail and helpfully breaks down the list with icons noting a beer's body, color, and level of hoppiness.

The brewing is now in the hands of Mike Yates, a former plant science major at the University of Massachusetts at Amherst. Before taking over at Amherst, Yates toiled for two and a half years at McNeill's Brewery in Brattleboro, Vermont, and spent time working for Will Meyers at Cambridge Brewing Company. He enjoys ample tank space at Amherst, allowing him a luxury most brewers do not bother even dreaming about: brewing lagers. When I visited Amherst, Yates had a true doppelbock gently hibernating for several weeks in the conditioning tanks.

Amherst is able to keep ten of its own beers on tap at all times. The pub's beers are each thoughtful and flavorful, including the omnipresent cask ale. A nice touch often available is the opportunity to sample different vintages of the house Scotch ale. With such a wide number of taps, do not expect to find your typical selection of yawn-inducing amber and pale ales. Dark-beer lovers will find a home at Amherst with the chocolate and smoked porters and the Two Sisters Russian Imperial Stout.

Perhaps the pub's most well-known beer is its two-time Great American Beer Festival award–winning Heather Ale. While many brewers have attempted this obscure style, where the heather plant replaces hops as the counterbalance to malt, Amherst's offering is one of few that results in anything other than an unpalatable experiment gone horribly wrong. The idea for the Heather Ale originated with Korpita, who was intrigued by the popular Fraoch Heather Ale. In creating the beer, Yates uses heather from Washington State in an amount three times greater than the hop level he uses in other beers. The resulting product is impressively well balanced and quite striking on the palate, bouncing from a tongue-teasing, minty flavor to an unexpected yet pleasing sweet malt finish. Due to its unusual flavor, the Heather Ale is perhaps not the ideal session beer for most people, but remains an intriguing and enjoyable one-off for sure.

Amherst Brewing's solid, simple, brick building in the center of town used to house a bank. The location was split into two levels after an expansion, with regular pub-seating downstairs and an even more relaxed lounge area upstairs, named plainly ABC Upstairs. The restaurant seats 150, while the lounge offers an additional 100 seats. Instead of simply leveling the upstairs and creating a lackluster, loud pool hall, the designers instead created a series of nooks for visitors to enjoy. There is also a 40-seat patio outside for summer dining.

The small brewhouse is located on the right, directly next to the entryway. The pub's decoration is vaguely eclectic, with scattered pieces of breweriana and an assortment of unusual gargoyles. Two particular notes are the attractive, original neon sign for Hampden Ale that hangs over the long, 30-seat wraparound bar, and the mosaic tile of two clinking beer mugs centered in the middle of the restaurant's floor.

Nashoba Valley Winery

100 Wattaquadoc Hill Road
Bolton, Massachusetts 01740
Tel. (978) 779–5521
www.nashobawinery.com

★ **Best Beer:** Imperial Stout. Brewer Ben Roesch is slowly trying to shake things up at this beautiful brewing location. His version of the classic imperial stout style represents such an attempt. The aroma is possessed of dark malts with hints of chocolate and a very reserved level of alcohol esters. The flavor mixes roasted and chocolate malts, light alcohol, and fruity hints. While lighter than some offerings in the style, Nashoba's version remains more drinkable and very enjoyable.

Opened: 1998.

Type: Brewery.

Owners: Richard and Cindy Pelletier.

Brewer: Ben Roesch.

Brewing system: 15-barrel World Brewing Systems brewhouse.

Amount produced: 400 barrels. Presently at capacity.

First beer: Heron Pale Ale.

Flagship beer: Heron Pale Ale.

Year-round beers: Heron Pale Ale and Bolt 117 Lager.

Seasonal beers: Imperial Stout, Barleywine, Summer Stout, Wattaquadoc Wheat, Oaktoberfest, and IPA.

Tours: Roesch is here five days a week, so stop in at the barn to see if he is around.

Beer to go: Bottles of Nashoba's beers are available in the gift shop in the main structure housing the restaurant.

Amenities: Parking is available in the lot near the main house and restaurant. A sizable outdoor pavilion hosts weddings and private events.

Other attractions: The Nashoba estate is a destination in and of itself. The estate sponsors several events during the year, including the Harvest Festival, Apple Festival, and an Oktoberfest featuring six of Nashoba's beers.

Directions: From Bolton Center, travel west on Main Street. At the blinking light turn left onto Wattaquadoc Hill Road. The brewery is located in a small building off to the side of the main restaurant.

In its idyllic country setting, surrounded by fifty-two rolling acres of apple orchard, the Nashoba Valley Winery estate is an inspiring place to visit. The estate first started producing fruit wines in 1978, and now produces more than twenty varieties, including Blueberry Merlot, Strawberry Rhubarb, and Cranberry Apple. The estate also includes an orchard with seventy kinds of apples, a popular restaurant, and a distillery.

With all of its attractions, too few people note the little barn off to the side of the main shop and restaurant. Just inside the simple exterior resides Nashoba's own brewery. Amid the beauty of the estate, winery, and new distillery, the brewery suffers the fate of the oft-neglected middle child. The system is manned by Ben Roesch, an intense guy with a resolute dedication to craft beer. A local, Roesch worked at the Wachusett Brewing Company and as the assistant brewer at the Cambridge Brewing Company before securing the head brewer position here.

The brewery started small, only producing a few kegs for on-site consumption at J's Restaurant and a limited number of swing-top bottles for sale in the farm's bottle shop. Nashoba slowly expanded its operation to include off-premise sales. In 2003, it received the first Farmer's Distiller license ever issued in Massachusetts. With the addition of the enthusiastic Roesch, the brewery now seems poised to continue its expansion.

Reserved on the outside, Roesch is a bit of a rebel on the inside. A while back, Nashoba was invited to attend a Boston beer festival focusing on extreme beers. While other breweries started dry-hopping their regular offerings with ungodly amounts of hops or threw their beers into a whiskey barrel to make them extreme, Roesch went medieval on it all, literally. Instead of simply tweaking a house recipe, he decided to recreate an ale as it would have tasted in the late thirteenth century. Modern ales ferment and condition an average of two weeks before consumption; Roesch brewed his Medieval Ale a mere five days before the festival. As historic ales were made solely from grain, water, and yeast, Roesch added no hops to his beer. Without any natural or artificial preservatives, the beers were designed for nearly immediate consumption. The resulting ale was disturbingly murky, smelled like A-1 Steak Sauce, and was not particularly palatable. Roesch himself admitted that the beer was beyond its prime by the time he served it at the fest. Despite its deficiencies in the taste department, I give the brewer credit for having the guts and creativity to produce such an unusual beer.

Beyond occasional experimentation, Roesch plans to reconnect the brewery and the estate by using some of the latter's fruits in his future releases. He hopes to cultivate some wood barrels to lay down a wheat beer on top of thirty pounds of locally grown peaches, inoculating the beer with a commercially available lambic yeast strain to create a distinctive, traditional fruit beer.

Beer Works

61 Brookline Avenue
Boston, Massachusetts 02215
Tel. (617) 536-BEER
www.beerworks.net

★ **Best Beer:** Back Bay IPA. While Beer Works brews many different beer styles, including several eccentric selections, this classic is a staple I enjoy every time I visit Beer Works. The aroma is sharply bitter, of no particular hop variety—just aggressive. With its distinctive, copper color, the Back Bay IPA is full of grapefruit and piney flavors, mixed with a hefty dose of caramel malt. Not over the top, the Back Bay IPA is a great example of the style. It won a bronze medal in the competitive India Pale Ale category at the 1997 Great American Beer Festival.

Opened: April 1992.

Type: Brewpub.

Owner: Steve and Joe Slesar.

Brewer: Jodi Andrews (Fenway), Herb Lindtveit (Canal Street), and Scott Houghton (Salem).

Brewing system: 16-barrel DME brewhouse (Fenway), 16-barrel JV Northwest brewhouse (Canal Street), and 16-barrel Pub Brewing Systems brewhouse (Salem).

Amount produced: 5,500 barrels.

First beer: Boston Red.

Flagship beers: Fenway Pale Ale and Boston Red.

Year-round beers: While many of the recipes are common to each location, the names change to reflect the environs. The following names correspond to the original Fenway location: Boston Red, Back Bay IPA, Bunker Hill Bluebeery, Curley's Irish Stout, and Bambino Ale.

Seasonal beers: Too many to attempt a complete list, but includes the 9 Alarm Amber, Accelerator Double Bock, Allston Mild, Bay State ESB, Beantown Nut Brown Ale, Biere De Mars, Boston Common, Victory Bock, Buck Eye Oatmeal Stout, Bullfinch Bitter, Centennial Alt, Double Vision (dubbel), Hub Dry Draft, Imperial Stout, Kenmore Kolsch, Haymarket Hefe-Weizen, Mad Hops Double IPA, Triple Gold Belgian Ale, Peanut Butter Porter, Watermelon Ale, and West End Wit.

Tours: By appointment only.

Beer to go: Growlers are available at all locations.

Food: While Beer Works focuses on beer, its owners also take food quite seriously; food accounts for 50 percent of sales. The Beer Works menu usually pitches straight down the middle of the plate, with an occasional curve ball. Lots of burgers, salads, pizzas, and sandwiches. Also, give the mako shark skewers, marinated in Raspbeery Ale, a try. The spicy chicken sandwich is excellent.

Amenities: Limited on-street parking available for both Boston locations. The subway (MBTA) is a good way to reach both the Fenway and Canal Street locations (see Directions). There is a small parking lot next to the Salem location and on-street parking is available. Full liquor licenses.

Other attractions: Each of the locations is near areas of interest. The Fenway location is of course located across the street from historic Fenway Park, home of the 2004 World Series champions, the Boston Red Sox. The lines are long before and after Red Sox games, but while the game is in progress, seating is available and the pub remains a lively place to watch the game. The Canal Street location is across from the TDBanknorth Garden, home to the Celtics and Bruins. The Salem operation is near Salem Common and has a front row seat for the madness of the Halloween season.

Pub hours: Fenway: daily, 11:30 A.M. to 1 A.M. Canal Street: daily, 11:30 A.M. to 2 A.M. Salem: daily, 11:30 A.M. to 12:30 A.M.

Directions: The Fenway location is directly across from Fenway Park. Take the Green Line of the MBTA to the Kenmore Square stop, then walk up Brookline Avenue toward Fenway Park. The Canal Street location is a short walk from both the North Station stop on the Green Line of the MBTA, and the TDBanknorth Garden (or whatever it's called by the time this book is released). 112 Canal Street, Boston, Massachusetts 02114, tel. (617) 896-BEER. The Salem brewpub is located a few blocks from Derby Wharf near the waterfront area. 278 Derby Street, Salem, Massachusetts 01970, tel. (978) 745–BEER.

Born and raised in Canada, the Slesar brothers watched their father drink Labatt's IPA and treat beer as an important part of the social fabric of life. Steve Slesar moved to Boston in 1987 after finishing his college degree. He took a job at Commonwealth Brewing Company as a busboy, eventually working his way up to head brewer. Across town, Joe Slesar, a graduate of Cornell with a degree in hospitality, was learning the brewing trade at Harpoon. While Commonwealth focused on traditional, English-style ales, Steve wanted to brew more assertive, American-style beers. The brothers slowly developed a plan to go out on their own.

They originally planned to name their brewpub the Planetary Fermentation Works and follow a world theme in the establishment. The pair eventually rethought the name and settled on Boston Beer Works. Almost immediately, they ran into a legal challenge from the Boston Beer Company, makers of the Samuel Adams beer brand. After eighteen months of litigation and more than one hundred thousand dollars in legal fees, the United States Court of Appeals for the First Circuit upheld the new brewpub's right to use the name.

The Slesar brothers now have the makings of a mini–brewpub empire in Eastern Massachusetts. In 1992, they renovated a vacant building across from Fenway Park and turned it into one of the nation's top ten brewpubs in total production. Building on this success, the brothers took over the ailing Old Salem Brewing Company in the Witch City and reopened it as the Salem Beer Works. By 2001, the company was so profitable that its owners bought a large, multifloor building on Canal Street near North Station. They installed a third location downstairs, a sprawling sixteen-thousand-square-foot restaurant spread over two floors, with the top floors used for office and leasing space.

The overall design theme in all Beer Works locations is a mix of natural and industrial elements. At the flagship Fenway location, the owners implemented a "naked and true" concept that keeps the space very open. The signature black-and-silver diamond plating covers much of the restaurant, from the bar to the bathrooms. The Salem location offers an open kitchen and lots of rich woods, including a U-shaped area with high-backed booths, called the Brewer's Den. The Canal Street location is wide open and full of brick, with perhaps the most industrial feeling of the three sites. At each site, the brewhouse is prominently displayed.

Each pub maintains an impressive assortment of fifteen beers on tap at any one time, born from more than fifty company recipes. As a result, the brewers remain tremendously busy and each location brews several days per week. While the company sets some standard recipes common to all three locations, the Slesar brothers prefer to give their brewers (whom Steve refers to as "the artists") opportunities to experiment. When Steve approached brewer Jodi Andrews with an idea for a peanut butter beer, she must have thought he was nuts. Concerned about the effects the fatty substance would have on the head retention in the final product, Andrews first tried dehydrated peanut butter. The resulting product was mildly reminiscent in the flavor but with no peanut notes in the aroma. For the second batch, she added store-bought Teddie Peanut Butter. The resulting beer, a porter, possessed subtle nut flavors with more obvious aromatics. As the beer was hellaciously difficult to clean up afterwards, the brewers now rely on African peanut oil added directly to the boil and conditioning tank to achieve the nuanced nut flavors and delicate aromas.

Beer Works's most famous beer, however, has to be its blueberry offering. The Bluebeery Ale possesses both a pleasing, fruit flavor and a fascinating visual element. The brewers age a base golden ale on top of a foundation of blueberries. To complete the process, the bartender pours two spoonfuls of fresh blueberries into each pint. The result is a cascade of dancing blueberries that bob up and down in the glass as they float against currents of carbonation. Though you might think it bad form after you finish the pint, put away your pride and dig into the bottom of the glass with a spoon to capture the final berries. As this ale accounts for 15 percent of total beer sales, you'll be in good company.

The Boston Beer Company

30 Germania Street
Boston (Jamaica Plain), Massachusetts 02130
Tel. (617) 368–5000
www.samadams.com

Take pride in your beer."

★ **Best Beer:** Double Bock. At nearly 9 percent alcohol, this version of the storied German style is a big, boozy customer made with half a pound of malt per bottle. It pours with a deep chestnut color and an intriguing off-beige, creamy head. The nose is all-malt with the slightest hints of German noble hops. The first sip shows this robust beer means business, with a full body and a maltiness that washes over your palate. As it warms, the beer exhibits some light, fruity flavors. Often said, but still a fact: this is a true meal in a bottle.

Opened: April 1985.

Type: Brewery.

Owner: Publicly traded corporation. Martin Roper, president and CEO.

Brewer: Jim Koch.

Brewing system: 12-barrel Liquid Assets Brewing Systems brewhouse.

Amount produced: 1.2 million barrels (including contract production).

First beer: Samuel Adams Boston Lager.

Flagship beer: Samuel Adams Boston Lager.

Year-round beers: Samuel Adams Boston Lager, Sam Adams Light, Cherry Wheat, Cream Stout, Hefeweizen, Pale Ale, Boston Ale, Black Lager, and Scotch Ale.

Seasonal beers: White Ale, Summer Ale, Holiday Porter, Winter Lager, Double Bock, Octoberfest, Cranberry Lambic, and Old Fezziwig Ale (winter warmer).

Tours: Regular tours run Thursday at 2 p.m.; Friday at 2 p.m. and 5:30 p.m.; Saturday at noon, 1 p.m., and 2 p.m. From May through August, there is an additional tour on Wednesday at 2 p.m.

Beer to go: None.

Amenities: For those who choose to drive, parking is available in the brewery's lot. The brewery can be a challenge to reach by car, so I recommend taking public transportation (see directions). The tour costs $2 and the money is donated to a local charity. The tour hotline can be reached at tel. (617) 368–5080.

Other attractions: Perhaps the most authentic Irish pub in Boston, Doyle's Café is a must-visit during any trip to the city. Doyle's is a short distance from the Boston Beer Company, whose tour staff will provide you with printed directions to Doyle's after your tour. Open since 1882, Doyle's has long been a favorite of city, regional, and national politicians; it also has the distinction of serving the first pints of Samuel Adams Boston Lager. A feel of authenticity reigns here, in stark contrast to the prefabricated pubs that litter downtown Boston. The restaurant is spread over four rooms, all named after politicians. Be sure to check out a large mural in the main room that depicts many colorful pols sharing a beer and a few laughs inside these very walls. Doyle's has a solid selection of tap beers, including several Samuel Adams products, and an impressive selection of reasonably priced, single-malt Scotches. Open daily, 9 a.m. to 1 a.m. 3484 Washington Street, Jamaica Plain, Massachusetts 02130, tel. (617) 524–2345.

Directions: The brewery is located in the Jamaica Plain neighborhood of Boston, and is near the Stonybrook stop on the Orange Line of the MBTA subway. A map is necessary to successfully traverse the confusing area by car.

You probably already know the story behind Jim Koch, the founder of the Boston Beer Company and Samuel Adams Boston Lager, the most popular craft beer in America, and how he transformed a small business into one of the largest brewing companies in America. After countless retellings, Koch's story is now firmly ensconced in beer lore. A sixth-generation brewmaster, Koch allegedly found the recipe for his Boston Lager in his family's attic, then began the company by peddling his new beer bar to bar in a briefcase. The company is the only craft brewery to have broken the one-million-barrel mark and now brings in more than two hundred million dollars annually in sales.

With its chosen name and location, the modern Boston Beer Company fuses together two storied brewing histories. The first incarnation of the Boston Beer Company opened in 1828, when a group of investors opened a brewery on D Street in the heart of South Boston; it was one of the first stable breweries to operate in the commonwealth. After Prohibition, the brewery started up again and operated for twenty years before folding in 1956. On the other side of the city, in the neighborhoods of Roxbury and Jamaica Plain, German immigrants flooded the neighborhoods during the early part of the nineteenth century. Their influence can be seen in such street names as Germania and Bismarck, and in the slew of breweries that once dotted this area. These immigrants also brought with them a love of lager beer, which the local breweries happily brewed for them. In 1870, Rudolf F. Haffenreffer began operating on the site now occupied by the modern BBC. Haffenreffer brewed lager beers for fellow German immigrants, using water from the aquifers of Stony Brook. The brewery was the oldest continually operated brewery in American before finally closing in 1964.

At the pilot brewery in Jamaica Plain, the modern Boston Beer Company pays homage to Boston's rich brewing history. When it moved to the location of Haffenreffer's brewery in the mid-1980s, Boston Beer found a long-neglected, dilapidated site. With the help of a neighborhood preservation group, Boston Beer rejuvenated the languishing structure, which is on the National Register of Historic Places. More than twenty-five thousand people—called "pilgrims" by Koch—visit the brewery each year. The tour starts in a small welcome room filled with thoughtful displays on the histories of both the company and brewing in Boston. A map shows the range of breweries, forty-five total at its peak, that made Jamaica Plain and Roxbury the true centers of brewing in the city.

The tour also does a nice job of illustrating the history of beer and brewing. In the brewhouse, tour guides encourage visitors to smell fistfuls of hops and to pop barley grains into their mouths. Visitors can also walk through a giant, glass-lined aging tank in the first room of the tour. During my tour, Koch excitedly points out various details of its construction and expresses amazement over how difficult a job it would have been to climb through the small manhole with a flashlight and a brush to clean the interiors after each batch.

When he passes by the portrait of the man who adorns every bottle of the brewery's beer, Koch pauses for a moment of reflection. Koch heralds Samuel Adams as a "forgotten figure of the Revolution" and he celebrates the patriot as "a provocateur who fanned the flames of the Revolution." Koch selected Adams as the icon for his brewery not only for his historic contributions, but also because of his ties to the brewing industry. Although there exists convincing evidence that Adams unsuccessfully ran a family malting business passed down through several generations, there is little to support the common misconception that Adams was a brewer himself. A maltster is a person who makes malt from barley and then provides it to brewers, who use it to make beer. The distinction is important, much like the difference between a miller and a baker.

Koch originally intended to brew Samuel Adams from the old Haffenreffer brewery, but a sober examination of the site and its largely residential location soon rendered that plan unfeasible. Because of the high start-up costs, Koch chose to contract brew his Samuel Adams Lager at the Pittsburgh Brewing Company—a decision that remains controversial more than twenty years later. Boston Beer continues to brew its beers at a handful of breweries around the country, including the Hudepohl-Schoenling Brewing Company in Ohio. Originally from the area, Koch purchased the Cincinnati-based brewery in 1997; it now produces about two-thirds of BBC's total barrelage.

Though the company occasionally takes flack, either from the industry for some of Koch's more colorful antics, or from beer geeks for allegedly selling out by contract brewing some of his beer, Boston Beer remains steadfastly dedicated to producing good beer. Beyond his unquestionable role as a pioneer of craft brewing, Koch remains driven by a desire to push the boundaries of beer. As the country's largest craft brewer, Boston Beer could simply withdraw from the world of beer geeks and settle for servicing its shareholders. Instead, it continues to play a leading, innovative role in advancing the good-beer scene.

The pilot brewery in Jamaica Plain is the headquarters for the company's research and development operations. The master brewers here perform a variety of tasks, from testing new shipments of malts and hops, to creating specialty releases. With the release of Triple Bock in 1994, Boston Beer started stretching the common understanding of what constitutes beer. The brewery's subsequent releases of Millennium and then Utopias, which boasts an alcohol level of more than 50 proof, continue to set new standards for the industry. The brewers here also produce occasional single-batch test products that are available only in the brewery's tasting room and for special accounts. During the tour, you can catch glimpses of wooden hogshead casks resting off in a corner, quietly aging upcoming releases.

Throughout the tour, colorful flags promote the company's many brewing awards. In the display cases, you can see artifacts of corporate history, including the first sales slip (from Doyle's) and bottles from the earliest batches of Samuel Adams. The tour ends in the brewery's well-appointed tasting room. Guides encourage visitors to sit together at the long, communal tables, while they pass out pitchers for pouring samples. The atmosphere is jovial and visitors thoroughly enjoy the anticipation of finding out what special treats the brewery has on tap for them.

Koch is quick to point out Boston Beer's unique position among American brewers. "We have all of the resources of a big brewery," he says. "Yet we can do the things a little brewery can't do and a bigger brewery doesn't want to do."

Harpoon Brewery

306 Northern Avenue
Boston, Massachusetts 02210
Tel. (888) HARPOON
www.harpoonbrewery.com

★ **Best Beer:** Harpoon Munich Dark. Introduced in 1998, the Munich Dark is one of the last remaining old-guard Harpoon beers. Aromas of toasted grain are met with similar flavors on the first sip. As the beer warms up, slight caramel flavors emerge and the slight hop bite fades away. Complex in flavor, the Munich Dark is a much-welcomed dark offering from Harpoon.

Opened: April 1987.

Type: Brewery.

Owner: Private corporation. Richard Doyle, chairman and CEO.

Brewer: Al Marzi, vice president of brewing operations.

Brewing system: 120-barrel Huppman brewhouse.

Amount produced: 59,000 barrels. 66,000-barrel total capacity.

First beer: Harpoon Ale.

Flagship beer: Harpoon IPA.

Year-round beers: Harpoon IPA, Harpoon UFO, Harpoon Ale, and Harpoon Munich Dark.

Seasonal beers: Summer Ale, Winter Warmer, Hibernian Ale, Octoberfest, and 100 Barrel Series.

Tours: The Boston facility is open year-round for tastings and guided tours from a platform overlooking the brewhouse. Closed Sunday and Monday. Tours are scheduled Tuesday through Thursday at 3 p.m; Friday and Saturday at 1 P.M. and 3 P.M. A small brewery store overlooking the brewhouse sells a variety of Harpoon-related merchandise. Closed Sunday and Monday. Open Tuesday through Friday, 11 A.M. to 6 P.M.; and Saturday, 11 A.M. to 5 P.M. Tastings, tours, and the brewery store are not available on major holidays and during Harpoon's beer festivals.

Beer to go: The whole range of Harpoon products are for sale at the brewery, including kegs, 64-ounce growlers, cases, 12-packs, and 22-ounce bottles. You can even pick up selections from Harpoon's line of handcrafted sodas, including root beer, orange and cream, and vanilla cream.

Amenities: For tours, limited parking is available in the brewery's lot. For festivals, when the brewery covers its parking lot with a large tent, you would be wise to take public transportation or park in the lot across the street from the brewery.

Other attractions: The Boston brewery hosts three widely attended events during the year to coincide with the release of three of its seasonal products: St. Patrick's Day for the Hibernian Ale, Brewstock for the Summer Ale, and Octoberfest for the Octoberfest Ale. Tickets, which presently cost $12, are available at the door for each event and come with a pint glass. The brewery sponsors a variety of musical acts for each festival and its beers are available for purchase, at a price strangely higher than you would pay in downtown Boston. Be advised, these festivals are not particularly safe-havens for beer geeks to sniff and swirl their beers. The music, especially at the summer festival, is often deafening, the place gets packed, and the young crowd is there to party.

Directions: Harpoon's Boston site is located on Northern Avenue on the waterfront at the Marine Industrial Park just after the Fish Pier and the Bank of America Pavilion. For the MBTA, head to South Station and follow signs for Silver Line-Waterfront. Take the SL2 or SL3 bus to the first stop.

When three Harvard classmates joined together in 1986 to open a brewery in an industrial section of Boston's waterfront, they had little idea their venture would wind up as the largest craft brewery in New England. With the release of their first Harpoon Ale in June 1987, Richard Doyle, Dan Kenary, and George Legeti became the first people to brew and bottle beer commercially in Boston since the Haffenreffer brewery closed in 1964.

From the start, the three young partners knew they wanted a bricks-and-mortar brewery physically located within Boston proper, a point of differentiation they would use to needle Jim Koch and the Boston Beer Company in their early days. With the general unavailability of suitable commercial space, the partners selected an old shipbuilding warehouse as their home. Despite the tight confines of the brewery on Northern Avenue, Harpoon has never known another home. As the company grew, the owners simply expanded the brewery. The company originally undertook its own bottling operations, but space issues forced it to contract out to the F. X. Matt Brewing Company in Utica, New York. Harpoon regained control of its bottling operations in 1994 and slowly enlarged its operation. As described in detail in the Vermont chapter, Harpoon purchased the Catamount Brewery's facility in Windsor in 2000 to bolster its production and ease the burden on its maxed-out home brewery.

Entering its second decade of life, Harpoon is trying to answer the familiar question of what it wants to be when it grows up. Between the Boston and Windsor, Vermont, facilities, Harpoon is second only to Anheuser-Busch in terms of production in New England. The brewery continues to grow at a fast clip, with 730 percent growth between 1992 and 2002, and it hopes to double production in the next five years. The brewery has pared down its offerings in recent years, eliminating a handful of niche products that were popular with beer geeks but didn't sell well to the general public. New Englanders and those in Harpoon's limited distribution markets continue to fuel the brewery's growth, while beer geeks have started to grumble that Harpoon is too "mainstream."

The Harpoon operation is indeed pretty slick, with striking artwork, catchy marketing slogans ("Love Beer. Love Life. Harpoon."), and professional execution from start to finish. While a small contingent of beer geeks might not think it cool for a brewery to talk about consistency and having a focused product portfolio, such an approach is necessary for a brewery seeking to progress from adolescence to adulthood. Few like to take on added responsibility, nevertheless beer drinkers hate a bad batch or, even worse, a closed brewery.

For his part, cofounder Rich Doyle laughs at the criticism. For him, Harpoon was born from his own dissatisfaction as a beer-drinking consumer. After college and before attending business school at Harvard, Doyle traveled around Europe. Like so many before him, Doyle discovered that American brewers failed to offer any real selection for consumers. Upon his return, he had trouble finding domestic products worth drinking. From this all-too-common experience, the idea for Harpoon was born.

It wasn't until the launch of a new product, however, that the brewery really found success. Doyle knew something special was happening when the Harpoon IPA made its debut as a summer seasonal in 1993. "Everything about it just clicked," Doyle says. Because of its popularity with consumers, the Harpoon IPA entered year-round production the next year and quickly overtook Harpoon Ale as the brewery's flagship product. Doyle notes with a laugh that the sudden success of the Harpoon IPA turned the brewery into an "overnight success—seven years late."

Doyle and his partners have great plans to take Harpoon into the future. In October 2002, the brewery held a dedication ceremony, presided over by Boston Mayor Tom Menino, for the arrival of its new $1.5-million brewhouse equipment. What the brewery lacks in ground space, it makes up for in vertical space; the huge, 120-barrel fermenters tower over the brewing floor. The brewery also reached out to the beer geek audience with its initiation of the 100 Barrel Series, a release of single-batch, specialty products. Harpoon remains the biggest craft beer player in New England. Its ability to navigate the next few years will prove crucial both to its own future and as a beacon for the health of the craft-brewing industry as a whole.

Rock Bottom Restaurant and Brewery

115 Stuart Street
Boston, Massachusetts 02116
Tel. (617) 742-BREW
www.rockbottom.com

★ **Best Beer:** Cinco de Mayo Jalapeno Lager. Brewer Scott Brunelle originally created the beer for a Cinco de Mayo beer dinner. I first discovered this spicy beer (brewed at the Braintree location) during the 2003 Great American Beer Festival in Denver. That year, beers from several Rock Bottom locations thoroughly impressed the crowd. The beers made an impression on the judges as well; Brunelle won a bronze medal in the competitive Herb and Spice Beer category for this particular beer. The Jalapeno Lager, brewed with actual jalapenos, shouldn't scare you. It's actually quite delicious, with a sharply piquant aroma, like nacho cheese, that tingles your nose and intense bursts of spiciness that gently needle your throat on the way down. The Jalapeno Lager is a real treat, very drinkable, and radically different than most any other beer you will ever have. It's also a great accompaniment for, of all things, spicy food. The two play off one another and serve to both confuse and delight the palate. Keep an open mind and give the beer a try. You might be surprised how much you enjoy it.

Opened: 2001 (under new ownership).

Type: Brewpub.

Owner: Rock Bottom Restaurants, Inc.

Brewers: Gerry O'Connell (Boston) and Scott Brunelle (Braintree).

Brewing system: 15-barrel Pub Brewing Systems brewhouse (Boston) and 15-barrel JV Northwest (Braintree).

Amount produced: 1,500 barrels (Boston) and 1,050 barrels (Braintree). The entire chain produces 40,000 barrels per year.

First beer: Munich Gold.

Flagship beer: Munich Gold.

Year-round beers: Lumpy Dog Light Lager, Munich Gold, Improper Hopper IPA, North Star Amber, and one rotating dark selection.

Seasonal beers: Boston Location: Big Foot Stout, Black Rock Porter, Blackberry Wheat, Scotch Ale, Bottoms Up Brown Ale, Bourbon Stout, Boylston Street Bock, Cleland's Scotch Ale, Double Barrel IPA, Freedom Trail Stout, Hubaweizen,

Liquid Happiness (strong ale), Mardi Gras Lager, Maximus Belgian Strong Pale Ale, Mid Winter Mild, Old Curmudgeon (barleywine), Old Ironside Stout, Rock Bottom Bitter, Rock Bottom Framboise, Rudolph Red (winter warmer), Shea's Extra Stout, Tea Party Porter, Up Town Brown, Whitey's Ale (witbier), and Winter's Over Wheat.

Braintree Location: American Dream IPA, Anniversary Ale (pale ale), Black Dolphin (schwarzbier), Burnie's Best Bitter, Czar's Nightmare Imperial Stout, Czechmate Pils, Cinco de Mayo Jalapeno Lager, Deb's Blueberry Ale, English Pub Draught, Five Malt Alt, Special Reserve Raspberry Lambic, Peach Lambic, Red Sock Bock, Sheehan Stout, and Whitey Belgian (witbier).

Tours: By appointment or if the brewer is on-site.

Beer to go: Table talkers announce the availability of growlers, which are popular here.

Food: The menus are pretty consistent from location to location, with traditional pub fare done in a clean fashion and with ample portions.

Pub Hours: Daily, 11:30 A.M. to 1 A.M.

Amenities: The Rock Bottom chain has two locations in the Boston area, one in the city's theatre district and the other in the southern suburb of Braintree. 250 Granite Street, Braintree, Massachusetts 02184, tel. (781) 356–2739. On-street parking near the Boston location is very difficult and the lots can be expensive. Public transportation is recommended (see directions). There is ample parking near the Braintree location, which is located next to the South Shore Plaza mall. Both locations have full liquor licenses. As Massachusetts law does not allow bars to offer happy-hour specials on alcohol, each Rock Bottom location simply reduces the price on one of its beers every week and this effectively becomes the beer-of-the-week special.

Other attractions: After a busy day marching the Freedom Trail or lounging around Boston Common, head to Jacob Wirth's, Boston's second-oldest restaurant. Located just down the street from Rock Bottom in Boston, this German beer hall dates back to 1868 and is more reminiscent of old Chicago saloons than classic New England taverns. Unlike many of Boston's historic sites, Jacob Wirth's retains much of its original character. From behind the restaurant's ornate, dark-wood bar, bartenders sling liters of twenty-eight different draft beers and serve a selection of well-crafted German dishes from the fine menu. The location also holds occasional beer dinners and other events. Jake Wirth imported Rhine wines from his homeland and served as the New England distributor for a range of beers, including Anheuser-Busch's lagers, Robert Smith's India Pale Ale, and the products of the local Narragansett Brewing Company. Before you step out the door, ask the staff for a free copy of *A Seidel for Jake Wirth*, a wonderful, small pamphlet detailing this institution's grand history and its faithful servant, Fritz Früh (who on the death of Prohibition reportedly counseled, "A good glass of beer never hurt anybody"). Jacob Wirth Co., 31–37 Stuart Street, Boston, Massachusetts

02116, tel. (617) 338–8586. Open Sunday and Monday, 11:30 A.M. to 8 P.M.; Tuesday through Thursday, 11:30 A.M. to 11:30 P.M.; Friday and Saturday, 11:30 A.M. to midnight.

Directions: The Boston location is near the Boylston Street stop on the Green Line of the MBTA. It sits on Stuart Street just off Tremont Street, one block south of Boston Common in the theatre district. The Braintree location is south of Boston, nestled in the South Shore Plaza Shopping Mall near the intersection of I-93 and Route 37.

With almost thirty U.S. locations and $264 million in annual sales, you could be forgiven for dismissing America's largest brewpub group as a soulless corporate giant comprised of cookie-cutter franchise restaurants. You might even think the food is average, the décor is all the same, greetings are scripted, and the beers are a mere gimmick. You might even be inclined to head somewhere else. And that works fine by Rock Bottom's loyal customers, myself included, as it assures us a table and a ready pint after a hard day of work.

Frank B. Day laid the groundwork for Rock Bottom when he opened his first Old Chicago restaurant in Boulder, Colorado, in 1976. When this location proved successful, Day slowly started building new outlets across the country. In 1991, near its headquarters in downtown Denver, his company opened the first Rock Bottom brewery. The concept proved quite popular and the company quickly expanded to other markets. As other breweries stumbled, Rock Bottom stepped in. One such company, the Brew Moon chain of brewpubs, had three locations in the Boston area before filing for Chapter 11 bankruptcy. The Brew Moon operations possessed a funky spirit, with abstract, artsy interior designs and an emphasis on the restaurant side of the trade. By contrast, Rock Bottom heavily focuses on the beer angle. In November 2000, Rock Bottom acquired the Brew Moon company and slowly converted the locations to fit its own design. With the exception of the June 2003 closure of its underperforming Harvard Square location, Rock Bottom's takeover of the fumbling chain was successful.

When Rock Bottom bought Brew Moon, it changed the concept but didn't totally clean house. Rock Bottom assumed the leases, retrained the staff, and created new beers on the existing brewing equipment. Irish-born brewmaster Gerry O'Connell of the Boston location is a holdover from the Brew Moon days. He reports that the company asks him to brew a few styles of beer but doesn't waste time looking over his shoulder on each batch.

Many people who visit Rock Bottom's Theater District location have no idea the place is a brewpub. Customers routinely ask for Budweiser and are puzzled when patient staffers explain why that beer, and others like it, are not available here. Both locations are open in design, with high ceilings, and decorated with a mildly outdoorsy theme. The bar area overlooks the gleaming brewing systems, with fermenters and conditioning tanks spread throughout other parts of the restaurant. The "Fresh Beers" chalkboards announce the available beers and describe their particular features, the days they were brewed, and their specific gravities and alcohol levels. The menus and beer sampler trays each do a laudable job of explaining the beers and suggesting pairings with the food.

Besides allowing the local brewers flexibility with the common corporate flavors, Rock Bottom also turns the brewing staff loose to create their own recipes under the Brewmaster's Choice offering. Both Scott Brunelle and Gerry O'Connell brew a wide variety of specialty releases throughout the year and there is usually something new on tap every week. Both have recently taken to experimenting with barrel-aging their beers and with the occasional assertive, tart, and lip-smacking fruit beer.

Cambridge Brewing Company

Hampshire Street—One Kendall Square
Cambridge, Massachusetts 02139
(617) 494–1994
www.cambrew.com

★ **Best Beer:** Benevolence. Perhaps no New England brewer ever deserved a medal more than when Will Meyers won silver in the Experimental category at the 2004 Great American Beer Festival with his awe-inspiring Benevolence. This Belgian-style dark ale is easily one of the brewer's best and most challenging creations. Created as part of Meyers's ongoing barrel-aged project, Benevolence is mind-numbingly complex with a wild array of hard-to-define characteristics. The beer plays on all keys, balancing acidity, oakiness, and dull fruit flavors such as cherries and dates. The aroma is rich and full of hot alcohol, and the beer manages a slightly tangy and intriguing finish. Benevolence is easily one of the best beers produced in New England.

Opened: May 1989.

Type: Brewpub.

Owner: Phil Bannatyne.

Brewer: Will Meyers.

Brewing system: 10-barrel Pub Brewing Systems brewhouse.

Amount produced: 1,500 barrels. 2,000-barrel total capacity.

First beer: Cambridge Amber.

Flagship beer: Cambridge Amber.

Year-round beers: Regatta Golden, Cambridge Amber, Tall Tale Pale, and Charles River Porter.

Seasonal beers: Great Pumpkin, Winter Ale, Vienna Gold, Hefeweizen, "The Wind Cried Mari . . ." Scottish Heather Ale, 80 Schilling Scottish Ale, Abbey Normal (dubbel), American Red Ale, Anniversary Ale (ESB), Bannatyne's Scotch Ale, Beantowne Espresso Stout, Benevolence, Best Bitter, Biere De Garde, Big Man Ale, Bitchin Bitter, Bitchin Special Bitter, Blackout Oatmeal Stout, Blunderbuss Barley Wine, BMF Stout, Bodacious Bitter, Cerise Cassee American Sour Ale, Dunkles Weizen, Endless Summer IPA, Half Wit, Honey-Ginger Ale, Red God IPA, Saison du CBC, Tripel Threat, Vienna Lager, Weekapaug Gruit Ale, and Winter IPA.

Tours: Tours by appointment or upon request if the brewer is around.

Beer to go: Growlers are available for purchase.

Food: Beer is often integrated into the pub's menu. A reduction of the porter is used as a sauce for the filet mignon tips. The create-your-own brick-oven pizzas are an especially solid choice.

Amenities: On-street parking is tight in this area. There is a pay parking lot next to the nearby Kendall Square Theater. You can quietly sneak into the movie theater's lobby and validate your parking ticket to receive a reduced price, but don't tell them I sent you. The brewpub is also a short walk from the Kendall Square stop on the Red Line of the MBTA. Full liquor license.

Other attractions: Although it isn't really located anywhere near the Cambridge Brewing Company, the funky and eclectic Other Side Café is one of Boston's great, unheralded beer bars. Located directly across from the Hynes Convention Center stop on the Green Line of the MBTA and at the crossroads of Massachusetts Avenue and Newbury Street, the pub is a short ride from Cambridge and well worth the trip. While nearby Bukowski's gets all the attention, the Other Side Café defines cool without the poseur's compulsion to flaunt it. The pub offers nine well-selected tap beers, equally split between imports and domestic craft beers, and a wide selection of bottled and canned beers. The beer menu is informative and well written, including this description of Lone Star Beer: "Originated in San Antonio in 1883; still yellow, cold, and wet." The staff is friendly and refreshingly honest, and the clientele, often comprised of students from the nearby Berklee School of Music, is always colorful. The menu features wonderfully fresh foods, including many vegetarian plates. 407 Newbury Street, Boston, Massachusetts 02136, tel. (617) 536–9477. Open Monday through Thursday, 11 A.M. to midnight; Friday, 11:30 A.M. to 1 A.M.; Saturday, 11 A.M. to 1 A.M.; and Sunday, noon to midnight.

Pub hours: Open Monday through Friday, 11:30 A.M. to 12:45 A.M.; Saturday, noon to 12:45 A.M.; Sunday, 11:30 A.M. to 9 P.M.

Directions: Located in the Kendall Square neighborhood of Cambridge. Look for the brewery in the back left corner of the complex at One Kendall Square near the intersection of Hampshire and Broadway Streets. From the Red Line MBTA station at Kendall, walk northwest up Broadway and veer to the right at the light after the train tracks.

★ ★ ★

A fitting slogan for the Cambridge Brewing Company might be, "Where beer geeks and real geeks meet for drinks." Set in the middle of Kendall Square's bustling high-tech corridor, the Cambridge Brewing Company has seen firsthand the transformation of this once heavily immigrant-occupied neighborhood. The circa-1890s building formerly housed the American Woven Hose Factory, a manufacturer of fire hoses. Retaining much of its original charm, the restored factory contains a mix of old brick, bare beams, and exposed ductwork.

While living in the San Francisco area, owner Phil Bannatyne saw the craft brewing movement develop from its infancy. He fell in love with brewpubs after a friend opened the Roaring Rock Brewery in Berkeley. Now known as the Triple Rock Brewery and Alehouse, that brewpub is the oldest surviving operation in America today. Bannatyne liked the funky feel of Berkeley and wanted to open an establishment in a neighborhood with a similar attitude. The owner eventually settled on Cambridge because of its young crowd and artsy atmosphere.

In the spring of 1989, few people had heard of the brewpub concept. After researching possible locations, Bannatyne selected the old factory building as much for its charm as for the local zoning board's polite suggestion that he locate his weird new restaurant-brewery in an industrial section of town. When Cambridge Brewing opened, it was the second brewpub in greater Boston and only the fifth in all of New England.

The crowd is an eclectic mix of students from the nearby Massachusetts Institute of Technology, young biotech professionals, dedicated beer lovers, and theatregoers seeking a quick meal and drink before the show. Under two large, convex skylights, the bartenders serve up popular 100-ounce towers of beer to parties of three or more, from which happy drinkers use a built-in spigot to pour their own pints. In the summer, seating extends to the outdoor patio in the Kendall Square courtyard.

The beer at Cambridge Brewing is among the best you'll sample in all of New England. Brewer Will Meyers has been here since 1993 and Bannatyne gives him free rein to create some distinctive beers. While the four primary beers remain pretty constant, the seasonal and specialty releases really spice things up, ranging from highly hopped American pale ales to wild takes on Belgian-style ales. Each one is well and thoughtfully crafted, casting aside experimentation simply for its own sake. The seasonals remain quite popular with patrons, including the annual Great Pumpkin ale for Halloween, which accounts for a whopping fifteen batches per year. Cambridge also frequently offers aged batches from years past, including vertical flights of the Blunderbuss Barleywine.

On the topic of experimentation, Meyers admits that he "gets to play around a lot." Tucked away in the basement, far from public view, Meyers conducts frequent experiments with a series of wood barrels, including French oak casks. It was here, on a dirt floor, that Meyers's classic Belgian-influenced masterpiece Benevolence was born.

Cambridge hosts a variety of special events throughout the year, including a series of brewer's dinners and a new cask ale every Tuesday evening. As a Cantabrigian, I am proud to call Cambridge Brewing my home brewpub.

John Harvard's Brew House

33 Dunster Street
Cambridge, Massachusetts 02138
Tel. (617) 868–3585
www.johnharvards.com

★ **Best Beer:** Three choices here, one for each location: Espresso Stout (Cambridge), Framingham Bock (Framingham), and Presidential Blonde Bock (Manchester). Brian Sanford's rich, malty bock won a gold medal in the Bock category at the 2000 Great American Beer Festival (GABF). Sanford's take on the rarely attempted style is spot-on and delicious. Geoff DeBisschop's delightful Espresso Stout won three straight medals at the GABF, including a gold in 2000 in the Herb and Spiced Beer category. During the brewing process, the brewers blend in espresso to give the well-received beer its distinctive coffee and nutty flavors. The Espresso Stout is the perfect accompaniment to chocolate. Chris Jacques's Presidential Blonde Bock is bright gold in color and loaded with German malt aromas and flavors. A pale bock by style, a touch of bitterness maintains the needed balance.

Opened: 1992.

Type: Brewpub.

Owner: Boston Culinary Group.

Brewer: Geoff DeBisschop (Cambridge), Brian Sanford (Framingham), and Chris Jacques (Manchester, Connecticut).

Brewing system: 14-barrel Pub Brewing Systems brewhouse.

Amount produced: Figures not available.

First beer: St. Valentine's Passion Ale.

Flagship beer: Pale Ale.

Year-round beers: Pale Ale, All American Light Lager, Nut Brown Ale, Dry Irish Stout, and Old Willy India Pale Ale.

Seasonal beers: List varies greatly at each establishment, but generally includes Mid-Winter's Strong Ale, Celtic Red, Queen Bee Honey Beer, Wheat Beer, Summer Blonde, Oktoberfest, and Holiday Red.

Tours: By appointment only.

Beer to go: Growlers are available at all locations, with tabletop signs and empty bottles promoting their sales.

Food: Ever-so-slightly upscale pub fare at reasonable prices, with occasional Asian influences.

Amenities: At the Cambridge location, on-street parking is almost nonexistent in Harvard Square. Take public transportation (Red Line MBTA, or number 1, 68, or 69 bus to Harvard Square). One John Harvard's restaurant is located in the Shopper's World mall in Framingham. 1 Worcester Road, Framingham, Massachusetts 01701, tel. (508) 875–2337. There is ample parking in the mall's lot. The Connecticut restaurant is in a stand-alone building near the Buckland Hills Mall. 1487 Pleasant Valley Road, Manchester, Connecticut 06040, tel. (860) 644–2739. Parking is available in the restaurant's lot. Full liquor license at all locations.

Pub hours: Harvard Square, Cambridge: Monday through Wednesday from 11:30 A.M. to 12:30 A.M.; Thursday through Saturday, 11:30 A.M. to 1:30 A.M.; and Sunday, 11:30 A.M. to midnight. Framingham: Monday through Thursday from 11:30 A.M. to midnight; Friday and Saturday, 11:30 A.M. to 1 A.M.; and Sunday, 11:30 A.M. to 11:30 P.M. Manchester: Monday through Thursday from 11:30 A.M. to 12:30 A.M.; Friday and Saturday, 11:30 A.M. to 1:30 A.M.; and Sunday, 11:30 A.M. to midnight.

Directions: In Cambridge, head north on Massachusetts Avenue (Route 2A) to Harvard Square. The brewpub is a few steps south of the center of the square and the MBTA station.

In Framingham, the restaurant is situated in the back corner of the Shoppers World mall adjacent to Route 9.

In Manchester, Connecticut, exit from I-84 and then go north on Buckland Street. The restaurant is directly across from an opening to the Buckland Hills Mall.

Residing in the heart of Harvard Square, the flagship location of the John Harvard's Brew House chain retains the most charm of all the operations. With its tall pub-table seating, dark woods, and cavelike basement setting, the pub oozes character, even considering the corporate design elements common to all John Harvard's locations. As far as chain operations go, however, John Harvard's at least took a different design route. Each restaurant has a series of backlit stained-glass windows featuring figures of varying cultural importance carrying odd symbolic implements. Grateful Dead leader Jerry Garcia clutches a copy of Tom Wolfe's hippie classic, *The Electric Kool-Aid Acid Test,* along with a staff topped by the arm of a guitar. Nearby, Bobby Orr grips his trusted hockey stick in preparation for another flying leap.

Founded in 1992 by Grenville Byford and Gary Gut, two Harvard graduates, John Harvard's started with a single location and a simple concept: provide a gathering place with good food and fresh beer. Business started slow and John Harvard's didn't even brew its own beer for the first few months, contracting out operations to Harpoon. The slow times didn't last long, however, and within five years Byford and Gut had opened twelve more brewpubs. When things were good, predictions were grand, and the owners planned to open three to five new locations every year. The pair smartly sold the business in 2000, the same year it won the Large Brewpub of the Year Award at the Great American Beer Festival.

After the sale, the corporate history gets pretty sketchy. What is clear, however, is that the brewery fell on bad financial times, closed several of its operations, and scrapped plans for expansion. In mid-2004, the chain quietly entered Chapter 11 bankruptcy, leaving many of its creditors awaiting payment. The chain is now owned by the Boston Culinary Group and presently has ten locations in five states and the District of Columbia.

While the brewing regimen remains scripted and doesn't often change, each brewer retains the freedom to create his own recipes. Each location has its own bright spots, from great stouts in Cambridge to solid lagers in Framingham. Check the restaurant for a sign announcing the offerings, the days the beers were brewed, and their original gravities. Use the board to discern which beers are freshest and order them for the best results.

Cape Ann Brewing Company

27 Commercial Street
Gloucester, Massachusetts 01966
Tel. (978) 281–4782

★ **Best Beer:** Fishermen's Brew. As the brewery's only beer, this is another easy choice. The initial batches of this lager released right after the brewery opened were surprisingly fruity and almost resembled an American wheat beer. Later releases have shown more consistency, with a mild caramel malt flavor mixed with touches of toasted sweetness.

Opened: 2004.

Type: Brewery.

Owners: Michael Beaton and Jeremy Goldberg.

Brewer: Jeremy Goldberg.

Brewing system: 20-barrel Pub Brewing Systems brewhouse.

Amount produced: Figures not yet available.

First beer: Fishermen's Brew.

Flagship beer: Fishermen's Brew.

Year-round beers: Fishermen's Brew.

Seasonal beers: None.

Tours: Tours available by appointment.

Beer to go: None.

Amenities: Limited parking is available near the brewery.

Directions: Commercial Street is located just off coastal Route 27 next to Gloucester's Western Harbor. The brewery is located just steps from downtown and the lost sailors memorial.

The joint effort of brothers-in-law Michael Beaton and Jeremy Goldberg, the Cape Ann Brewing Company is one of the newer production breweries profiled in this book. Located in the heart of Gloucester, behind Beaton's real estate office, the brewery draws upon the town's rich heritage and connection with the sea. From the packaging materials to the logo to the name of the flagship beer, Cape Ann Brewing closely associates itself with the local fishing industry and its courageous tradesmen.

Both Beaton and Goldberg arrived at the idea of opening a microbrewery by very different avenues. As a local businessman, Beaton believed Cape Ann, and specifically Gloucester, deserved its own beer. When he purchased a building in downtown Gloucester, he knew that it would be the perfect place for a small brewery. Though he had the idea in mind, he never acted upon it.

At the opposite end of the Atlantic seaboard, Goldberg was developing his own interest in good beer. Along with four friends, Goldberg participated in a quirky project that allowed him to visit thirty-eight breweries in forty days in a minivan. Captured on film, the beer adventure was chronicled in the documentary, *American Beer*, produced and directed by Paul Kermizian. Departing from New York City in June 2002, the group traveled over twelve thousand miles drinking their way across America. Along the way, the cast met with and interviewed many of the pioneers and leading proponents of the craft-beer movement. The movie does not attempt any compelling narrative on the craft-brewing industry or impart any philosophy of brewing or life; it is simply an entertaining romp through some of America's best-known breweries. Any such film is going to include some drunken exploits and this film is no exception. It mixes the tried-and-true elements of drunkenness, debauchery, and flatulence, often to comedic effect. Along the way, however, the troupe manages to conduct some great interviews and provide glimpses of classic breweries. The vignettes from the trip include some very personal and compelling moments with some brewers, including a haunting segment where brewer and cellist Ray McNeill of McNeill's Brewery in Brattleboro provides some chilling theme music for the film. Goldberg features prominently in the movie, taking part in some disturbing, yet hysterical moments and providing great comic relief.

After he completed the journey, Goldberg returned to Massachusetts and started talking about beer. When Goldberg admitted that he was intrigued by the idea of owning his own brewery, Beaton revealed his own thoughts on the subject.

The partners eventually combined efforts to bring life to their respective ideas. The resulting product, the Fisherman's Brew, is an American Amber Lager brewed literally steps away from America's oldest seaport.

Barrington Brewery and Restaurant

Jennifer House Commons
Route 7
Great Barrington, Massachusetts 01203
Tel. (978) 937–1200
www.barringtonbrewery.com

★ **Best Beer:** Barrington Brown Ale. This often-ignored style is one of the great traditional varieties associated with English brewing. Barrington's version is an enjoyable session ale, with a more-pronounced bitterness and balance of roasted malts than most versions. The flavors are sometimes reminiscent of maple syrup.

Opened: April 1995.

Type: Brewpub.

Owners: Andrew Mankin and Gary Happ.

Brewer: Andrew Mankin.

Brewing system: 7-barrel Stainless Steel Specialists brewhouse.

Amount produced: 800 barrels. Presently at capacity.

First beer: Blonde Ale.

Flagship beer: Blonde Ale.

Year-round beers: Berkshire Blond Ale, Hopland Pale Ale, Barrington Brown Ale, and Black Bear Stout.

Seasonal beers: Barrington brews a variety of seasonal ales, many in traditional styles, including the Vienna, Alt, India Pale Ale, ESB, Raspberry Ale, and Barrington Yuel Fuel.

Tours: Tours available by appointment.

Beer to go: To help build their off-premise sales, Mankin and Happ began the Berkshire Mountain Brewers. The pub's outside sales in Massachusetts and Connecticut now account for 15 percent of total production. You can also take home very reasonably priced 22-ounce bottles and growlers from the pub itself and the Yuel Fuel is an especially nice pick-up. Kegs are also for sale every day of the week.

Food: The menu here includes few surprises, with staples of sandwiches and burgers. The dinner menu offers a wider variety of dishes, ranging from free-range chicken to Maryland crab cakes and shepherd's pie.

Amenities: There is ample parking in front of the brewpub and around the Jennifer House Commons facility. Wine and beer only. Outdoor seating in warmer months.

Other attractions: The Jennifer House Commons is a complex of century-old barns that now house hundreds of antiques dealers. Jennifer House Commons, U.S. 7, Great Barrington, Massachusetts 01203, tel. (413) 528–9282. In the town center of Stockbridge, a short drive up the highway from the brewpub, lies the historic Red Lion Tavern. Immortalized in Norman Rockwell's painting *Main Street*, the inn has been in continuous use since 1773. 30 Main Street, Stockbridge, Massachusetts 01262, tel. (413) 298–5545. As the summer home of the Boston Symphony Orchestra for more than 60 years, Tanglewood in Lenox is one of America's preeminent outdoor music venues. 297 West Street, Lenox, Massachusetts 02140, tel. (413) 637–1600.

Pub hours: Open Monday through Thursday, 11:30 A.M. to 9:30 P.M.; Friday and Saturday, 11:30 A.M. to 10 P.M.; and Sunday, 11:30 A.M. to 9 P.M.

Directions: Traveling on Route 7 through Great Barrington, look for the WSBS radio tower. The Barrington Brewery and Restaurant is across the street in the Jennifer House Commons complex.

Tucked away in the scenic, rolling Berkshire Mountains of western Massachusetts, a small roadside brewpub serves fresh, simple beer to thirsty antiquers and locals. Walk beyond the doors of the red barn and you enter a relaxed taproom with low-hung ceilings and hardwood floors so old the pub feels as if it has been in business forever. Or at least since 1995, when brewer Andrew Mankin and his partner Gary Happ decided to convert this former art gallery and restaurant into a full-time brewhouse. Happ previously owned another restaurant in the Great Barrington area for many years, where he met a customer who bugged him about opening a brewpub. After selling his restaurant in 1993, Happ took some time off and thought about Mankin, the customer, and his idea.

The brewpub originally opened as the Berkshire Beer Works. The name, however, didn't last long, since Boston Beer Works owns a trademark on the Beer Works moniker. A few months after opening, the owners changed the name to the Barrington Brewery and Restaurant. An original sign using the old name still hangs over the brewhouse as a testament to the early days.

Before firing up the kettles as a professional, Mankin spent several years as a homebrewer. As his interest in brewing developed, he aggressively pursued an apprenticeship at the now-closed Vaux Brewery in Sunderland, United Kingdom. After convincing the brewing manager that he was not an industrial spy, Mankin spent four months learning the trade. He returned to New England and spent two weeks at the Vermont Pub and Brewery learning the less sexy side of small-batch brewing, namely cleaning and sanitation, before setting to work at Barrington.

In a creative use of limited vertical space, the pub's 7-barrel system towers on a raised platform over fermenters and conditioning tanks, standing in altarlike fashion across from the tavern's bar, in full view for all patrons. A small grain storage area is off to the left and the entire open operation is almost within reaching distance. The brewpub consists of three distinct sections: the dining room, the pub, and a lofted billiards room. The dining room, with its uneven brick floor, is lightly touched with elements of country kitsch décor and local, historic breweriana, including pieces from the original Berkshire Brewing Association, which operated in Deerfield, Massachusetts, from 1891 until Prohibition.

With its hard, unfinished, natural wood floors and solid wood beams, the place feels like it was destined to become a tavern and is happy to have achieved its true purpose. Mankin notes that, while he loved English pubs, he didn't really want to replicate an English-style pub in Barrington. "The barn helped set the tone for [the design]," Mankin says. The small, hand-made, L-shaped mahogany bar begs for you to pull up a stool and nurse a beer. Tall-backed booths in the bar support both friendly conversation and quiet pints alone. You can often find the reserved and polite Mankin tending bar or filling a mug club member's ceramic tankard, each of which is handcrafted by a member of the waitstaff.

Although you might not think kindly of beers made in a barn, Barrington's offerings are faithful recreations of traditional and well-known English beer styles. Each of the simply named beers is well constructed and entirely drinkable. Mankin does occasionally stray from tradition, brewing a Belgian witbier and an annual barleywine. The popular Yuel Fuel weighs in at 8 percent alcohol by volume and borrows from both English and Belgian brewing traditions.

The People's Pint

24 Federal Street
Greenfield, Massachusetts 01301
Tel. (413) 773–0333
www.thepeoplespint.com

> ★ **Best Beer:** Extra Special Bitter. A classic offering often available on cask at the People's Pint. The beer is richly aromatic and possessed with multiple floral and herbal notes from the English hops. A solid malt backbone provides stability for this ESB and balances the ale's fruitiness.

Opened: January 1997.

Type: Brewpub.

Owners: Alden Booth and Dan Young.

Brewer: Jeremy Krusas.

Brewing system: 15-barrel Pub Brewing Systems brewhouse.

Amount produced: 350 barrels. 1,200 barrels total capacity.

First beer: Provider Pale Ale.

Flagship beer: Pied pIPA.

Year-round beers: Provider Pale Ale, Farmer Brown, Pied pIPA, Extra Special Bitter, Brakeshoe Porter, Oatmeal Stout, and Xtra Ordinary Ale.

Seasonal beers: Broadfork Stout, Erebus Imperial Stout, Honey Wheat, Ordinary Bitter, Poets Seat Pale Ale, Schweat, Slipper Slope, Spring IPA, and Winter IPA.

Tours: By appointment.

Beer to go: Growlers and some bottles are available to go.

Food: The Pint is dedicated to serving locally produced foods, often organic, and even some items from the owner's personal farm. The menu changes seasonally and focuses on fresh, clean food. The bartender makes some of the excellent cheese and bread platters directly at the bar.

Amenities: On-street parking is available. The People's Pint sponsors local music, with jazz on Thursday evenings and Celtic music on Sundays.

Pub hours: Daily, 4 P.M. to close.

Directions: At Exit 26 off I-91, go east on Route 2A into Greenfield and then turn left onto Federal Street. The People's Pint is located near the center of downtown Greenfield.

Located in the heart of downtown Greenfield, the People's Pint is one of those places that makes you smile while also putting a tear in your eye. Entering the unrivaled environs of this perfect community pub is always a greatly anticipated prospect. Unfortunately, for many reading this guide, the Pint is not in your neighborhood. That's where the tears are shed.

The People's Pint blends a social mission with a community consciousness to a near-perfect end. If there is a common theme to be found here, it is that the Pint focuses on all things local. From the beginning, co-owners Alden Booth and Dan Young wanted to create a meeting place for locals. Beyond its simple storefront exterior, the doors open onto a small, narrow room with worn, wooden floors, a series of free-standing tables, some unadorned booths, and a no-frills bar. Colorful local artwork adorns the walls and brightens up the space. The Pint opens at 4 P.M. and within an hour, it's packed full of locals deep in conversation, celebrating life, and tilting back glasses of the pub's own beer.

The owners' dedication to the philosophy of local focus extends far beyond merely providing a meeting space for friends and neighbors. The menu heavily emphasizes the importance of supporting local food producers. The Pint provides desserts from the nearby Ambrosia Bakery, the veggie burgers are made by Lightlife in Turners Falls, and the seasonal dishes include produce from local farmers.

The owners also promote a sustainable living agenda, which includes recycling, reusing, and reducing waste. Other brewpubs simply provide spent grain for local farmers, which is done more out of necessity than as an environmental statement; the Pint offers no disposable plastic items, such as straws, a minimum of paper items, and all food scraps are composted. In another link in the sustainable chain, Booth takes the compost home and feeds it to his pigs, which are eventually brought for slaughter and returned to the Pint as a pork offering. After a busy night of serving nearly two hundred meals, the Pint produces about one barrel of trash.

While The People's Pint is rich in goodwill, it is short on physical space. Due to size restrictions, the owners relocated the brewery to a space on nearby Hope Street and expanded the brewing system. They replaced their original system, a quirky melange of cider and milk tanks, with a brewing system torn from the now-defunct Northeast Brewing Company in Boston.

The pub runs five to nine taps at any one time, with half of the offerings rotating seasonally. To match its casual pub atmosphere, The People's Pint specializes in English-style ales, including a variety of India pale ales, bitters, and stouts. Following this line, the Pint also offers three dedicated cask beer engines that play host to some beers with spectacular flavors.

As I look around the pub, everyone seems pleased to be here. The place possesses a friendly, inviting vibe that can only be achieved off the beaten brewpub path. Pubs in larger city environments strive to create the feeling of a local pub, but they cannot match the ambience of a true community meeting place, such as The People's Pint. Local groups advocating bicycle travel meet here. Members of the local Green Party discuss the group's environmental agenda while sipping cask ales. Coworkers laugh as fellow Franklin County neighbors—lawyers, farmers, teachers, students—celebrate this local treasure.

The Tap Brewpub

100 Washington Street
Haverhill, Massachusetts 01832
Tel. (978) 374–1117
www.tapbrewpub.com

★ **Best Beer:** Leatherlips IPA. Though only 5 percent alcohol, this India pale ale is a bruiser and one of the most aggressively hopped beers in all of New England. Leatherlips is packed with pungent hop aromas and earthy, citrusy, and mouth-puckeringly bitter flavors from the mix of Centennial, Nugget, and Chinook hops.

Opened: 2003.

Type: Brewpub.

Owner: John Fahimian.

Brewer: Stephen Bernard.

Brewing system: 10-barrel Century Manufacturing brewhouse.

Amount Produced: Figures not available.

First beer: Haverale.

Flagship beer: Haverale.

Year-round beers: Haverale, Merrimack Mild Ale, Leatherlips IPA, Bootblack's Extra Stout, and Hannah's Weizen.

Seasonal beers: Alt Uberschuh, Apple Ale, Blonde Bombshell (strong ale), Merry Mac, Christmas Spirit, Cobbler's Thumb (pale ale), Golden Slipper (tripel), Gouden Schoen (Belgian pale ale), Haverale Summer Brew, King's Slipper (Belgian dark ale), Marynka Pils, Octoberfest, Old Farmhouse Porter, Pentucket Porter, Plug's Pond Pale Ale, Printemps D'abord (amber), Scherezade (oud bruin), Special Bitter, and Merry Mac (old ale).

Tours: Tours available by appointment.

Beer to go: Growlers available for purchase.

Food: Well-rounded menu balances pub food and more upscale entrees, including seafood and pasta dishes.

Amenities: Parking is available on the street or in the large lot behind the brewpub next to the river. Full liquor license.

Pub hours: Closed Monday. Open Tuesday through Saturday, 11:30 A.M. to 11 P.M.; and Sunday, noon to 11 P.M.

Directions: From I-495, take Exit 49 and travel east on River Street. The Tap is on the right side of the road after it changes names to Washington Street just past the train overpass.

Resting on the banks of the Merrimack River, Haverhill is a city caught in a moment in time. Established in 1640 as Pentucket, the rural community evolved into a major manufacturing center by the early eighteenth century. Filled with tanneries, boatyards, and mills, Haverhill was best known as one of the world's leading manufacturers of shoes.

Walking down Washington Street in Haverhill's historic downtown shoe manufacturing district, you can still get a feel for the period architecture of the time. The facades of many buildings remain pristinely intact, including the historic building housing the Tap brewpub. This space has long served as a bar and restaurant, with the first such recorded use coming in 1897. Located in the J. M. Hickey Shoe and Leather Exchange building, the original restaurant was half the present size until 1967, when the owners purchased the Goodman Building next door. They broke through the brick wall and created access arches between the two structures, thus doubling the size of the restaurant.

The Tap is a real throwback in terms of atmosphere, with architecture dating from the turn of the century. With floor-to-ceiling, half-moon–shaped arching windows, old and creaky floors, and solid and well-aged brick, the Tap sometimes gives you the feeling you've stepped into an old speakeasy photo colorized for the modern age. The owner has done a nice job of letting the building's design set the tone. The dazzling, stainless-steel brewhouse sits quietly off to one side, gleaming down on the restaurant, but not in a distracting way. An enormous new deck jets off the back of the building, allowing great views of the flowing Merrimack River. Beautiful frescoes depicting scenes of boats and New England cover the walls of the bar area, reportedly produced in the 1940s by an artist who worked for beer.

Despite plentiful parking and a location only a few steps from a commuter rail stop, Haverhill is an out-of-the way destination for many beer lovers. It remains questionable how much dedication local drinkers have to craft beer. On any given day, lots of macro beers go across the bar, along with a slew of flavored martinis. The place also clears out very early, even on weekend nights, resulting in the early closing time.

In its short existence, the Tap has seen a string of very talented brewers work on its beautiful system. Brewer Tod Mott, now of the Portsmouth Brewery, served as a consultant and the head brewer here for the first few months of operation. He set some of the early recipes, mainly English-style offerings. Mott turned the boots over to brewer Dann Paquette, formerly of the now-closed Northeast Brewing Company and the Concord Brewing Company. Paquette's influence here cannot be understated. In a short period of time, he created some of the most expressive and inspiring beers in New England, generating great excitement among beer geeks. Paquette experimented with obscure Belgian beer styles, crafted some style-bending twists on American classics, and produced several beers that could easily vie for the crown of best in New England.

In early 2005, Paquette left his position with the Tap. His departure saddened many beer lovers and it remains to be seen whether Stephen Bernard, the new brewer, formerly of the Mercury Brewing Company, will continue Paquette's experimental ways or settle for producing less expressive beers.

Paper City Brewery Company

108 Cabot Street
Holyoke, Massachusetts 01040
Tel. (413) 535–1588
www.papercity.com

★ **Best Beer:** Blonde Hop Monster. Paper City does a variety of wild ales, but none can top the Hop Monster's explosion of flavor. The aroma is a sharp smack in the nose with earthy hop and hugely sweet malt notes. The beer is gloriously unbalanced, with the ultimate battle for control waged between citrusy, bitter hops and an almost cloying malt sweetness. As it warms, the Hop Monster tames a bit and shows some lighter flavors, including passion fruit. With its rough, unpolished edges, the Hop Monster bears great similarity to Dogfish Head's flagship 60 Minute IPA and it clearly breaks out of the mold set by other IPAs in New England.

Opened: November 1996.

Type: Brewery.

Owner: Jay Hebert.

Brewer: Ben Anhult.

Brewing system: 20-barrel DME brewhouse with open fermenters.

Amount produced: 3,000 barrels. 5,000-barrel total capacity.

First beer: Holyoke Dam Ale.

Flagship beer: Holyoke Dam Ale.

Year-round beers: Banchee Extra Pale Ale, Ireland Parish Golden Ale, Winter Palace Wee Heavy, India's Pale Ale, Riley Stout, and Cabot Street Wheat.

Seasonal beers: Blonde Hop Monster, Denogginator (doppelbock), Dorado Cerveza Lager, ESB, Goats Peak Bock, Nut Brown Ale, One Eared Monkey (peach ale), Riler's Mothers Milk Stout, Smoked Porter, Spring Ale (brown ale), Summer Brew (pilsner), Summer Haze (witbier), Rage N' Razzberry, Summit House Oktoberfest, Winter Lager, and Winter Solstice Old Ale.

Tours: Paper City has hosted visitors to its brewery on Friday evenings for many years. From 6 P.M. to 8 P.M., you can visit and walk around the old warehouse brewery while local bands play. Admission is $5 and that buys you unlimited samples and a mixed 4-pack of beer to take with you. Tours otherwise by appointment.

Beer to go: 6-packs are for sale in the small store at the brewery.

Amenities: Limited on-street parking around the brewery. Paper City also produces a line of sodas under the Rollie's brand name, including root beer, cream soda, and watermelon. As noted below, Holyoke's economy is not in great shape. The area around the brewery can sometimes be a little sketchy.

Directions: From I-90, take Exit 5 (Route 33) to Chicopee, go right at Montgomery Street, which becomes Yelle Street. Go left at Prospect Street and then right at Chicopee Street (Route 116), which becomes Cabot Street. The brewery is located on the fifth floor of a converted manufacturing warehouse in the industrial section of town.

Located at the top of an enormous old manufacturing warehouse in an industrial section of Holyoke, the Paper City Brewing Company rocks on Friday nights. On my visit, I can't seem to find the brewery on Cabot Street, but I know I'm in the right place when I see several college-aged kids walking around with four-packs of Paper City beer. Upon entering the building, you start the first leg of a long, arduous journey up four steep flights of stairs.

When you finally reach the top, you emerge into a whole new world of beer. The warehouse is beautiful, running about 200 feet in length with well-preserved brick on all sides and vaulted ceilings. Before the sun sets, the large windows afford striking views of the area. Visitors for the Friday night event congregate in the main pub area, occasionally ambling up to the bar for another sample of Paper City's slightly eccentric offerings. A two-piece jazz band, comprised of two local college kids, plays a form of fusion jazz that would make Ornette Coleman smile.

Off to one side, a series of antique motorcycles sit idly by while a man quietly builds and fills beer containers for his departing guests. With his prodigious work ethic, it's no surprise the man turns out to be a big Jimmy Carter fan. As unusual a statement as that may be, I promise the two subjects are related. It can be said that if it wasn't for the former president and Senator Alan Cranston of California, Paper City and a host of other craft breweries might not exist today.

In 1978, President Carter signed legislation introduced by Senator Cranston that legalized homebrewing in America. After his government performed this patriotic act, Paper City's founder, Jay Hebert, started brewing beer for his own personal consumption. Until that time, Hebert had been disturbed by the state of domestic beers. From the start, he knew he wanted eventually to own his own brewery and bring good beer to his home city of Holyoke.

In the 1840s, a group of Boston industrialists devised a plan to build factories powered by the Connecticut River's Hadley Falls. By 1847, they started on their plan to replace the existing agricultural village near the falls with a new industrial city, complete with a dam, three levels of canals, and fifty factories. The resulting factories produced a variety of goods, including woolens, cotton, thread, and silk. Before long, Holyoke became well known for its high-quality paper.

By the 1920s, however, the city's economy started to decline as companies followed cheap labor to the South. The city's paper manufacturers faced stiff competition from cheaper, wood pulp papermakers, and the development of steam and electric power allowed factories greater freedom from water-based power supplies.

Modern Holyoke's population is two-thirds what it was in the 1920s, and the city's economy is in poor condition. Holyoke's dams and canals continue to generate hydroelectric energy, though many of its mills and factories sit vacant. Several city and business groups are now in the process of trying to revitalize the city and its flagging economy. They are presenting Holyoke as a "living industrial museum," complete with beautiful, historic architecture and attractive canals. There are plans to create a canal walk, which would take visitors right past the brewery and serve as a catalyst for the restoration of vacant warehouses.

Long before the renaissance talk came up, Hebert saw value in the old buildings. He purchased this mammoth warehouse, which used to manufacture wool jackets, with hopes of transforming it into a brewery. In 1995, he incorporated the Paper City Brewery Company and then spent most of his time transforming the fifth floor of the warehouse into a functional, federal- and state-approved microbrewery.

Paper City's attractive brewery often flies under the radar of beer enthusiasts in New England. It produces a diverse selection of flavorful ales and lagers, along with some quirky beers in its Limited Brewer's Offering specialty series.

Cape Cod Beer

720 Main Street
Hyannis, Massachusetts 02601
Tel. (774) 836–2121
www.capecodbeer.com

> ★ **Best Beer:** Channel Marker Red. Brewed with five varieties of English malts and three types of American hops, this offering combines two historic brewing cultures to form a nice amber ale. Possessing session ale strength, the medium-bodied Red strikes a balance between slightly toasted malt flavors and a touch of hop bitterness.

Opened: April 2004.

Type: Brewery.

Owners: Todd and Beth Marcus.

Brewer: Todd Marcus.

Brewing system: 7-barrel DME brewhouse.

Amount Produced: 500 barrels. 1,000-barrel total capacity.

First beer: Channel Marker Red and Sharkstooth I.P.A.

Flagship beer: Channel Marker Red and Sharkstooth I.P.A.

Year-round beers: Channel Marker Red and Sharkstooth I.P.A.

Seasonal beers: Stellwagen Stout.

Tours: Tours available by appointment.

Beer to go: Growlers are for sale at the brewery.

Amenities: Parking is available in the lot in front of the brewery.

Directions: The brewery is adjacent to the now-closed Hyport Brewing Company restaurant at the end of Main Street in downtown Hyannis.

With its beautiful beaches, marshy expanses, and picturesque clapboard houses, Cape Cod attracts millions of people to this idyllic extension of land separating Nantucket Sound, Cape Cod Bay, and the Atlantic Ocean. Despite its overwhelming popularity as a prime vacation destination, Cape Cod is remarkably wanting in breweries and brewpubs. Excluding the operations on the nearby islands of Nantucket and Martha's Vineyard, the Cape proper has exactly one brewery and no brewpubs.

In Hyannis, Todd and Beth Marcus are working hard to bring the cause of good beer to the residents of Cape Cod. Their Cape Cod Beer company, whose slogan is "A Vacation In Every Pint," is located in a small space attached to the now-closed

Hyport Brewing Company on Main Street. A big, colorful sign in the window over-looking the fermenters lets you know you've found the right place. Come around to the side door and prepare to see the entire 525-square-foot operation laid out before you.

Marcus has long brewed on the system in place here, having previously served as brewmaster when the location was part of the adjoining restaurant. The history is a bit convoluted, as the operation has gone through several iterations. Brewing first began in this location in 1995, when the place opened as the Cape Cod Brewhouse. It later became the Hyannisport Brewing Company, followed by the Hyport Brewing Company. The location still suffers from a mild case of identity confusion as the signs out front and on the building itself continue to advertise the conflicting names. The scene was more confounding when you consider that, while the restaurant no longer operated as a brewpub and closed in early fall 2005, Cape Cod Beer still occasionally brewed a beer or two for its former partner.

Realizing both the potential for consumer confusion and the need for a larger operation, Cape Cod's owners are in the process of building a new brewery across town. Todd Marcus also plans to downplay the individual product names and turn the brewery's focus more toward spreading the Cape Cod brand name. The owners also hope to produce their IPA in cans for consumption in places where bottles are not allowed, such as campgrounds and golf courses.

After taking in the intoxicating atmosphere at a brewers' dinner at Redbones in Somerville, one filled with barleywines and strong ales, Todd Marcus made the decision to enter the brewing game. He looked around at the crowd of assembled brewers and said to himself, "I'm home and I've found my people." Until that point, Marcus was merely an enthusiastic homebrewer and a gainfully employed electrical engineer. After leaving his job, he worked at the Long Trail Brewing Company and the Sunday River Brewing Company before landing at a John Harvard's location in Pennsylvania. When the new owners of this former Hyannis-based brewpub decided to hire a full-time brewer, Marcus applied and won the job.

Marcus and his wife are betting hard on the viability of craft beer in the local marketplace. The couple operates the brewery year-round and focuses on building strong local support for the brand. In the off-season, when many restaurants and pubs close, Cape Cod Beer tries to cultivate close relationships with the merchants who provide services to the hardy locals. Whether you're in Plymouth or Province-town, keep an eye out for Cape Cod's local beer.

Mercury Brewing Company

23 Hayward Street
Ipswich, Massachusetts 01938
Tel. (978) 356–3329
www.mercurybrewing.com

★ **Best Beer:** Ipswich Original Ale. The original is still the best. The Ipswich Original Ale is one of the first craft beers I tried after moving to New England from Chicago. Coming from the land of lagers, I remember being a little disappointed over what I perceived to be the similar flavor profiles of many locally produced beers. This beer single-handedly changed my outlook. Enjoyed directly from the bottle or in a glass from a fresh growler, the Original Ale is a raw and thoroughly enjoyable English-style pale ale. The beer is hazy and unfiltered and harkens back to the earliest days of brewing, with its pastoral charms. Ipswich's flagship beer is full of toasted, biscuity malt flavors and aromas, grainy to the taste, and very lightly hopped. An unwavering New England classic.

Opened: August 1992 (under new ownership in 1999).

Type: Brewery.

Owner: Rob Martin.

Brewer: Rob Martin.

Brewing system: Not known.

Amount produced: Not known.

First beer: Ipswich Original Ale.

Flagship beer: Ipswich Original Ale.

Year-round beers: Ipswich Original Ale, Ipswich India Pale Ale, Ipswich Dark Ale, Ipswich ESB, Ipswich Oatmeal Stout, Ipswich Commemorative 1722 Porter, Stone Cat Ale, Stone Cat Blonde Ale, Stone Cat IPA, Stone Cat Blueberry, Stone Cat ESB, Farmington River Mahogany Ale, and Farmington River Blonde Ale.

Seasonal beers: Stone Cat Barleywine, Stone Cat Wheat, Stone Cat Winter Ale, Stone Cat Scotch Ale, Stone Cat Octoberfest, Stone Cat Pumpkin, 1084 Barley Wine Ale, and Ipswich Winter Ale.

Tours: Tours not available.

Beer to go: None.

Other attractions: If you get turned away at the brewery, why not drown your sorrows with Cape Ann's other favorite product: fried clams. Woodman's of Essex claims to be the originator of this epicurean delight; the Clam Box claims to have the best food. Visit both and decide for yourself. Woodman's is located at

Route 133, 121 Main Street, Essex, Massachusetts 01929, tel. (800) 649–1773, www.woodmans.com. The Clam Box is located at 246 High Street, Ipswich, Massachusetts 01938, tel. (978) 356–9707.

Directions: From Route 1, turn onto Ipswich Road. Head toward Ipswich. When the road becomes Topsfield Road, keep an eye out for Hayward Street on the right.

If the New England brewing scene were a theatrical performance, the Mercury Brewing Company would shun the stage in favor of playing the role of "anonymous benefactor" listed deep in the pages of the program. Long a staple on Cape Ann and in the Eastern Massachusetts marketplace, Mercury quietly goes about brewing thousands of barrels of beer and soda every year. While other breweries desperately seek the spotlight, Mercury prefers the quiet anonymity of its brewhouse near Route 1. Despite repeated attempts to contact Mercury, it remains the only brewery with whom I had no direct contact in writing this guide. The information contained herein is taken from the company's Web site, discussions with other beer lovers, and previously published media accounts of the company and its history.

Originally opened by Jim Beauvais and Paul Sylva as the Ipswich Brewing Company, the partners sold the brewery to their once-intern and current owner, Rob Martin, in 1999. While Ipswich was in its infancy, Martin busily developed the idea for opening his own craft brewery as part of a class project while attending the Rensselaer Polytechnic Institute. After graduation, he briefly worked as an architect before leaving in 1995 to work for Ipswich. After acquiring the brewery, Martin rechristened it the Mercury Brewing Company (after the Roman messenger to the gods). When he assumed control of the business, the rights to Ipswich's flagship ales were actually owned by U.S. Beverage, a beer-marketing company based in Chicago. The company contracted the production of bottles to the Clipper City Brewing Company in Baltimore, Maryland, while the home facility in Ipswich continued to produce the growler versions.

In April 2003, Martin finally achieved his goal of regaining control of the brands and moving their production entirely in-house. Mercury also runs a successful contract brewing operation. It produced the critically acclaimed, but now defunct, Dornbusch line of German-style beers, which won a bronze medal in the alt category at the 2000 Great American Beer Festival. Mercury also brews small-batch, specialty house beers for more than a dozen restaurants in Boston and the North Shore. The brewery continues to produce its signature growlers, which account for approximately one-fifth of the company's business.

The Concord Brewery

199 Cabot Street
Lowell, Massachusetts 01854
Tel. (978) 937–1200
www.concordbrew.com

★ **Best Beer:** I'm keeping it simple with this choice. While it would be easy to select the much-discussed and inventive Rapscallion offerings, Concord's IPA is a nicely balanced beer, with a light hop bite that is quite drinkable and does not abuse the palate.

Opened: 1998.

Type: Brewery.

Owner: David Asadoorian.

Brewer: David Wilson and Karl Baldrate.

Brewing system: 20-barrel DME brewhouse.

Amount produced: 4,000 barrels. 10,000-barrel total capacity.

First beer: Pale Ale.

Flagship beer: Pale Ale.

Year-round beers: In the Concord line: Pale Ale, IPA, Porter, and Stout. In the Rapscallion line: Blessing, Creation, and Premier. In the Boardinghouse line: Harvard Lager.

Seasonal beers: Grape Ale (spring to summer) and North Woods Ale (fall to winter).

Tours: The brewery recently added a regular Friday-evening open house between 5 P.M. and 7:30 P.M. Call ahead to confirm the hours.

Beer to go: The brewery offers cases, 6-packs, and 4-packs of its beers. Generally open from 4 P.M. to 6 P.M., but call ahead to confirm as this is subject to change.

Amenities: Metered street parking is available near the brewery.

Other attractions: Once the second-largest city in New England and an American industry powerhouse, Lowell is now a city trying to fight its way back from post–Industrial Era obscurity. The city is quite attractive, flanked on all sides by a series of canals and filled with many buildings of great architectural character. After a stop at the brewery, head to LeLacheur Park where, for a fraction of the cost of Red Sox tickets, you can watch the wildly popular Lowell Spinners, the Single A affiliate of the Sox, play. Tel. (978) 459–1702, www.lowellspinners.com.

Directions: Head out from downtown going west on Merrimack Street. Take a right on Cabot Street and look for the Brewer's Exchange complex, fronted by outdoor patio seating. The brewery is located down the street from University of Massachusetts–Lowell.

In its short seven-year existence, the Concord Brewery has had four different names, three different owners, and three different homes. Originally incorporated as the Concord Junction Brewing Company, the name refers to the brewery's first home in Massachusetts, where brewers developed the idea for the unusual Concord Grape Ale. After former brewer Mike Labbe purchased the brewery from its original owners, he changed the the name to Concord Brewers. When the brewery left its Concord home for Shirley, it reopened as the Concorde Brewery. Soon after taking over, Labbe discovered that he preferred being a brewer to being an owner; the brewery fell on hard financial times, and it nearly closed. In the most recent twist, the company's accountant, David Asadoorian, purchased the brewery, renamed it the Concord Brewery, and relocated operations to the old Brewery Exchange complex in Lowell. To add a little more to the convoluted history, the brewery also produces beers under three different brand names.

Concord's beers remained fairly consistent during the frequent changes in ownership and address, and the brewery now enjoys a new measure of stability and direction under Asadoorian. Concord produces nearly 4000 barrels per year; the new owner is looking to double that amount in the near future. For his part, Asadoorian never dreamed of owning a brewery. While working with small businesses during his accounting career, Asadoorian always kept his options open about starting his own business when the time was right. When the brewery opportunity presented itself, he accepted it.

Concord's location is another interesting facet of the brewery: although the brewery is attached to a restaurant in the complex, and its expansive operating space is a focal point for diners (thanks to the restaurant's large, glass windows), the brewery is not associated with the restaurant. The brewery's beers, of course, are the house beers served at the restaurant.

To broaden its appeal, Concord employs a two-tiered approach to promoting its products. For Budweiser drinkers, it offers the Brewery Exchange's house beer, the Harvard Lager, as a timid step into the world of craft beer. For those who already enjoy bolder beers, the Concord line of ales remains very approachable while not backing down in terms of flavor.

Developed by a former brewer as an artisanal line, the Rapscallion line has perhaps been the brewery's most visible project and it continues to push the definitional boundaries of beer. Born in the spirit of beers that are intentionally different from batch to batch, the Rapscallion line defies the notion that consistency in flavor profile is the brewer's main goal. The three Rapscallion brands—Blessing, Creation, and Premier—have varied in consistency and flavor from batch to batch, but have been widely lauded by beer enthusiasts. As the operation stabilizes, the brewery plans to expand and further promote the Rapscallion line as "America's sipping beer."

Experimentation at Concord is not limited to Rapscallion, as demonstrated by the kitschy Grape Ale. In selecting this beer for its Best of Boston in 2000, *Boston Magazine* offered a backhanded compliment by saying the beer was actually not as "icky" as it sounded. That's actually a pretty fair assessment. The nose is dead-on Concord grapes, but the aromas do not transcend into the body of the beer, which remains a balanced, if slightly malty, ale.

Cisco Brewers

5 Bartlett Farm Road
Nantucket, Massachusetts 02584
Tel. (508) 325–5929
www.ciscobrewers.com

★ **Best Beer:** Captain Swain's Extra Stout. Named for one of the brewer's ancestors who originally settled on Nantucket in the 1600s, this beer is most often found in Cisco's signature 750-milliliter bottles. It possesses a very rich and creamy flavor, a beautiful, tan head, and loads of roasted malts. Dry-hopped with Chinook hops, there is a earthy aroma that translates to a slightly piney finish, balancing the dark malt flavors.

Opened: July 1995.

Type: Brewery.

Owners: Jay Harman, Randy Hudson, and Wendy Hudson.

Brewer: Randy Hudson.

Brewing system: 7-barrel self-fabricated system.

Amount produced: Figures not available.

First beer: Whale's Tale Pale Ale.

Flagship beer: Whale's Tale Pale Ale.

Year-round beers: Bailey's Ale, Captain Swain's Extra Stout, Moor Porter, Sankaty Light, and Whale's Tale Pale Ale.

Seasonal beers: Celebration Libation, Baggywrinkle Barleywine, and Summer of Lager.

Tours: Tours by appointment. The brewery, winery, and distillery are open daily, 10 A.M. to 6 P.M. A small shop has some fun, Cisco-related goods, from well-worn hats to comfortable t-shirts.

Beer to go: Bottles are available for purchase from the brewery.

Amenities: Parking is very limited at the brewery site so consider taking a taxi or riding a bike if you plan to visit.

Directions: Follow Hummock Pond Road south toward Cisco Beach, and find Bartlett Farm Road on the left.

Dean and Melissa Long founded the Nantucket Vineyard on this sweeping property in 1981. After many years of fighting to grow their own grapes on the site, the owners finally accepted Mother Nature's fickle ways and the winery now imports grapes from out-of-state growers.

Across the country in California, Wendy Hudson took up homebrewing with friends. When she moved back to Nantucket in 1992, she met her future husband, Randy, and bought him a homebrewing kit. Randy had experience working with yeasts and grains as an employee at Something Natural, a bakery on Nantucket.

The two couples eventually met on the island and the Hudsons moved into the loft over the winery. When they started Cisco, which was actually located outdoors (except for the cold-conditioning room), they called it a nanobrewery because it wasn't big enough to qualify as a microbrewery. Tight surroundings demanded a new structure to house both operations. Construction was delayed, resulting in a complete absence of Cisco's beer for a two-month period of time. The black time led to the brewery's humorous motto: "Nice beer, if you can get it."

In 2000, Dean Long secured a distilling license, which allowed him to open the Triple Eight Distillery. The company's first product, a whiskey aging in sixty three oak barrels, took five years to hit the market. To raise money to support the distillery, Triple Eight sold futures to the public on each barrel of its whiskey. To make up for the delay, the distillery decided to produce the Triple Eight Vodka—the release of which has been a business-altering event for the three operations. Made from organically grown corn blended with sand-filtered island water from well number 888 (thus the name), the triple-distilled vodka has proven wildly popular with consumers and very lucrative for the owners.

Because of the popularity of the Triple Eight Vodka, there has been some concern about the future of Cisco as a brewery. Much of the company's promotional energy and attention are directed at the growth of the liquor operation. Since 2001, a marketing team has been seen around Boston promoting the liquor from a souped-up, pale blue 1975 VW camper van. The brand is now available at more than two hundred accounts and is a mainstay liquor in Boston-area bars. Triple Eight remains busy branching out with new products, including an orange vodka, a rum, and a gin.

Located a fair distance from town, Cisco couldn't be a nicer place to spend an afternoon. With the three alcohol-based operations, it's a veritable playground for adults. In the brewery, a ramshackle tasting room with a small bar beckons you to pull up a tall stool, have a seat, and order a taste of fresh Whale's Tail. A decidedly laid-back atmosphere exists here. It is Nantucket, of course, so what's the rush? The tasting room looks out into the brewery and you are usually welcome to show yourself around. On the exterior of the structure, hop vines climb their way from the ground toward the roof. With a sample or two of Cisco's beer in your system and the warm sun of a Nantucket summer day on your face, all your cares seem to quickly fade away.

Owen O'Leary's

319 Speen Street
Natick, Massachusetts, 01760
Tel. (508) 650–1976
www.owenolearys.com

319 Speen Street • (Hampton Inn)
Natick, MA 01760

★ **Best Beer:** Irish Sunsetter. This beer definitely lives up to its billing as a rich, hoppy, full-bodied red ale. The Sunsetter's impressive hop profile, which includes three different varieties and a fair dose of dry hopping, balances well against the brewer's use of four select malts.

Opened: January 1997.

Type: Brewpub.

Owner: Kevin Gill.

Brewer: Dan Kramer, head brewer. Dave Thompson, assistant brewer.

Brewing system: 10-barrel JV Northwest brewhouse.

Amount Produced: 400 barrels. 1,000-barrel total capacity.

First beer: Irish Red.

Flagship beer: Irish Sunsetter.

Year-round beers: Golden Ale, IPA, Light, Irish Stout, and Irish Sunsetter.

Seasonal beers: Marzen.

Tours: By appointment.

Beer to go: None.

Food: Generally uninspired pub fare. Though it's a restaurant and not a grade-school cafeteria, sandwiches are literally served with a bag of chips on the side of the plate.

Amenities: Parking lot next to hotel and pub. Full liquor license.

Pub hours: Daily, 11:30 A.M. to 12:30 P.M.

Directions: Look for the Hampton Inn off Route 9 in Natick. Owen O'Leary's is attached to the hotel.

In my five years of shopping in the many stores in this part of Natick, I never knew there was a brewpub other than John Harvard's in the area. Although I regularly travel around in search of good beer, I managed to miss the Owen O'Leary's brewpub, tucked away inside a Hampton Inn near the mall. From its dank, cold interior to its uninspired cuisine, it's easy to see how the place has failed to register with the local beer community.

From the outside, O'Leary's looks like a typical chain restaurant with its white brick exterior and simple signage. Beyond the front entryway, the rest of the pub resembles a rundown, underground sports bar, complete with lottery ticket systems and a multitude of flickering televisions. Patrons quietly sit at the bar, sip Budweisers, and watch life go by. As a cross between a Bennigan's and a neglected Irish pub, there was little to be said about Owen O'Leary's.

Then brewer Dan Kramer brought a little sunshine to the place. Kramer, whose other job involves making the beer at the delightful Opa Opa Steakhouse and Brewery in Southampton, is slowly turning Owen O'Leary's around in terms of beer. He is assisted by brewer Dave Thompson, who also works at the Deja Brew Beer-on-Premise in Shrewsbury.

Considering the dank, dive-bar atmosphere, I can only imagine what the beers must have been like before Kramer appeared on the scene. The pub's layout is disjointed, with the large, main bar area feeding off into several smaller, distant feeling sections, including a pool and video game room. The vaguely Irish theme comes and goes throughout the place, giving way in the back room to gloriously cheesy décor, including a funny wooden beer keg. The brewing set-up is sizable, but blocked off from any real public view by the clumsy layout.

The situation remains in flux, with some obvious miscommunication between the brewing and service sides of the operation. When I ask for a sample of the marzen, a style defined by a deep garnet or reddish color, a substantial body, and rich, malty flavor, the waitress brings me a light pale beer, thin in body, and slightly hoppy, with no discernible malt flavors. When I ask if she brought the right beer, she says yes, but that the beer is weird and no one at the pub really likes it. Having sampled Kramer's quality offerings at both Maplewood and more recently at Opa Opa, I'm left to guess whether this is a holdover beer from a previous brewer or the mistake of an inexperienced or ill-informed staffer.

It's hard to gauge how much passion the owner has for the brewing side of the business here. While the beer is not prominently featured or promoted anywhere in the pub, the owner made a solid choice in securing Kramer's services. As Kramer becomes more familiar with the system at Owen O'Leary's, I look forward to charting his progress with future batches.

Northampton Brewery

11 Brewster Court
Northampton, Massachusetts 01060
Tel. (413) 584–9903

NORTHAMPTON
BREWERY
BAR + GRILLE

> ★ **Best Beer:** Black Cat Stout. Pouring with a deep black color and a frothy white head, this creamy, dry Irish stout mixes roasted flavors and aromas with tangents of cocoa and light malt notes. The complex, roasted flavors include a touch of smoke and light chocolate. A colorful take on a traditional style.

Opened: August 1987.

Type: Brewpub.

Owner: Janet Egelston.

Brewer: Chris O'Connor.

Brewing system: 10-barrel JV Northwest brewhouse.

Amount Produced: 850 barrels. Presently at capacity.

First beer: Golden Lager.

Flagship beer: Northampton Pale Ale.

Year-round beers: Hoover's Porter, Northampton Pale Ale, Old Brown Dog Ale, Paradise City Gold, Daniel Shay's Best Bitter, Black Cat Stout, Blackberry Porter, Raspberry Brown Dog, Red Headed Stepchild (Irish red), and Unquamonk Amber Lager.

Seasonal beers: The list of around 25 special releases grows every year and includes the Decadent Ale (double IPA), Maggie's Wee Heavy, Nonotuck India Pale Ale, Golden Lager, Oatmeal Stout, Raspberry Weizen, Simeon Jones River Amber Ale, Snowshovel ESB, Graduation Ale (wheat fruit beer), Spring Bock, Steamer (California common), Windbreaker (hefeweizen), Weizenheimer, Alternator, Humbug Ale (IPA), and Octoberfest.

Tours: Tours available by appointment.

Beer to go: Growlers and 22-ounce bottles available for purchase.

Food: A sizable menu covering all of the regular bases, but with a noted dedication to cooking with beer and preparing items from scratch. Meals are well considered and presented with obvious thought.

Amenities: There are two sizable parking lots directly adjacent to the brewpub. Full liquor license.

Other attractions: The excellent Table and Vine Liquors is located a short drive from the brewpub. Taking a decidedly upscale approach to food and liquor,

T&V offers a wide selection of cheeses, chocolates, wines, glassware, and, of course, beers. Mix-and-match 6-packs are available, as well as tasteful displays and a sizable library of books. 122 North King Street, Northampton, Massachusetts 01060, tel. (800) 474–2449, www.tableandvine.com.

Pub hours: Open Monday through Saturday, 11:30 A.M. to 1 A.M.; and Sunday, noon to 1 A.M.

Directions: The brewery is one block off Main Street in downtown Northampton, next to a city parking lot.

The Northampton Brewery has a lot to brag about, with its enviable history and long-standing levels of excellence and success. Perhaps the most inspiring facts about the brewpub, however, are its vibrant spirit and its ceaseless ability to better itself. As the second craft brewery to open in Massachusetts, the fourth in all of New England, and the oldest operating brewpub in the region, Northampton is pretty impressive on paper. But after nearly twenty years in business, what is truly amazing is how much vibrance the Northampton Brewery retains. With each new addition to the building or the tap list, you get the feeling the brewpub is just beginning to hit its stride.

While on a trip to California with her brother, Janet Egelston stopped into the Front Street Brewpub in Santa Cruz on a lark for a drink. The pair quickly became entranced with the place and with the notion of owning their own brewpub. They scouted locations on the West Coast before settling on their mother's hometown of Northampton, Massachusetts. At the time, Janet was considering a master's degree program at the University of Massachusetts–Amherst, while her brother Peter was a homebrewer living in New York City.

At the young age of twenty-four, a brash and bold Janet Egelston returned to Massachusetts and prepared to become one of the youngest entrepreneurs in the nascent craft brewing movement. When it opened in the fall of 1987, the Northampton Brewery became the second brewpub to open in New England, bested only by the Commonwealth Brewing Company. Brewpub openings today are treated as commonplace, so it is mind-boggling to consider that there were less than twenty such operations in existence in the United States when Janet and her brother opened this place. In 1991, the brother-sister team opened the Portsmouth Brewery in New Hampshire, which eventually spawned the Smuttynose Brewing Company. In 2000, Janet and Peter split the operations, with Janet maintaining control of the Northampton brewpub and Peter becoming sole owner of the Portsmouth brewing operations.

Every time I visit, something new is happening at the Northampton Brewery. The restored carriage house, which dates from 1894, looks very little like it did the day the Northampton Brewery opened. The owners converted the structure, located appropriately on Brewster Court, from an office building into a restaurant and brewery. Northampton opened with a small kitchen, poor storage, and a simple menu. A ground-level, outdoor beer garden opened in 1988, followed by a major expansion in 1995, which included a basement, a new kitchen, and 150 outdoor seats on a rooftop beer garden complete with its own bar. In spring 2004, an attractive sunroom opened. The rooftop beer garden, with its innovative, mist cooling system, and the glorious sunroom, with its mahogany ceilings and tasteful beer artwork, remain two of the nicest places to enjoy a beer in all of New England.

The brewer, Chris O'Connor, joined Northampton's team after working on his own at the Triple Rock Brewery and Alehouse in Berkeley, California. During his years here, O'Connor has developed many long-standing relationships, including his marriage to Janet Egelston. The gregarious O'Connor is a fitting analogue to Egelston, who, with her pigtails and ebullient disposition, brings a distinct sparkle to the brewpub. O'Connor brews twenty-five styles of beer every year, using mostly English 2-row malt and hops from the Pacific Northwest. After working in the kitchen and behind the bar, O'Connor assumed the head brewing position in 1994 and later attended the Siebel Institute of Brewing.

The Egelstons initially styled their new brewpub as a place where members of the local Northampton community could meet and enjoy good food and drink. Though it is located in a valley of colleges, the Northampton Brewery has an upscale feel and remains welcoming for both students and families. The brewpub has also become a bit of a hangout for otherwise-reclusive members of the American literati. In 2000, O'Connor befriended author Kurt Vonnegut, who taught advanced writing at nearby Smith College. In discussing beer with the writer, O'Connor learned that Vonnegut's grandfather had been a brewer at the Indianapolis Brewing Company. After discussing the project with the author, O'Connor brewed a beer similar to a style brewed more than one hundred years ago by Vonnegut the elder.

It's easy to see how O'Connor and the notoriously ribald Vonnegut became friendly with one another. Just because the brewpub is located smack in the middle of one of the most progressive-minded communities in America doesn't mean its owners aren't above a little politically incorrect humor. The popular Paradise City Gold is as much an inside joke about the town's penchant for political correctness (thus PC Gold) as it is named for O'Connor's appreciation of Eighties hair metal. For the annual Halloween party, go-go dancers gyrate behind the brewhouse windows. O'Connor proudly reminisces about the time his band won a "Battle of the Brewery Bands" contest with beer-soaked, lesbian-accompanied renditions of Meat Loaf songs.

Offshore Ale Company

Kennebec Avenue
Oak Bluffs, Massachusetts 02557
Tel. (508) 693–2626
www.offshoreale.com

> ★ **Best Beer:** Rye Knot?. I am tempted to choose the delightfully hoppy Stonewall IPA served on cask, or one of Steinberg's specialty reserve beers, but this beer trumps the others. Once forgotten as a long-discarded brewing ingredient, rye is making a comeback. Rye is a strongly flavored grain that imparts a slightly spicy, zesty note when used at moderate levels in brewing. While most brewers use rye as a gimmick, Offshore's version boasts a distinct, intriguing spiciness imparted by additions of caraway seeds, orange peel, and white pepper. The Rye Knot? is a remarkably crisp beer that zings with flavor.

Opened: August 1997.

Type: Brewpub.

Owner: Robert Skydell.

Brewer: Matthew Steinberg.

Brewing system: 10-barrel Liquid Assets brewhouse.

Amount produced: Figures not available.

First beer: Amber Ale.

Flagship beer: Amber Ale.

Year-round beers: Amber Ale, Stonewall IPA, and American Pale Ale.

Seasonal beers: Belgian Trippel, Barley Wine, Bryggiemann Paquette, Beetlebung Porter, Dry Irish Stout, Euro Pils, Fond de Tiroir, Inkwell Imperial Stout, Kilt Lifter (Scottish-style ale), Oatmeal Stout, Rye Knot?, Nutbrown Ale, Menemsha Mild, Munich Helles, Rye Pilsener, and Spring Bock.

Tours: Tours by appointment.

Beer to go: Growlers available for sale. Offshore contracts with Casco Bay Brewing of Portland, Maine, to produce its Amber Ale and IPA in bottles for off-island distribution.

Food: Upscale pub fare with some island prices to match. Fancy, wood-fired pizzas are the best value and flavor on an intriguing and nourishing menu.

Amenities: You probably just took the ferry to the island, but if you were crazy enough to drive, there is very limited street parking near the brewpub. Full liquor license.

Pub hours: Unlike many attractions in Oak Bluffs, Offshore stays open year-round. From November through April, the pub is open Monday and Tuesday, 5 P.M. to 1 A.M.; and Wednesday through Sunday, noon to 1 A.M. From June through October, the pub is open daily, noon to 1 A.M.

Directions: The Offshore Ale brewery in the town of Oak Bluffs, near Ocean Park and down the street from the Flying Horse Carousel, the country's oldest working carousel.

Nestled in the heart of Oak Bluffs on Martha's Vineyard, a few steps from the ferry, Offshore is a noteworthy destination for beer lovers. Putting aside the great summer weather, relaxed vibe, and island locale, a trip to Offshore is a must, even in the middle of winter. The brewpub combines a welcoming environment, well-considered food, good company, and, of course, excellent beers.

Visitors to the Victorian-era looking barn often mistake the brewpub for a piece of original architecture. Owner Bob Skydell, an architect by training, designed and built the charming structure on the site of a former laundromat. Constructed in part with reclaimed dock wood, the building is wide open on the inside with vaulted, wood-beamed ceilings almost three stories high. An enormous, stone fireplace anchors the far wall, flanked on the other side by an open kitchen with a wood-fired, brick oven. On the attractive, lofted second floor, fermenters and grain bags overlook the main room. The highlight of the design is the striking copper brewing system that stands proudly behind the pub's bar.

Rustic is a good way to describe the feel here. Peanut shells cover the floor and a series of small, cozy booths line one side, with a smattering of big, round tables in the center. Despite a large window overlooking the street, Offshore remains cast in dim light much of the day, creating an insular, focused drinking experience. With all of the dark woods, Offshore gives the impression it has been a part of the community for longer than anyone can recall.

Brewer Matthew Steinberg first arrived at Offshore in 2003 after working at several breweries in Massachusetts. While employed at a brew-on-premise in Colorado, Steinberg received a phone call from a friend in Boston who suggested he apply for a job opening at Harpoon. After an intense five-month training at Harpoon, Steinberg moved to John Harvard's in Cambridge, working as an assistant brewer for several years before moving into a sales job at Concord Brewing. There he met Robert Skydell, the owner of Offshore, who was looking for a contract brewery to produce his Amber Ale. As Concord's business grew more chaotic and unfocused, Skydell suggested to Steinberg that he take over the brewing operations at Offshore. After some soul searching, Steinberg agreed to take the permanent ferry to the island.

The brewer now runs the brewing system here and serves as the brand manager for the pub's burgeoning off-premise business (Offshore contracts its bottle production to Casco Bay Brewing). Steinberg spends several days each week off the island, cruising between package stores and tap accounts in the promotion of Offshore's beers. When he is on-island, Steinberg remains one of the friendliest and most approachable brewers in New England. He frequently invites friends and strangers to the Vineyard to sample his beers and happily chats with customers about Offshore and upcoming releases.

While the off-island brewed bottled beers are solid offerings, Offshore is best experienced in the heart of the operation on Martha's Vineyard. Steinberg freely experiments at the brewery, often using unusual ingredients and wood barrels to create some stellar beers. His brewing efforts are hardly art for its own sake. He carefully considers the recipes and tends to brew and present a solid stable of beers that age well over years. While Steinberg occasionally throws out a new, special beer, like the Fond de Tiroir, much of his efforts focus on tweaking his portfolio, including his Kilt Lifter Scotch Ale and his Inkwell Imperial Stout, in an attempt to better them. Offshore has two hand pumps for cask-conditioned beer, and the Stonewall IPA is not to be missed. Steinberg often alters the recipe, sometimes with new hop additions or by simply doubling the hop dose, leading to a different pint every visit.

Berkshire Brewing Company

12 Railroad Street
South Deerfield, Massachusetts 01373
Tel. (413) 665–6600
www.berkshirebrewingcompany.com

Berkshire Brewing Company, Inc.

★ **Best Beer:** Raspberry Strong Ale. In an industry filled with fruit beers flavored with extracts, syrups, and sugary substances, it's refreshing to find a brewery dedicated to making its beers with actual fruit. Few breweries actually take the time and bear the expense of employing real fruit in the process of making their beers. For those who equate fruit beers with wimpy, Zima-drinking sissies, Berkshire's Raspberry Strong Ale will slap you back into line. The beer pours with a substantial, well-sustained, off-white head and smells strongly of raspberries and sharper acidic notes. Add to the mix its radiant, reddish orange hue and you know this is no average fruit beer. The flavor is a mix of big malts, a sizable alcohol presence, and a slightly mouth-puckering balance of sweet and tart flavors from the fruit. Simply one of the best fruit beers in New England.

Opened: October 1994.

Type: Brewery.

Owners: Chris Lalli and Gary Bogoff.

Brewer: Chris Lalli.

Brewing system: 24-barrel DME kettle and self-fabricated brewhouse.

Amount produced: 10,600 barrels. 25,000-barrel total capacity.

First beer: Steel Rail Extra Pale Ale.

Flagship beer: Steel Rail Extra Pale Ale.

Year-round beers: Steel Rail Extra Pale Ale, Berkshire Ale, Drayman's Porter, Lost Sailor India Pale Ale, "Shabadoo" Black & Tan Ale, Imperial Stout, River Ale, Coffeehouse Porter, and Golden Spike Ale.

Seasonal beers: Maibock Lager, Raspberry Strong Ale, Cabin Fever Ale, Oktoberfest Lager, and Holidale.

Tours: Tours available Saturdays at 1 P.M.

Beer to go: None.

Amenities: Limited parking available at the brewery.

Directions: Take Exit 24 (Route 10/US-5) from I-91 and follow State Road into South Deerfield. After the road becomes Greenfield Street, turn right onto Elm Street. Cross over the train tracks and look for Railroad Street on the left.

Owners Chris Lalli and Gary Bogoff are living the homebrewer's dream in western Massachusetts. Together they started brewing larger and larger batches of beer until ten gallons at a time simply wasn't enough. So the partners spent three years carefully planning their brewery and preparing test batches. The local community was also very welcoming to the aspiring brewery owners; the head of the local Chamber of Commerce drove Bogoff and Lalli around to scout possible locations. After finding a home in historic Deerfield, Massachusetts, and winning the unanimous approval and backing of the town selectmen, the owners started renovating an old cigar factory into the craft brewery of their dreams.

When I say the owners started renovating, I mean exactly that. Before dreaming up the brewery, Bogoff worked as a general contractor and master tradesman, while Lalli was employed as a laser technician doing custom welding. When I visit, Berkshire is in the process of completing its third major expansion. Both of the owners wear matching maroon Berkshire Brewing Company sweatshirts with the word "staff" on them. When they shake, there is dirt under the fingernails of their worn hands. Halfway through the interview, Bogoff excuses himself to attend to the brewery. A worker has called in sick, so he is headed out to pour the concrete floor that will soon sustain the new bottling line.

The brewery itself is now a sprawling, twenty-three-thousand-square-foot mammoth, though it remains far from a slick, turnkey operation. Virtually nothing here is brand new, and the owners and workers pride themselves on their abilities to improvise. The operation works with great precision, as product moves swiftly from the brewhouse to fermentation to conditioning to packaging. One of the newest additions allows the delivery trucks to pull right up to an enormous, well-designed cold room to retrieve the next shipment.

The original 7-barrel system is still on display, and sometimes in use, in the brewhouse. Fashioned by Bogoff and Lalli from parts from another brewery, "the little brewery that could," as Lalli calls it, produced an astounding 6,000 barrels per year at its peak. The brewery also boasts an enormous 100,000 BTU hot water tank capable of running twenty-four hours a day without a break.

In what would become a trademark of the brewery, Bogoff and Lalli enlisted friends, associates in the trades, volunteers, and family members to help transform and run the brewery. The owners are quick to thank all those who helped build the brewery and kept it running in the early days, including three retired gentlemen the owners affectionately refer to as "the three mugs of beer." Along with stray local college kids, these three pillars of the brewery helped Lalli and Bogoff bottle their early releases. Even though Berkshire finally gave up hand-bottling after more than nine years, the guys still come around once in a while to check on the place.

Berkshire is also noteworthy because it brews a huge variety of year-round beers that other breweries won't even produce on a seasonal basis. The brewery produces up to fifteen styles of beer throughout the year, running the gamut from a light ale to a deeply roasted imperial stout. The owners remain very dedicated to brewing beers within their traditional styles, including a few quality lagers. They also do not believe in using artificial ingredients, and their powerful Raspberry Strong Ale is brewed with real fruit and no flavorings.

The owners talk a lot about their desire to create a brewery built upon the classic European model, where communities once had their own local breweries. So although the Berkshire brand is very familiar to those in western Massachusetts, it remains a bit of an unknown to drinkers in Boston—and the owners like it that way. Lalli and Bogoff are intensely focused on their local markets, selling almost 95 percent of their more than 10,000 barrels a year within sixty miles of the brewery. With four refrigerated trucks, Berkshire self-distributes its brands to more than a thousand accounts in Massachusetts, and the owners try to develop a personal relationship with their retailers.

Berkshire has also pioneered the practice, which is now catching on with some other breweries listed in these pages, of restricting their packaged sales to 22-ounce bottles. To this day, you won't find a six-pack of Berkshire's beer for sale. Berkshire also offers growlers, a package the owners laughingly refer to as "the hillbilly six-pack."

As Berkshire looks to the future, Lalli and Bogoff remain dedicated to maintaining a slow pace of growth. A lot of unused space remains at the brewery, including a large, beautiful, lofted area that eventually may house the brewpub the guys have been dreaming of for years. But given all of their current balancing jobs, the brewpub plan remains a distant one. Lalli is also in the process of reopening the Windham Brewery in Brattleboro, Vermont, where he will brew some smaller, experimental beers. Berkshire beer, of course, will come along for the ride.

Opa Opa Steakhouse and Brewery

169 College Highway
Southampton, Massachusetts 01073
Tel. (413) 527–0808
www.opaopasteakhousebrewery.com

> ★ **Best Beer:** Warthog Double IPA. Kramer wasted no time in brewing an absolute stunner of a souped-up India pale ale. The nose is a mixture of various fruit esters and wine notes, with distinct, fresh hop aromas. The flavor is a perfect balance of hop bitterness and malt that showcases hop flavor above all else. One of the best American strong ales I have sampled in a long time.

Opened: September 2004.

Type: Brewpub.

Owners: Themis and Tony Rizos.

Brewer: Dan Kramer.

Brewing system: 10-barrel Century Manufacturing brewhouse.

Amount produced: 600 barrels. 1,500-barrel total capacity.

First beer: Red Rock.

Flagship beer: Opa Opa.

Year-round beers: Adonis Gold, Buckwheat IPA, Honesty 47 Pale Ale, King Oak Milt Stout, Opa Opa (helles), Opa Opa Light, Red Rock (amber), Southampton Porter, and Kix Brew (blonde ale).

Seasonal beers: Warthog Double IPA.

Tours: Tours available by appointment.

Beer to go: Growlers available for purchase.

Food: The food at Opa Opa is among the best you'll find at a New England brewpub. The restaurant focuses on steaks and barbecue dishes and is not really a place for vegetarians. The menu has a humorous touch: if you want your steak rare, you're advised that you "better keep a rope on it," and fans of well-done steak are told not to "mistake it for your boot." The menu is upscale but the prices are fair and everything is presented in a casual fashion.

Amenities: Parking is available in the pub's lot. Full liquor license.

Pub hours: Open Monday through Thursday, 4 P.M. to midnight; Friday and Saturday, 11 A.M. to 1 A.M.; and Sunday, 11 A.M. to midnight.

Directions: College Highway (Route 10) is the main artery through the town of Southampton. The brewery is located at the intersection of this road and Pomeroy Meadow Road.

Absolutely nothing prepared me for the surreal experience of visiting the Opa Opa Steakhouse and Brewery. When I pull into the parking lot of this new and oddly named brewpub, I don't really know what to expect. With its boxy architecture, Opa Opa looks like your average, small-town roadside eatery. After a long weekend of traveling to nearly a dozen other places, I secretly hope to make a quick stop. When I exit the pub nearly three hours later, I immediately wish I had never left.

The story begins in a little town a few hours north of Athens, where two young Greek boys spent many hours soaking up American culture. Like so many others around the world, Themis and Tony Rizos loved to watch Westerns on television and at the movies. The boys grew up idolizing John Wayne and dreaming of the United States. When they later moved here, the Rizos boys opened up a little pizza and sandwich shop in Southampton. The business grew a little bigger each year and they expanded the restaurant a half-dozen times, but the owners weren't fully satisfied. Although certainly a good start, the pizza restaurant was not the dream. After scouting around, the Rizos found the perfect location to open a true American steakhouse.

Opa Opa is perhaps New England's single greatest undiscovered brewpub treasure. From the moment you walk through the ornate entryway, you embark on a gustatory and visual romp. With the help of a local designer, the owners created a true Texas steakhouse with an unmistakable country-and-western theme that is wonderfully kitschy. The whole scene inspires amazement, with the restaurant's décor wavering between tacky and classy. It takes a true fondness for the classic age of Westerns to create a place as detail-oriented as Opa Opa. There are striking, laser-cut metal cowboy engravings on the railings, cowboy-themed showpieces made from rope and spurs, and hand-sewn Wild West murals covering the booth seats. A large stone hearth anchors it all.

Though they never expressly say so, I'm pretty sure the owners selected this particular building as much for its location as for the fact that it also once hosted a Hollywood film shoot. In 1965, Elizabeth Taylor and Richard Burton shot a critical scene here for the film, *Who's Afraid of Virginia Woolf?* At the time, the restaurant was known as the Red Basket. The groundbreaking film won multiple Academy Awards and scored a historical note as the first film to receive an R rating from the Motion Picture Association of America. The film's tagline, "Drop in for drinks and brace yourself," is an invitation and piece of advice that clearly applies here at Opa Opa.

In the swirl of cowboy madness, it's easy to miss the brewhouse that sits off to one far side of the pub. The oversight is quickly rectified when I meet with brewer Dan Kramer under a sign reading, "Cowgirls are forever." His beers, which include several lagers, are served on a tasting tray made by his father. Each of the beers is very clean and flavorful, with a few crossing over to true excellence. The variety of beers on offer at Opa Opa provides choices both for novices and for the most ardent beer geeks alike.

Formerly of the now-closed Maplewood Farms Restaurant and Brewery in nearby Amherst, the Siebel-trained Kramer worked with his boss to fine-tune the recipes. The brewer notes that while Themis may lack experience in the technical minutiae of brewing, the owner clearly knows what flavors he wants in his beers. When the pair was testing potential beers, Themis would sample Kramer's newest batch and offer simple critiques until they found the right formula. While Themis usually maintains a solemn and serious exterior, the big guy occasionally lowers his guard to reveal a warm smile while he shares a laugh and a story. Themis likes to joke that he is one-quarter German, so he knows what beer should taste like.

With his owner's direction in mind, Kramer is then free to craft the final products. The lager beers typically tie up three of his tanks, so Kramer spends part of his time trying to arrange the logistics of the operation. The beers reflect a global appreciation of beer, with representatives from German, English, and American brewing styles. The mildly English pale ale, Honesty 47, is named after the reputation and badge number of a local police officer who is a long-time customer. Some offerings are filtered, while many are not. While the beer here is in its infancy, the first batches are impressive and bode well for future releases.

Named after the traditional Greek exclamation of joy, Opa Opa covers all the elements necessary to make it a true destination. The service is thoughtful and efficient, the food is well prepared and flavorful, the design is eye-catching and well executed, and the beer is top notch. There is only one thing I could find missing at Opa Opa. Although Themis was clad in a leather vest and bolo tie, I was shocked to see him wearing shiny wingtips instead of cowboy boots. However, considering the rest of the place, I imagine even John Wayne could forgive him for that.

Hyland Orchard and Brewery

199 Arnold Road
Sturbridge, Massachusetts 01566
Tel. (508) 347–7500
www.hylandbrew.com

★ **Best Beer:** Dark Harvest ESB. At the outset, this is admittedly not an ESB by any conventional style guideline. While ESBs traditionally tend towards light amber in color, the Dark Harvest possesses a deep garnet hue. ESBs usually weigh in at session-ale alcohol levels, while the Dark Harvest tips the scales at 8 percent alcohol by volume. Full of deep, roasted malts; light, smoky hints; and a balance of Galena bittering hops in the finish, the Dark Harvest ESB portends good things for future releases under the new Pioneer Brewing Company label.

Opened: 1996 (under new ownership in May 2004).

Type: Brewery.

Owners: Tim Daly and Todd Sullivan.

Brewers: Tim Daly and Todd Sullivan.

Brewing system: 20-barrel Criveller brewhouse.

Amount produced: 2,000 barrels. Presently at capacity.

First beer: Amber Ale.

Flagship beer: Amber Ale.

Year-round beers: Amber Ale, Farmhand Ale, American Pale Ale, and Sturbridge Stout.

Seasonal beers: Octoberfest and Dark Harvest ESB.

Tours: Tours given on Saturdays and Sundays at 2 P.M.

Beer to go: 64-ounce growlers and 22-ounce bottles.

Food: Limited snacks, ranging from nachos to chicken wings, are available during Friday-evening taproom sessions.

Amenities: Limited parking is available near the brewery.

Other attractions: Only a short distance from the brewery, you find an astounding selection of beer at Yankee Spirits. While the store focuses on wine, the beer section here is larger in size than some liquor stores are in total. The store carries the full range of Hyland's products, along with a sweeping selection of beers from New England, the United States, and beyond. Yankee Spirits, 376 Main Street, Sturbridge, Massachusetts 01566, tel. (508) 347–2231, www.yankeespirits.com.

Directions: The brewery and Tap Room are only minutes away from Old Sturbridge Village; head out Main Street and turn on Arnold Road.

Todd Sullivan was destined to become a brewer. Look closely behind the tasting bar at the picturesque farm brewery and you'll see an old, faded photo of a thirteen-year-old Todd standing in front of his sizable beer can collection. While pursuing an art major as an oil painter in college, Todd received a homebrew kit and was immediately hooked. After stints at several New England breweries, the gregarious Sullivan met his quieter alter ego, Tim Daly, while the two brewed together at the Mill City Brewing Company in Lowell. While Sullivan eventually ended up at Hyland, Daly left to brew at various other locations in New England.

Hyland is located in one of the most picturesque settings for a brewery in New England. Located on 150 acres of the Damon family farmstead, Hyland originally opened as an apple orchard. The family eventually saw an opportunity to expand its business as a local attraction by opening a microbrewery. In 2004, the family decided to exit the beer business and offered their head brewer, Sullivan, the opportunity to take over the brands and lease, to own the entire brewery. With Daly's help, Sullivan accepted the offer.

From there, the two partners couldn't seem to get enough of one another. As the brewery's only two employees, they brew, bottle, and distribute the beer together in the company's rickety old van. They live down the street from one another in this beautiful, hilly section of southern Massachusetts and even spend their only day off from the brewery together. With a laugh, Sullivan insists the similarities end there. As an example, Sullivan offers that he is a man dedicated to the German purity law of brewing, which strictly limits the ingredients used in brewing to the four traditional offerings of barley, hops, water, and yeast. Conversely, Daly has expressed interest in brewing fruit lambics.

The 150-acre site is shared by three different businesses: a brewery, a bakery, and the orchard. It takes each of the three entities working cooperatively to make the overall location a success. It's an enviable model. In the summer and fall high seasons, the orchard sponsors festivals every weekend, with live music, apple picking, a petting zoo, and hay rides. The family-friendly events usually draw around two thousand visitors, where kids play with Colleen the cow and Thelma the pygmy goat, while the adults sneak off to sample Hyland's beer. The events are so successful that the brewery sells nearly one-quarter of its beer on site.

While Hyland's distribution once stretched across Massachusetts, the brewery's focus is now one of intense dedication to the local market. The co-owners model their brewery on the model from smaller European cities, where the brewery is firmly rooted in the community and serves as a meeting place for its people. The brewery aims to fully serve the Sturbridge community, including its restaurants, bars, and package stores. "If you come to our town, you get our beer," Sullivan says with a big smile. "Plus, we don't want to drive too far in that van."

To better connect the brewery and the town, Hyland expanded its tasting bar into a full, welcoming bar, called the Tap Room. On Friday evenings, the brewery opens its doors and taps to anyone looking to unwind from a long week. Last call occurs at 6:30 P.M.

Hyland's beers each have a distinctive crispness to their flavor, a character Sullivan attributes to the pure well water located deep below the brewery. The beers are uniformly clean and well made, if not adventurous in flavor. Recognizing that the brewery's main lineup of beers may not necessarily excite finicky beer geeks, Daly and Sullivan are in the process of developing their own special line of beers under the new Pioneer Brewing Company brand. Comprised of small-batch, special releases, the new beers will allow the two brewers to experiment and put their own mark on the company, without alienating Hyland's existing customers. Sullivan envisions Pioneer as an artisanal brewery, producing unusual styles and experimental, high-gravity batches.

Watch City Brewing Company

256 Moody Street
Waltham, Massachusetts 02453
Tel. (781) 647–4000
www.watchcitybrew.com

★ **Best Beer:** Moody Street Stout. While every brewpub offers a yawn-inducing, dry Irish stout, Watch City comes to the table with a terrific version of the venerable and often-neglected export-stout style. Often found in tropical regions, the export-stout style is best characterized by its higher alcohol content and substantial malt base. With its strong, roasted-malt aroma, sweet coffee and mocha flavors, and slight bitterness, the Moody Street Stout is no exception to the style guidelines. I only wish more brewpubs looked to this style for their stout offerings.

Opened: March 1996.

Type: Brewpub.

Owner: Jocelyn McLaughlin.

Brewer: Aaron Mateychuk.

Brewing system: 14-barrel Peter Austin brewhouse.

Amount produced: 800 barrels. 2,500-barrel total capacity.

First beer: Orient Pale Ale.

Flagship beer: Hops Explosion IPA.

Year-round beers: Tick Tock Ale (golden), Totem Pale Ale, Hops Explosion IPA, Moody Street Stout, and Titan Ale (brown).

Seasonal beers: 38 Schilling Scottish Ale, Beet The Clock Amber Ale, Biere De Bordel, Biking Bob's Bohemian Pilsner, Blackdogg Oatmeal Stout, Bombed Blondeshelle Tripel, Buster Nut Brown Ale, Chocolate Thunder Porter, Clockwork Orange Cream Ale, Colossus Big Brown, Diamond Pilsner, Dubbel CrossxD, Frostbite Winter Ale, Gunther (dunkel), I Got Your Doppelbok, Jack Horner's Plum Wit, Kingpin Imperial Stout, Legerete Belgian Strong Ale, Lunar Shine Burley Whine, Mach Marzen, Mia Bock Spring Lager, Midnight Munich Lager, Mongrel Pale Ale, Monky Monk Saison, Mr. Dexter's Very Vanilla Cream Ale, My O' Maibock, Nuptial Ale, Obscurite Tripel Brown, Opening Day IPA, Oriten Ten-Seater Ale, Peace Pipe Pale Ale, Pie Eyed Pumpkin Ale, Primetime IPA, Privateer IPA, Rabbie Burns Quintesensual Ale, Rites of Spring IPA, Road Rash Raspberry Wheat, Saturnalea Grand Cru, Saturnalea Solstice Ale, Schwartz Bier Lager, Shillelagh Irish Red Ale, Skye High Scotch Ale, Spring Saison, The Gourd and Sheaf Ale, Vanguard Stout, Wit's End Wit, Uber Oktolager, Yellow Jacket Belgian Pale Ale, Zok's Baltic Porter, and Zuper Eisbock.

Tours: By appointment.

Beer to go: Growlers are filled here, and pricey 22-ounce bottles of the pub's higher alcohol offerings are available for purchase.

Food: The menu is slightly upscale pub fare, with an emphasis on sandwiches, wraps, and seafood.

Amenities: On-street parking is available or park in the lot behind the nearby movie theater. Watch City is also located in close proximity to a commuter rail stop. Wi-Fi connection available.

Pub Hours: Monday through Saturday, 11:30 A.M. to 12:30 A.M.; Sunday, 4:30 P.M. to 11:30 P.M.

Directions: Watch City is on Moody Street near the commuter rail station and the Charles River Museum of Industry, and directly next to the movie theater.

In the 1850s, two artisans sought a clean, dust-free environment in which to assemble their precision-built watches. After scouting some locations, the partners settled on the city of Waltham and built the world's largest brick structure on the banks of the Charles River. Their business, the Waltham Watch Company, ascended to great international acclaim, producing more than forty million timepieces and mastering the intricacies of crafting complex, mechanized products on a mass level.

While the Waltham Watch Company didn't survive past the late 1950s, its host city was forever deemed "the Watch City." In a large storefront on a corner of downtown's Moody Street, a brewpub bearing the city's popular nickname continues the artisanship of its ancestors. On Waltham's Restaurant Row, brewer Aaron Mateychuk works in the brewhouse overlooking Moody Street. During his time as head brewer at the Watch City Brewing Company, Mateychuk has produced more than 140 different beers. After interning at Harpoon, he knew he wanted to strike out on his own. "It's like being in a kitchen," he says. "You want to be in charge."

The pub's owners provide the young brewer, who has been here nearly from the beginning, with the ultimate freedom to ply his craft.

Watch City originally contracted with Alan Pugsley's consulting company to provide it with a brewing system and the Ringwood house yeast strain. Very early on, Watch City's brewers were displeased by the flavors produced with the yeast. Soon after opening, the brewery discontinued its use of the Ringwood strain and replaced it with six or seven other varieties, including two different Belgian and lager strains. The familiar, brick-clad brewing kettle and open fermentation tanks remain; Mateychuk praises the system for its versatility with other strains, including his lager yeasts. The lengths to which the brewery has gone to shed its affiliation with the Ringwood strain are sometimes amusing, including the employment of a purple, plastic, child's outdoor pool turned upside down as a giant cover for one of the open 14-barrel fermentation tanks.

The variety of offerings brewed by Watch City is impressive. The pub always runs at least one lager beer, including the wildly popular Uber Oktolager. The beer is labor intensive, requiring six weeks of lagering; Mateychuk laments how quickly his customers finish it off. "It's a favorite," he says. "I work for months on it and then put it on and it's gone." He takes a small quantity of each batch of Oktolager, freezes it, removes the water (as alcohol freezes at a lower temperature), and makes a souped-up Zuper Eisbock. Weighing in at 15 percent alcohol by volume, the Eisbock packs an intense, malt punch and a slight hop spiciness, with notable alcohol and fruit aromas. In the spring, Mateychuk brews a handful of different IPAs to celebrate a hoppy Easter.

The space at Watch City is wide open, with two dining areas wrapping around the centralized main bar, which anchors the establishment. The décor has a muted but slightly upscale tone, with pieces of original artwork and reproductions of antique French liquor ads. A young crowd, mainly professionals from the Route 128 belt area, congregate in the main bar and chat over pints after work.

Wachusett Brewing Company

175 State Road East
Westminster, Massachusetts 01473
Tel. (978) 874–9965
www.wachusettbrew.com

★ **Best Beer:** IPA. No doubt about it, this is one of the great, underappreciated India pale ales in New England. The IPA is aged longer than the rest of the Wachusett line, filled with tantalizing additions of Amarillo, Centennial, East Kent Goldings, and Magnum hops, and heavily dry-hopped with 40 pounds of Cascade hops per batch. The aroma is wonderfully hoppy, with earthy and citrus hints and a touch of malt sweetness. The resulting beer is not designed to punish but rather reward your palate. The IPA is very well balanced; the raw hop flavor is kept in check by a healthy dose of malt. It finishes with a clean, crisp tang and a lingering dose of hop bitterness. The only downside here is that the IPA's enticing hop aroma discourages you from actually drinking the beer, out of the realization that each sip sadly diminishes the delicate, pungent olfactory experience.

Opened: December 1994.

Type: Brewery.

Owners: Ned LaFortune, Kevin Buckler, and Peter Quinn.

Brewer: Dave Howard.

Brewing system: 50-barrel Briggs of Burton brewhouse.

Amount produced: 10,800 barrels. 25,000-barrel total capacity.

First beer: Country Ale.

Flagship beer: Country Ale.

Year-round beers: Country Ale, IPA, Blueberry Ale, Black Shack Porter, Nut Brown Ale, and Green Monsta (double IPA).

Seasonal beers: Quinn's Amber Ale (spring), Summer Breeze (wheat), Octoberfest (fall), and Winter Ale.

Tours: Very informative and spirited tours are available Wednesday through Saturday, noon to 5 P.M. Call ahead for Monday and Tuesday tours.

Beer to go: Growlers and 6-packs are available for sale at the brewery.

Amenities: Parking is available in the brewery's lot. The tours are especially kid-friendly, with free samples of Wachusett Root Beer.

Directions: Head east from the center of Westminster on Route 2A, and find the brewery on the right near the stone railroad bridge.

Beyond politics and religion, geographical designation is perhaps the issue on which residents of the commonwealth share the least amount of common ground. In the Hub, there is Boston and there is western Massachusetts, the latter term referring to any community, business, or destination located outside the Route 128 belt. For the populace of the mythical place known as central Massachusetts, it can sometimes feel like you're dwelling in a hidden vortex, uncharted on any map. Living in the pleasant towns and valleys of Worcester County, you can either develop an inferiority complex over your more famous siblings of Boston and the Berkshires, or you can shrug it off and hope your secret doesn't get out.

Located in a small industrial park, the Wachusett Brewing Company is having a hard time keeping its brewery a secret. The product of three local guys, all friends who attended the Worcester Polytechnic Institute together, Wachusett is a local-oriented brewery. Founders Ned LaFortune, Kevin Buckler, and Peter Quinn are each from the area and grew up drinking cheap beer together in college. After graduating—Ned and Kevin are engineers and Peter is a microbiologist—the trio started drinking better beers. As their passion for craft beer flourished, the future brewery founders started road-tripping to the various breweries in New England to sample beers and learn more about the business.

Possessed by the entrepreneurial spirit, LaFortune knew he wanted to work for himself. On the trips, he spent a lot of time talking with some of the early pioneers of New England craft brewing, including Lawrence Miller of the Otter Creek Brewing Company and Ray McNeill of McNeill's Brewery. While Miller encouraged the upstart homebrewers, McNeill actively attempted to dissuade them from turning their hobbies into a commercial operation. During each trip to McNeill's colorful pub, the trio would offer the brewer samples of their homebrewed test batches and he would return with blistering judgments about their quality. Despite the criticism, the guys continued to brew; they kept coming back with new samples. McNeill eventually gave up trying to discourage the young brewers.

After traveling throughout New England, LaFortune knew he wanted to start the brewery in his own backyard of Worcester County. He did just that, brewing on his parents' farm in Westminster until the well dried up and his family kicked him out. By the time the trio got serious about brewing, the craft beer movement was already plowing ahead. Hundreds of new breweries opened each year during the 1990s, which led to a dearth of cheap, used brewing equipment. Strapped for start-up capital, the founders put their engineering backgrounds to work and fabricated their first brewhouse. Many breweries showcase their brewing systems, often boasting shiny copper kettles or gleaming stainless-steel vessels. Not so for Wachusett, whose early, 7-barrel system was far from easy on the eyes. As the brewery grew, the system expanded, eventually becoming what is perhaps the ugliest brewhouse in New England. When I first visit, I can't determine which piece is the brewing kettle. The horizontal kettle resembles less a place to create flavorful ales than a discarded heating and cooling system ripped from some decades old, industrial boiler room.

Thankfully, this ugly duckling is scheduled for a thorough makeover. The owners recently installed a 50-barrel brewhouse built by Briggs of Burton and taken from a defunct Scottish brewery. Of course, the guys at Wachusett can't do anything the easy way, so their new system actually hasn't been used in more than twenty years. With an eye to the brewery's future, the owners also purchased a gleaming, 120-barrel behemoth Ziemann system built in 1951. They treat the system as part of a carrot and stick approach to growth: if they continue to perform well and grow the business, they plan to build a new brewery in the coming years that will showcase the copper-clad kettles.

True beer lovers know better than to simply skip through central Massachusetts on the way to somewhere else. While Wachusett may appear to be a small brewery, and in the grander scheme of things it is, it's actually the second-largest brewery in Massachusetts behind Harpoon. Wachusett runs neck-and-neck in terms of production and growth with fellow "western Mass" brewery, the Berkshire Brewing Company, which lies forty miles due west in East Deerfield. Like Berkshire, Wachusett focuses its efforts on its local area, selling 99 percent of its beer in Massachusetts and 70 percent in Worcester County alone.

While most of the beers brewed by Wachusett won't bowl you over with unconscionable levels of hops or malt, they are each solid, flavorful, and enjoyable. The ales are easy-drinking, while the IPA and the stand-out Green Monsta, a self-described strong amber ale whose name is trademarked by the brewery, should please even demanding beer geeks.

Buzzards Bay Brewing

98 Horseneck Road
Westport, Massachusetts 02790
Tel. (508) 636–2288
www.buzzardsbrew.com

★ **Best Beer:** Lager. The heart of the brewery's portfolio, the Lager is a positively radiant, golden-hued beer. Brewed close to the Dortmunder style, the beer's aroma is grainy, with a touch of German hops. The flavor is clean, with biscuity notes and the lightest touch of butter. Full flavored, the Lager is a good, low-key accompaniment to summer activities for craft beer enthusiasts. A very drinkable and easy-going session beer.

Opened: July 1998.

Type: Brewery.

Owners: Robert and Carol Russell.

Brewer: Kurt Musselman.

Brewing system: 50-barrel Newlands Systems brewhouse.

Amount produced: 7,100 barrels (includes 1,700 barrels contract brewed for other breweries). 30,000-barrel total capacity.

First beer: Pale Ale.

Flagship beer: Lager.

Year-round beers: Lager, Pale Ale, and Golden Ale.

Seasonal beers: West Porter.

Tours: By appointment on Saturdays and Sundays. The small brewery shop is open Wednesday through Sunday, 11 A.M. to 5 P.M.

Beer to go: 6-packs and cases are for sale at the brewery.

Amenities: Parking is available next to the brewery.

Other attractions: While in the area, stop by the Westport Rivers vineyard and winery, Buzzards Bay's sister company. It produces a variety of sparkling and table wines from grapes grown in the Southeastern New England appellation. The tasting room and shop are open May 1 through December 31, daily, 11 A.M. to 5 P.M; January 2 through April 30, weekends only, 11 A.M. to 5 P.M; closed major holidays. Guided tours on weekends at 1 P.M. and 3 P.M. Buzzards Bay is also affiliated with the Long Acre House Wine and Food Center, a culinary education center that sponsors wine, beer, and food events throughout the year. 417 Hixbridge Road, Westport, Massachusetts 02790, tel. (800) 993–9695.

Directions: The brewery is located on Horseneck Road near popular Horseneck Beach. From I-195 East, take exit 10 (Route 88 south) and go left/east at Hix Bridge Road, and right/south on Horseneck Road. The brewery is on the left.

Owner Bob Russell spent many years scouting for the perfect place to build his winery. He traveled abroad, checking out possible sites, before returning home to find the right parcel of land in the town of Westport, near Cape Cod. His eldest son, Rob, started the vineyard by planting forty acres of Chardonnay, Pinot Noir, and Johannisberg Riesling vines. While the vines took root, Russell's second son, Bill, graduated from Boston College and returned home to start work as the family's vintner.

By the time the winery opened to the public in 1991, Bill's mind had started to wander to other yeasty experiments. In addition to making wine, he started baking bread before finding another outlet for his microbiological passion: home-brewing. When a local shop gave him a beer kit, the offbeat Bill Russell fell in love with his college sweetheart all over again. His interest quickly grew from passing to professional. Russell soon found himself taking occasional days off from working in the winery—not to relax, but to work in the Union Station brewpub in nearby Providence. While there, Russell learned how to mash-in, run a lauter tun, filter beer, and understand the nuances of the product's flavor profiles.

When a nearby 140-acre farm became available, the Russell family purchased it. By that time, Bill was suffering from a full-blown addiction to brewing beer. The family started considering the idea of opening its own brewery on the newly purchased plot of land. At the same time, the Benzinger Family Winery was planning to start its own brewery in the heart of California's wine country. When the Russell brothers learned about the California winery's plans, they decided to hop a plane and pay a visit.

At the Sonoma Mountain Brewing Company, brewer Chris Atkinson was busy keeping the tanks filled and running the brewing side of the business. He was more than a little nervous when one of his employees rushed in to tell him two inspectors from OSHA had come calling on the brewery. Atkinson met the pair, who didn't strike him as government officials, and dutifully showed them around the place. The inspectors kicked the proverbial tires, checking out the equipment and the set-up before finally revealing that they were winemakers from Massachusetts, sent over to the brewery by their friends at Benzinger.

After the initial shock of the prank wore off, Atkinson became quick friends with the Russells, and spent a lot of time discussing their plans for building a brewery. As the project came to life in 1998, Atkinson agreed to work as a consultant for the family. The brewer's tenure at Sonoma Brewing was short-lived, however, as the operation folded two years after it opened. "It was a dream brewery," he says. "But eventually we woke up from the dream." Every few months, Atkinson would travel to Westport to keep an eye on the place, answer questions, and give general assistance. Each time, the Russells would offer him a job, which he always refused. When Atkinson finally started thinking about the offer, his wife thought he was nuts for even considering going back to work for another brewery owned by a winery.

The Russells originally intended Buzzards Bay to function as an ale brewery. Within two years, the sole lager product started gaining headway as the brewery's flagship product, a position it maintains to this day. By the time Atkinson came aboard full time, the brewery was offering eight different beers. Buzzards Bay soon thereafter scaled back its offerings and focused on pushing the lager. The decision paid off: the brewery won a gold medal in the European-Style Pilsner category at the 2000 Great American Beer Festival.

With its oversized 50-barrel brewing system, it doesn't take long to churn out 5000 barrels of Buzzards Bay beer. In order to keep the system running, Buzzards Bay has taken to contract brewing for other smaller operations, including Cisco Brewers and the Coastal Extreme Brewing Company. The owners have dreams of transforming Buzzards Bay into the true craft lager brewery in the Northeast. The brewery has recently started brewing some specialty releases, including a very promising German pilsner.

It remains to be seen where the next few years will take Buzzards Bay. The brewery had suffered from a decided lack of focus, leadership, and management, and staff changes have proven to be a serious distraction. A new president was hired and almost immediately fired Atkinson, only to quit himself a few weeks later. Bill Russell recently resumed direction of the wayward brewery. I hope to see the brewery rebound with a renewed focus on high-quality lagers.

Enjoying Beer

There is a difference between drinking beer and enjoying beer, much like the distinction between hearing and listening to music. People often approach drinking beer with a roteness akin to purchasing hot-dog buns or selecting a type of gas for their cars. "It's all the same, so why bother?" some believe.

Most drinkers probably don't think they need any lessons in how to drink beer. I'm not talking about the mechanics of the physical act of drinking, but about the experience of enjoying beer and how to make the most of it. Certain styles of beer best express their full flavors at specific temperatures, while other styles benefit from the use of particular types of glassware. While I'm not advocating that you sniff, swirl, and spit, with pinky extended at the proper angle, here are a few time-tested suggestions to improve your beer drinking experience.

The first guiding principle of enjoying beer is that there are no inviolable rules other than to treat beer and brewers with respect and to follow your own personal tastes. One lady's delight is another guy's dislike.

Second, take a second to consider the beer in front of you. Enjoying beer should be a pleasing experience for all of the senses, including sight. Anyone who has ever seen a German-style hefe-weizen—a beer brewed with ample amounts of barley and wheat malts—can attest to the potential beauty of beer. When it is served in a shapely, gently sloping glass, with a sizable, bright white head, the result is striking. Deep, dark, and stormy pints of imperial stouts are equally mesmerizing to the eyes. Looking at your beer can also tell you a lot about what to expect from its flavor and freshness. Does the beer have a nice, sustained head or does it simply fall away because of poor construction or a dirty glass? Is the beer hazy and unfiltered, or is it radiantly clear so that you can see through it? While looks are sometimes deceiving—with their stocky builds, dry Irish stouts can look intimidating, but most remain very light to the taste—a quick peek at your pint is part of the experience.

Third, not every beer should be consumed ice cold; in fact, very few beers are best enjoyed at near-freezing temperatures. Whenever I read a food writer casually conclude, "This dish would go well with a big, bold California cabernet or a really cold beer," I want to reach through the paper and strangle the scribe. Varying temperature levels greatly affect the aromas and flavors of most beverages, including beer. When served very cold, most beers resemble commuters at Minnesota bus stops in the middle of January—very bitter. Cold beers hide delicate aromas and suppress carbonation levels, leaving drinkers with a sharp, unpleasant, and uncharacteristically bitter result. As a beer warms, it tends to open up, revealing aromatic notes and flavors that would otherwise remain hidden under abusive temperatures.

Certain styles of beer, often including those with higher alcohol levels, or cask-conditioned ales, require warmer temperatures to guarantee proper enjoyment. Sampling the same beer at different temperatures, one very cold and the other ten degrees warmer, is the best way to demonstrate this lesson. Take an example of the classic Dortmunder style of beer, a pale golden lager with mild bitterness and nice, biscuity malt flavors. Taken straight from the fridge, the beer possesses very little aroma and tastes of strong, bitter flavors foreign to the style. With the change of a few degrees, the lager is transformed into its characteristically complex and malty self. You usually don't want your beer to be Rocky Mountain cold and you should probably pass the bar offering the coldest beer in town.

Fourth, glassware influences the aromas and even the flavors in beer, while enhancing the ceremony. Long, narrow flutes, like those used for champagne, help maintain carbonation levels. Tall pilsner and weizen glasses help sustain the majestic, foamy heads characteristic of both styles. Rounded snifters, often used for cognac and brandy, allow drinkers to swirl the contents vigorously to agitate delicate aromas, which then funnel through a narrow opening. As the masters of beer ceremony, many Belgian breweries design unique glassware to flaunt the nuances of their distinctive beers. American craft breweries are slowly beginning to pick up on the benefits of providing specialized glassware for their products, and try to stock the appropriate glassware to match their beer lists.

For drinkers of all experience levels, beer is best enjoyed at a slow pace, with time taken to stop and smell the beer. Beer is a fluid product, with aromas frequently evolving from the first pour to the last sip. Every once in a while, give the glass a swirl and don't be embarrassed to stick your nose in and take a good whiff. A beer's aromas are sometimes even better than its flavors.

Finally, taste and smell are perhaps the most obvious components to enjoying beer, but also remain the most elusive. To novice drinkers who have only sampled macrobrewed products, all beers may very well taste alike. For these timid souls, the experience of trying more full-bodied beers can be nothing short of shocking. Many don't know what to make of a truly expressive beer. The most popular awakening beer is the ever-popular pub-standard Guinness. This gateway beer is a great product for the initial awakening, but Guinness operates more as a rite of passage than a pathway to lifelong beer exploration.

After taking a sip, roll the beer around in your mouth, covering every part of your palate. Consider the mouthfeel, the fancy phrase given to the relative body of the beer on your tongue. Does it feel thin and watery or is it thick and rich? Hops, malt, yeast, water, and a host of other ingredients may be at play in beer, with each contributing different features and characters. Bitterness and sweetness are the two most obvious components involved in most beers and there usually should be a balance between both. While recent forays into extreme brewing seem to have forsaken the delicate art of balance for the blunt power of brute force, harmony between all ingredients is the sign of a great brewer. While certain notes may predominate at various times, none should totally eclipse the rest and therefore hijack the beer's flavor profile.

Always remember to let your palate be your guide. With an open mind and these suggestions in your thoughts, enjoy the exploration.

New Hampshire

Often overlooked in terms of brewing in New England, New Hampshire is the picture of stability and consistency. Though the colossal Old Man of the Mountain recently fell to his final resting place, many of New Hampshire's breweries survived the industry's own tumble in the late 1990s. While the shakeout claimed some big names, including the notable loss of the Nutfield Brewing Company, the enduring New Hampshire breweries remain among the oldest in New England. Of the fourteen breweries and brewpubs, more than half have been open for ten years, and all of them for at least five years. New openings are rare here; the existing breweries are well established and spread to all corners of the Granite State.

While the breweries are stable in terms of their market share, New Hampshire drinkers still heavily support macroproducers. Local brewers sometimes joke that New Hampshire citizens can be counted on for two things: hating taxes and drinking Budweiser. Fittingly, New Hampshire is home to Anheuser-Busch's only brewery in the region, which is by far the largest brewery in New England.

Establishing themselves primarily in tourist destinations and along major highways, craft breweries and brewpubs provide respite from domestically brewed, American-style lagers (the polite term for Bud). Of the four craft breweries based in the state, Smuttynose appears best positioned to become New Hampshire's home brand. While Smuttynose offers a wide variety of beers, ales and lagers, the brewery is really tearing up the industry with its popular, earthy IPA. An hour to the north of Portsmouth, another pale ale is also growing in reputation: for people vacationing in the White Mountains, the Tuckerman Pale Ale is by far the beer of choice. Tuckerman only produces one beer on a regular basis; its pale ale has developed a truly organic cult following among beer lovers.

While some describe New Hampshire as a desert for good beer, pockets of hope exist throughout the state and are more than mere mirages. Though lacking the flash exhibited by the other brewing regions profiled in this guide, New Hampshire's small, craft brewers consistently produce beers worthy of praise and enjoyment. The brewers here are generally reserved, though many possess a quiet passion for their craft and the art of brewing. The casual, inviting, and laid-back atmospheres that pervade both the Moat Mountain Smokehouse and Brewing Company and the Portsmouth Brewery are entirely distinct from those of any other place in New England.

Tuckerman Brewing Company

64 Hobbs Street
Conway, New Hampshire 03818
Tel. (603) 447–5400
www.tuckermanbrewing.com

★ **Best Beer:** Headwall Alt. A rather limited-edition offering from Tuckerman that the brewers sneak in when they have a little extra tank space. The brewers use dark Belgian specialty malts and domestic whole hops to create their own take on the traditional brown ales of Dusseldorf. Boasting a radiant chestnut color and a light hop bite in the aroma, the flavor is slightly peppery, with a balance of tempered malt sweetness and sustained hop bitterness.

Opened: 1998.

Type: Brewery.

Owners: Nik and Kirsten Stanciu.

Brewer: Jeremy Fall, head brewer. Melissa Perreault, assistant brewer.

Brewing system: 25-barrel DME brewhouse.

Amount produced: 3,500 barrels. 6,000-barrel total capacity.

First beer: Pale Ale.

Flagship beer: Pale Ale.

Year-round beers: Pale Ale.

Seasonal beers: Headwall Alt.

Tours: Tours available Saturdays at 3 P.M., or by appointment.

Beer to go: 6-packs and cases are available for purchase.

Amenities: Parking is available next to the brewery.

Directions: Heading away from Conway Center on Route 16, turn left onto West Main Street, and then make another left onto Hobbs Street.

The Tuckerman Pale Ale is an enigmatic beer whose challenging and curious flavor profile draws on a variety of brewing methods. Part ale and part lager, the pale ale confounds as much as it pleases. In the few, short years of its existence, Tuckerman's Pale Ale has developed a cult following for quality and a reputation that comes from its limited distribution.

Tuckerman's owners, Nik and Kirsten Stanciu, met during college but didn't start dating until they were serendipitously reunited after both separately moved to New Mexico. The couple shared a common love of craft beer; they spent time together enjoying pints at the local Santa Fe Brewing Company. At the time, Nik worked for the Los Alamos National Laboratory and his bosses wanted him to study for a doctorate. Originally from New Hampshire, he decided, along with Kirsten, to move back home and spend a winter trying to decide his next step in life.

In the welcoming embrace of Conway and the White Mountains, the couple decided to stay permanently and open their own small business. They quickly focused on starting their own brewery, then began writing a business plan and homebrewing test batches. During their experiments, they scored good results brewing a crossbreed product. Borrowing from many disciplines, the flagship pale ale is a curious take on the American pale ale style. The style-bending recipe uses English and Belgian specialty malts and four varieties of whole leaf hops, including American Cascade, British Goldings, and two secret varieties, one of which may be German Hallertau.

In an unusual twist on the common ale-brewing method, the brewers lager the beer for a week at thirty-two degrees in horizontal conditioning tanks and then dry-hop it again with whole leaf hops. When the Tuckerman Pale Ale is ready for packaging, the brewers inject a small amount of fermenting wort with German lager yeast into the finished beer to provide a secondary fermentation that naturally carbonates the beer. The resulting product is a dull, straw color and possesses a slightly tangy aroma mixing citrus and wheat notes. The flavor remains dry and wheaty, revealing a mild, apricot fruitiness as it warms.

In contrast to the approach of the majority of craft brewers, Tuckerman has focused its efforts on promoting a single product from its earliest days. While the first plan included the Headwall Alt as the second offering, the popularity of the Tuckerman Pale Ale, which accounts for nearly 100 percent of the company's business, precluded any real push for the sibling brand.

Tuckerman takes its name from the famous steep-walled glacial basin located on the southeastern flank of nearby Mt. Washington. Popular with adventure skiers, the Tuckerman Ravine contains forty- to fifty-degree steep pitches that attract daredevils to its backcountry ski environs. Nik and Kirsten love the place and wanted to associate their new brewery with the local legend. Their original brewery was located a few blocks away, in the middle of Main Street in Conway. With its low ceilings and weak floors, the brewery was ill suited to meet growing demand. When delivery trucks arrived to take away fresh product, the owners personally had to stop street traffic and carefully guide the truck into their cramped environs. The new brewery is located a short distance away in a more industrial complex. The space affords the brewery plenty of room for growth and, hopefully, the capacity to produce a few new beers to keep the popular flagship ale company.

Elm City Brewing Company

Colony Mill Mall
222 West Street
Keene, New Hampshire 03431
Tel. (603) 355–3335
www.elmcitybrewing.com

> ★ **Best Beer:** No Name IPA. A strongly hopped beer weighing in at 72 IBUs and 6.5 percent alcohol. With its hazy, unfiltered appearance and thick head, this IPA sets itself apart before the first sip. The aroma is strong with piney notes and the first sips follow the aromas. A well-balanced IPA that manages strong, floral bitterness and solid, pale malt flavors.

Opened: December 1995.

Type: Brewpub.

Owner: Debra Rivest.

Brewer: Bill Dunn.

Brewing system: 7-barrel Stainless Steel Specialists brewhouse.

Amount produced: 380 barrels. 700-barrel total capacity.

First beer: Lunch Pail Ale.

Flagship beer: No Name IPA.

Year-round beers: Keene Kolsch, Peachy Keene Kolsch, Raspberry Wheat, No Name IPA, Elm City Altbier, Tilt Yer Kilt (Scottish-style ale), Pothole Porter, and Lunch Pail Ale.

Seasonal beers: ESB, Amber Ale, Cherry Stout, Espresso Porter, Hefeweizen, Honey Brown Ale, Irish Potato Ale, Belgian Wit, Mai Bock, Ordinary Bitter, Roggen Bier, Wing Nut Oktoberfest, Espresso Stout, and Belgian Tripel.

Tours: "If you see a guy behind the glass in the brewhouse, you'll get a tour," says brewer Bill Dunn. Ask at the bar or by appointment.

Beer to go: Growlers available for purchase.

Food: An above-average menu that ranges from burgers to steaks and seafood. The kitchen makes its own desserts on-site, including the Chocolate Stout Mousse.

Amenities: Parking is available in the Colony Mill Marketplace's parking lot. Full liquor license.

Other attractions: Take a walk through the Colony Mill Marketplace, a rambling, brick structure that possesses a great deal of character and offers 40 shops selling an intriguing mix of antiques, books, and other goods. Built in 1838 by the prominent Faulkner and Colony families to house their wool mill, the business closed in 1953. Thirty years later, locals purchased and restored the mill as a showcase for their businesses. The restoration was true to the original design and the building retains much of its architectural charm. Open Monday through Saturday, 10 A.M. to 9 P.M.; and Sunday, 11 A.M. to 6 P.M.

Pub hours: Open Monday through Thursday, 11:30 A.M. to 11 P.M.; Friday and Saturday, 11:30 A.M. to 1 A.M.; and Sunday, 11 A.M. to 9 P.M. Happy hour is Monday through Friday, 4 P.M. to 6 P.M.

Directions: From Main Street, head north to West Street and go left. The brewery is located a few blocks up in the Colony Mill Marketplace on your left, with parking around back.

It had been Debra Rivest's lifelong ambition to open a small pub of her own, emphasizing handcrafted products. Rivest discovered homebrewing in the early 1990s, and decided to add good beer to the concept and open a beer bar. When she teamed up with two other homebrewers to make the dream happen, her partners suggested they open a brewpub instead. So the would-be brewers piled into the car and traveled up to Vermont many times on research exhibitions. After multiple pints and several visits to the town's two local brewpubs, McNeill's Brewery and the Windham Brewery, the partners cemented the idea.

After completing the licensing, ordering the equipment, securing the subcontractors, and signing a lease, the partners had to bail out of their intended location because of unspecified complications. Across town, the directors of the Colony Mill Marketplace were looking for a restaurant to replace a recently closed establishment in the beautifully restored structure. The brewpub partners liked the space, so after several months of renovations, the Elm City Brewing Company opened for business just before Christmas 1995.

Rivest eventually bought out her partners and now runs the attractive pub along with her helpful staff. One prominent staffer, head brewer Bill Dunn, knows a little something about the knocking of opportunity. After brewing stints at the Long Trail Brewing Company, the Broadway Brewing Company in Colorado, and two John Harvard's locations, Dunn and his wife returned here. When the couple decided to move to Keene, where they had met in college, Dunn sent his résumé to Elm City only to learn it wasn't hiring. "Well, there goes my brewing career," he says with a laugh, recounting the experience. So Dunn started working some bartending shifts while trying to figure out his prospects. In the meanwhile, Elm City's head brewer left and Rivest busied herself trying to locate the résumé of the brewer who had called a few months back. She searched all over for Dunn before finally tracking him down, much to the brewer's surprise.

Dunn is now happily ensconced in Elm City's long, narrow brewhouse. Tucked behind a glass partition, the brewhouse benefits from a great deal of sunlight, which serves as an attractive backdrop for diners watching the brewing process. In the middle of the restaurant, a sign announces the present tap list, and also creatively promotes the beers happily bubbling away in the fermenters or planned for the near future.

Elm City typically runs six to eight different, unfiltered beers on tap, with up to twelve beers on special occasions. After many years in the beer business, Dunn remains a passionate and enthusiastic ambassador for his craft. The brewer is excited about producing a variety of beers, twenty-four in all, brewed close to style so that his customers can learn more about beer and the brewing process. Always quick with a joke, Dunn takes a light approach to up-selling his customers from macroproducts to craft-brewed beer. "You can't say you haven't found the one," he says to people who claim not to like beer. There is no beer snobbery here—Dunn works hard to create a welcoming learning environment. "You can't know everything about beer," he muses. "It always changes. The first time you meet someone who says he knows everything about beer, that's the day you've met someone who knows nothing about beer."

The owner gives Dunn nearly complete freedom to brew what he pleases on the attractive, copper system. On the day I show up, Dunn is busy brewing a special beer to celebrate the pub's tenth anniversary. Released on December 10, 2005, the imperial stout scored a series of perfect tens: it's brewed with ten different malts, ten ounces of ten different hops pitched every ten minutes, conditioned for ten months, contains ten percent alcohol with 100 IBUs, and is served in ten-ounce snifters.

Located in the heart of the Monadnock Region, Elm City melds with this thoughtfully restored mill setting. With brick archways, lots of bright windows, wood ceilings, and simple décor, Elm City remains a perfectly pleasant place to enjoy a meal and a quality beer.

Franconia Notch Brewing Company

260 Dells Road
Littleton, New Hampshire 03561
Tel. (603) 616–9788
www.notchbrew.com

★ **Best Beer:** Grail Pale Ale. A curious offering from Franconia Notch. The beer pours with a luminous, orange color and offers an aroma of tangy citrus, reserved hops, and lightly toasted malts. The flavor of this classic British-style ale is quite complex and a little hard to place. It's a pleasing mix of biscuity malt flavors and lightly bitter hops that slowly build into more pronounced bitterness in the beer's long finish.

Opened: 1996. (Closed 2005).

Type: Brewery.

Owner: John Wolfenberger.

Brewer: John Wolfenberger.

Brewing system: 24-barrel self-fabricated brewhouse.

Amount produced: Figures not available.

First beer: Grail Pale Ale.

Flagship beer: Grail Pale Ale.

Year-round beers: Grail Pale Ale, River Driver Ale, and Mountain Stout.

Seasonal beers: Bavarian Weissbier, Mead Ale, and Cloud Nine Barley Wine.

Tours: Tours available by appointment. If the door is open and the flag is out, then stop in for a tour.

Beer to go: 1-liter swing-top bottles, growlers, and kegs are for sale.

Amenities: Parking is available in the lot next to the brewery.

Directions: Take Exit 42 off I-93 and immediately look for The Clam Shell Restaurant, which shares a parking lot with the brewery.

In the modern age of craft brewing, brewers throw around phrases like "brewed by hand" and "handcrafted" to such an extent as to render them nearly meaningless. While it remains true that the brewing systems used by craft brewers pale in comparison to the industrial monsters in operation in macrobrewing facilities, the typical process hardly resembles anything you would qualify as handcrafted. With the larger craft breweries in New England, very little work is done by hand any more, with much of the automated brewing process controlled by the push of a few buttons or the click of a mouse.

Small-batch brewing is not in any realistic way preferable to large-batch brewing, and bigger operations are as respectable as smaller operations. It's simply to say that when you come across a place where nothing is automated and the brewery is solely powered by human involvement, it's both refreshing and deserving of the "handcrafted" label.

Regardless of your definition, there can be no argument about the set-up at the Franconia Notch Brewing Company. Located in the middle of a parking lot right off of I-93, the brewery is housed in a freestanding, faded green garage. Inside the brewery, the environs are so cramped that many of the brewing implements, including the auger and the wort chiller, are suspended from the ceiling. Owner John Wolfenberger enjoys working with his rudimentary brewing system. Instead of using steam or gas to power his kettle, he uses direct fire, which he credits for increasing the caramelization of the malt sugars during the brewing process. In Wolfenberger's self-made brewery, there is very little automation. Without the benefit of electronic arms, Wolfenberger stirs the mash himself. This remains entirely a one-man operation.

After quitting college at age twenty, Wolfenberger moved to London and discovered good beer. While working in the nascent computer business in the mid-1980s, he would often follow his coworkers to the pub at night. It was at his local pub that Wolfenberger first discovered real ale, the beginning of a lifelong love. Upon his return, Wolfenberger was so disheartened by the state of American beer that he revisited the homebrewing hobby he had toyed with during college. Without having made the conscious decision to open his own brewery, Wolfenberger slowly began to accumulate equipment, including old stainless-steel dairy vessels and maple syrup tanks. By 1994, he realized he owned half the equipment he would need to start the brewery, so he slowly began assembling the rest of the system.

While Franconia Notch offers only a small portfolio of beers, Wolfenberger applies strict rules to the production of his beers. His two dueling flagship beers, the Grail Pale Ale and River Driver Ale, are straightforward interpretations of English-style ales. All of the beers remain unfiltered and manage to meet both the strict requirements of the German Purity Law and the standards to qualify as real ale.

Wolfenberger is especially proud of the hard-fought right to self-distribute his beers throughout New Hampshire. After the New Hampshire Supreme Court nullified the law prohibiting breweries from distributing their own beers, small breweries such as Franconia Notch suddenly had the opportunity to work outside of the traditional three-tier system. In getting what he always hoped for, Wolfenberger now spends much of his time driving around the state delivering kegs out of the back of his minivan. "It's been great except for all the work," he says with a laugh.

The new arrangement is a boon for both the brewery and its customers. As a small brewer, it's very difficult to secure the attention and consideration of a distributor. Wolfenberger found that his beers often sat wasting away in hot warehouses—less than ideal conditions for any beer, but especially bad for beer containing live, active yeast. In the worst case he can recall, Wolfenberger notes that he gave one of his distributors a few casks of his Grail Ale to be delivered to a regular account. Despite his covering the kegs with warnings that the contents were for immediate delivery, the casks disappeared. The stale, heat-damaged, and potentially explosive casks resurfaced a year later at New Hampshire's largest beer festival, where one was tapped before Wolfenberger could prevent it.

By self-distributing his beer, Wolfenberger is often able to keg fresh beer and deliver it to an account all in the same day, providing one of the freshest drinking experiences a consumer could ever want. Working by himself, he now sells twice as much beer as his distributors did under the old system. By remaining true to traditional brewing methods and his desire to remain local, Wolfenberger happily sustains his tiny, green brewhouse. "I would miss it terribly if I ever had to give it up," he says.

Unfortunately, as this guide was in production, there was late word that Franconia Notch had lost its lease. Wolfenberger confirms that following the death of the Clam Shell Restaurant's owner, the brewery received a notice to vacate the premises to make way for new development on the site. Wolfenberger is reviewing his options and hopes to find a new location to house his small brewery.

Italian Oasis Restaurant and Brewery

127 Main Street
Littleton, New Hampshire 03561
Tel. (603) 444–6995

★ **Best Beer:** Black Bear Stout. Served with a mild nitrogen push, this stout is as creamy in appearance as Guinness could ever hope to be. The aroma is lightly fruity but mainly bounds with roasted-malt notes. Beyond a slightly fizzy carbonation level, this stout possesses a mix of sweet, malt flavors upfront, followed by a long, slow fade into a finish of roasted bitterness.

Opened: 1994.

Type: Brewpub.

Owners: Lisa and Wayne Morello.

Brewer: John Morello.

Brewing system: 2-barrel Horeca brewhouse.

Amount produced: 120 barrels. Presently at capacity.

First beer: Cannon Amber Ale.

Flagship beer: Cannon Amber Ale.

Year-round beers: Oasis Golden Ale, Cannon Amber Ale, and Black Bear Stout.

Seasonal beers: Scottish Ale, Barleywine, IPA, Honey Wheat, and Imperial Stout.

Tours: Tours by appointment.

Beer to go: None.

Food: Despite the restaurant's name, the reasonably priced menu does not exclusively focus on Italian food. Italian Oasis offers seafood, burgers, and inexpensive pizzas.

Amenities: Parking is available in the lot behind the brewpub. Full liquor license.

Pub hours: Open daily, 11:30 A.M. to midnight.

Directions: From I-93 take Exit 42 and travel east into Littleton on Route 302/Main Street.

Backed by a whopping 62-gallon brewing system tightly packed into a storage space in the restaurant's basement, the tiny Italian Oasis Restaurant and Brewery is easily one of the smallest brewpubs in the country. With a system capable of brewing four regular-sized kegs per batch, with a limit of 120 gallons per week, to call the operation "handcrafted" is to state the obvious.

In an intriguing complex of small shops, the Italian Oasis Restaurant came under the ownership of Wayne and Lisa Morello in 1992. While the couple ran the restaurant, Wayne's brother John was developing a love of homebrewing. Although he knew space was tight at the restaurant, John suggested that the Morellos add a brewpub component to the operation. Having followed both restaurant industry trends and the development of John's brewing skills, the owners quickly endorsed the idea. In surveying the restaurant, the Morellos all knew there wasn't enough room to add a big, showcase brewery; the only acceptable brewing space would be in two six-by-six-foot rooms in the basement.

With those specifications in mind, John sought a brewing system to fit the impossibly small brewhouse. After traveling around the country for six weeks, he settled on a 2-barrel system designed by Pierre Rajotte of the Cheval Blanc brewpub in Montreal, Canada. After purchasing the system, John trained with Rajotte in Canada to learn how to run his supersized homebrew set-up. When he fired up the kettles for the first time in 1994, Italian Oasis became the first commercial brewery in the history of northern New Hampshire.

Amid a light haze of cigarette smoke and clinking glasses of macro beer, you might not peg Italian Oasis as a place where craft beer had any chance of survival. With various winter sports antiques adorning the walls, including old skis and toboggans, the tavern looks like your average New Hampshire bar. Beyond the name, the only clues that this place is a brewpub can be found in a few words on the menu or by eyeballing the funky tap handles slotted next to the familiar Budweiser line.

After more than a decade in business, the Morellos have clearly beaten any long odds. They firmly believe that small-batch brewing creates better beers; and the unembellished products here are remarkably clean. The Cannon Amber Ale is strong bodied with a surprising hop bite that ends with a balancing touch of residual sweetness. The Scottish Ale is another assertive offering that shows great poise in balancing the ample malt portions with a touch of bitterness.

Once a year, Italian Oasis celebrates its roots by cosponsoring the local Littleton Homebrew Competition, where amateur brewers vie for more than mere ribbons and medals. In a great twist on the traditional competition, Italian Oasis allows the winning brewer to recreate his recipe on a commercial level at the pub. After tweaking the winning beer to fit the bigger system, the champion beer is served at Italian Oasis as a special release.

Milly's Tavern

500 Commercial Street
Manchester, New Hampshire 03101
Tel. (603) 625-4444
www.millystavern.com

★ **Best Beer:** General John Stark Dark Porter. This creamy, slightly bitter, brown porter is named for New Hampshire's first elected governor and Revolutionary War hero. The roasted malts build from sweet to bitter, offering a complex interaction in this very approachable porter.

Opened: January 2002.

Type: Brewpub.

Owner: Peter Telge.

Brewer: Mike Roy.

Brewing system: 15-barrel DME brewhouse.

Amount produced: 600 barrels per year. 2,500-barrel total capacity.

First beer: Mt. Uncanoonuc Golden Cream Ale.

Flagship beer: Mt. Uncanoonuc Golden Cream Ale.

Year-round beers: Mt. Uncanoonuc Golden Cream Ale, Amoskeag Harvest Ale, Tasha's Red Tail Ale, General John Stark Dark Porter, Milly's Oatmeal Stout, Manch-Vegas IPA, Bo's Scotch Ale, and Monarch Lager.

Seasonal beers: Pumpkin Ale, Goat's Breath Double Bock, Hefeweizen, and Brown Noser.

Tours: By appointment or ask at the bar.

Beer to go: 64-ounce and stylish 2-liter growlers available for filling.

Food: The reasonably priced menu will be familiar to anyone who regularly eats in a bar, offering the required troika of nachos, mozzarella sticks, and hot wings. Entrees rarely exceed $10–$12 in price, with very moderately priced appetizers.

Amenities: Free parking in lot next to and behind the brewpub. The quiet brewpub environment transforms into a club during the evenings, with live music every Tuesday, Friday, and Saturday; local DJs cover the rest of the nights. Milly's also offers some mind-boggling happy hour specials. While most New England states prohibit liquor-related specials in bars, New Hampshire happily discards such Victorian attitudes. The regular happy hour extends from 4 to 7 P.M., Monday through Friday, offering half-price appetizers and $1 draft beers. If you're embarrassingly cheap or an unemployed craft beer enthusiast, however, the pub's Beat the Clock special is perfect for you. On Tuesday evenings starting at 7 P.M., the pub lowers beer prices to a mere quarter per pint (yes, 25 cents per glass), and raises the price by a quarter every half-hour until it tops out at $2.

Pub hours: Daily, 11 A.M. to 1 A.M.

Directions: Tucked away in the basement of the old Stark Mill, Milly's is located on the east bank of the Merrimack River in Manchester, just under the Bridge Street bridge.

Lurking in the shadows of the towering Bridge Street overpass are the beers of Milly's Tavern. After finally locating the entrance on the side of the building, you descend the stairs and enter the dark, well-worn environs of the former textile mill turned brewpub. Milly's occupies the location of the former Stark Mill Brewing Company, which operated here in the 1990s. Present owner Peter Telge, who was involved with the original brewery before selling his interest in 1999, bought the pub back in 2002 and rechristened it after the historic mill.

The staffers at Milly's are some of the friendliest around. Take a seat at the large, L-shaped bar overlooking the open brewhouse and you'll likely be offered a sample or two of the house beers. A large sign behind the bar and in front of the kettles announces the daily listing of eleven available beers brewed on-site. The friendliest member of the Milly's family is the brewer, Mike Roy. A former home-brewer and brew-on-premise worker, Roy has been involved with the liquor business for many years. He spent time in New Orleans working for bars on Bourbon Street before moving to the promotions side. During his homebrewing days, Roy occasionally borrowed specialty malts from Milly's and stopped in on his own for pints. In August 2004, he took over as head brewer, and in his off time, he writes a beer column for a local magazine.

Roy sees his job as part brewer, part salesman. He frequently calls upon his marketing background and love of beer to promote Milly's line of beers. The energetic and engaging brewer relishes opportunities to interact directly with his customers. He often moves around the bar, offering samples to customers or stopping to discuss a particular beer or upcoming releases. Roy acknowledges he has a tough mission, as Manchester's citizens are not known for their passion for craft beer. He directly tackles the challenge, often pressing his customers on their likes and dislikes. "I hate vagueness," he says. "When someone says, 'I like light beer,' I want to know why. Is it the light flavor, the light body, the color, what?" Roy sends a lot of samples across the bar in his attempts to break Manchester's drinkers out of their rote Budweiser routines.

In New England craft brewing circles, beer enthusiasts don't often hear much about Milly's, which is too bad considering its spirit and quality. The Manch-Vegas IPA, whose title is derived from the loving nickname locals have given to their home city, is a nice play of malts and hop bitterness, with a pleasant yeast bite in the finish. The brewer has an appreciation for brewing history and often creates new, milder beers from the second runnings of stronger beers. Milly's also offers an intriguing manner of serving its popular Pumpkin Ale seasonal beer. I am simultaneously horrified and fascinated when the bartender rims my pint glass, as one might do with salt on a margarita glass, with a mixture of cinnamon, sugar, and other spices before filling it with the popular Pumpkin Ale seasonal beer. The resulting mixture is delightful and complements the base ale incredibly well.

Anheuser-Busch Brewing Company

221 Daniel Webster Highway
Merrimack, New Hampshire 03054
Tel. (603) 595–1202
www.budweiser.com

ONE OF THE ANHEUSER-BUSCH COMPANIES

> ★ **Best Beer:** Bare Knuckle Stout. Brewed by the company and served on nitrogen to compete with Guinness. The beer's light, roasted flavors are pleasant and the nitrogen delivery system softens the finished product, making it creamier to the taste. Available in select markets and brewed exclusively at this location.

Opened: 1970.

Type: Brewery.

Owner: Publicly traded company.

Brewer: Hans Stallmann, Senior Resident Brewmaster.

Brewing system: 630-barrel Huppmann and Anheuser-Busch brewhouse.

Amount produced: 3.3 million barrels. Presently at capacity.

First beer: Budweiser.

Flagship beer: Budweiser.

Year-round beers: Budweiser, Bud Light, Michelob, Michelob Light, Michelob Amber Bock, Michelob Honey Lager, Michelob Ultra, Bud Dry, Bud Ice, Bud Ice Light, Busch, Busch Light, Busch Ice, Busch NA, Natural Light, Natural Ice, King Cobra, Hurricane, O'Douls, O'Douls Amber, and Bare Knuckle Stout.

Tours: Tours available on a regular schedule. January through April: Thursday to Monday, 10 A.M. to 4 P.M. May, and September through December: daily, 10 A.M. to 4 P.M. June through August: daily, 9:30 A.M. to 5 P.M.

Amenities: Parking is available in the brewery's lot.

Directions: Take Exit 10 off Route 3 and head east on Industrial Drive. Go left onto Daniel Webster Highway for the entrance to the A-B plant.

Of Anheuser-Busch's twelve mammoth breweries around the country, its Merrimack plant is by far the smallest. But when you're talking about America's largest brewery, context and perspective are important things to consider. This small brewery produces more than 3.3 million barrels of beer per year, dwarfing New England's next-biggest brewery by more than 3.2 million barrels. As one of the world's largest breweries, and probably the best known, Anheuser-Busch produces America's top-selling beers, Bud Light and Budweiser, brews more than 100 million barrels worldwide, and controls a startling 50 percent of the domestic beer market.

With size and success, criticism necessarily follows. Mention Bud or A-B's corporate tactics to your favorite beer geek and prepare yourself for an ear-splitting onslaught of opposition and a cacophony of naysaying. "Budweiser tastes like cat pee," whines one. "A-B is the devil," sniffs another.

Beer geeks perhaps focus too much energy crusading against America's biggest brewer. Anheuser-Busch's brewers rank among the most highly trained and technically competent in the industry. Order a Budweiser and you are guaranteed of at least two things: it will be fresh and it will taste exactly like the last one you had. While technically sound, A-B's beers generally lack much creativity or notes of interest for its customers. The beers are specifically brewed to be nonoffensive, simple products.

As its popularity grew, Anheuser-Busch's executives realized that it was neither feasible nor in the interest of product freshness for the company to produce all of its beer in the home brewery in St. Louis. Opened in 1970, the Merrimack brewery is the oldest brewery in New England and brews all its beers for drinkers in the region. The brewery sits on three hundred sculpted acres, its enormous copper brewing kettles gleaming through large windows for all potential visitors to see. The Merrimack location is also home to a paddock of the iconic Clydesdale horses, which are equally popular with kids and adults.

Anheuser-Busch offers all beer drinkers the opportunity to learn more about the brewing process at its Merrimack plant. The tour is comprehensive and laid out to maximize visitor enjoyment. Through displays and a guided walking tour, visitors learn how the company's two signature families united to permanently change the face of American brewing. More than eighty thousand visitors take the tour each year, which begins in an old world–style chalet, more Swiss than German in design. With its wooden beams, hop vines etched in stained glass, and corporate communication displays with reproduced breweriana, the tour lodge strikes a slightly cold and soulless note. The tour starts here and moves through the brewing floor and the beechwood aging tanks, to the bowels of the facility, past the enormous bottling line, and finishes in the simply appointed tasting room.

Of note for beer geeks, the Merrimack plant was once home to a small, pilot brewery in the early days of the craft beer movement. In an effort to create more flavorful products to compete with the new craft beers, Anheuser-Busch's brewers were given a longer leash to brew new beers. Many of these brews never reached the market, but some now appear in the brewery's Michelob specialty series, including the Amber Bock.

Martha's Exchange

185 Main Street
Nashua, New Hampshire 03060
Tel. (603) 883–8781
groups.msn.com/MarthasExchangeBrewingCompany

> ★ **Best Beer:** Macleod's Scotch Ale. Weighing in at 7.7 percent alcohol by volume, this potent winter seasonal is served in a 12-ounce snifter glass. While the Macleod's possesses a deep, rich malt nose, the body is much lighter with a slight hop bite rounding out the well-considered flavors.

Opened: August 1993.

Type: Brewpub.

Owners: William and Chris Fokas.

Brewer: Greg Ouellette.

Brewing system: 7-barrel DME brewhouse.

Amount produced: 400 barrels. 1,000-barrel total capacity.

First beer: Volstead '33'.

Flagship beer: Volstead '33'.

Year-round beers: Volstead '33', Dark Rosaleen Stout, Golden Perch IPA, and Steeplechase Porter.

Seasonal beers: Arkenstone Alt, Back in Business Amber Ale, Baggins Best (bitter), Barrelrider Stock Ale, Belgian White, Biscuit City Pale Ale, Brandy Buck Oud Bruin, Choco-Good Oatmeal Stout, Indian Head Red, Macleod's Scotch Ale, Magi Winter Warmer, Martha's Belgian White, Martha's Hefeweizen,

Martha's Oktoberfest, Martha's Peculiar Brown, Mona Lisa Mild, Muggles ESB, Raven Stout, Revolution Red, Spy vs. Spy Rye, Velvet Elvis Vanilla Stout, Vow of Silence (imperial stout), and Weathertop Doppelbock.

Tours: Tours by appointment or if the brewer is available.

Beer to go: Growlers are available for purchase.

Food: Typical pub fare with a focus on creative sandwiches.

Amenities: Parking is available in the lot behind the brewpub and on-street. Full liquor license.

Pub hours: Open Monday through Friday, 11 A.M. to 1 A.M.; Saturday and Sunday, 9 A.M. to 1 A.M.

Directions: Martha's is on Main Street in Nashua just a few blocks south of the river.

Nowhere else in New England can you sample fresh craft beer while browsing through a turn-of-the-century candy shop. As ownership of the property here passed through successive generations, each required the next to keep the candy store in operation. The site developed into a soda fountain, then a restaurant, and finally a brewpub in 1993. To this day, the little candy counter in Martha's Sweet Shoppe survives and offers homemade chocolates, truffles, and fudge.

With its big windows looking out onto historic Main Street in downtown Nashua, Martha's Exchange brims with small pieces of history. The restored building, which has been in the family for more than fifty years, contains a restaurant and bar on the first floor and a meeting area on the second floor. The restaurant once housed a money exchange, which explains the vague, bank lobby–feel in the bar. There are charming touches throughout the pub, including marble floors, half–moon shaped booths, and an eclectic collection of statues. The sometimes-ornate wooden bar weaves throughout the dining sections. Continuing the historic theme, a dark-wood section of the bar purportedly comes from a speakeasy owned and operated by Al Capone.

In the circa-1887 Merchants Exchange Building, brewer Greg Ouellette works on the brewpub's gleaming, copper brewhouse, which stands remarkably open to the restaurant. A large mural behind the attractive brewing system depicts Main Street life in the early part of the twentieth century. Ouellette developed an interest in good beer when his brother brought him a homebrewing kit. Despite making a self-described awful first batch of beer, Ouellette remained focused on brewing. After college, he started working at a local brew-on-premise operation as his first professional job, where he helped novices brew batches from preformulated recipes.

When Ouellette assumed the head brewer position at Martha's Exchange, he basically started from scratch with the recipes. Unlike other brewpubs, Martha's offers very few year-round beers. Of those listed here, only the Volstead '33' is available every day. The other regular offerings listed here are among the most consistently available on the beer menu, but even they often change in composition. Ouellette enjoys tinkering with each batch, by using more or less hops or different types of malt. Only the Golden Perch IPA, named after a tavern in Tolkien's *Lord of the Rings,* remains the same after much experimentation.

The historical theme continues with the pub's flagship, Volstead '33', a beer named for the Minnesota congressman who authored the bill creating the legal enforcement mechanism for Prohibition. Andrew J. Volstead introduced the National Prohibition Act in May 1919. Though standing for nearly fourteen years, the law did not prove popular with Volstead's local district, however, as Minnesotans voted him out of office in 1922. While advocates of good beer might see this as a justly deserved reward for the teetotaling congressman, Volstead's defeat likely had more to do with abysmal farm prices than proliquor forces back home.

In crafting his seasonal releases, Ouellette brews a variety of beers, including a handful of true lagers. Ouellette often ages a few of his stronger beers, with word traveling quickly among regulars just before their respective releases. The lager releases, including the doppelbock and the Oktoberfest, remain wildly popular with patrons at Martha's Exchange.

Flying Goose Brew Pub and Grille

40 Andover Road
New London, New Hampshire 03257
Tel. (603) 526–6899
www.flyinggoose.com

★ **Best Beer:** Crockett's Corner Oatmeal Stout. Named for the original family dairy and ice cream shop that previously operated on this site, this oatmeal stout also offers many creamy notes. Pours a deep ruby color with lightly roasted notes, the flavor mixes roasted malts and a decided smoothness to achieve a very drinkable stout.

Opened: 1997.

Type: Brewpub.

Owner: Tom Mills.

Brewer: Kevin Kerner.

Brewing system: 7-barrel New England Brewing Systems brewhouse.

Amount produced: 350 barrels. Presently at capacity.

First beer: Hedgehog Brown Ale.

Flagship beer: Perley Town IPA.

Year-round beers: Split Rock Golden Ale, Perley Town IPA, Weetamoo Raspberry Wheat, Hedgehog Brown Ale, Flying Goose Pale Ale, Potter Place Porter,

Alexandria Alt, Ragged Mountain Red Ale, Long Brothers Strong Ale, Robert Strong Brown, Hominy Pot ESB, Loon Island Lighthouse Ale, Wildflower Honey Ale, Crockett's Corner Oatmeal Stout, and Isle of Pines Barleywine.

Seasonal beers: Harvest Wheat, Blueberry Wheat, Christmas Treaty of 1914 Stalt, Flying Goose Bock, and Oktoberfest.

Tours: By appointment or ask for the brewer.

Beer to go: Growlers available for sale.

Food: The chefs make a lot of their own ingredients on-site and pit-style barbeque is a house specialty. The menu includes ample servings of seafood, steaks, and pasta dishes. A sister company, the Kearsarge Mountain Coffee Roasters, roasts and blends its own coffee beans.

Amenities: Parking is available in the pub's lot. Full liquor license. Special kid's menu.

Other attractions: At 2,937 feet, Mount Kearsarge is clearly a dominant peak in central New Hampshire. Derived from a Native American word meaning "notch-pointed mountain of pines," Kearsarge has several trailheads and a bare summit that is manageable for all classes of hikers, including children. Winslow State Park, Route 11, Wilmot, New Hampshire 03287, tel. (603) 526–6168. Open weekends only from mid-May to mid-June, and daily from mid-June to November.

Pub hours: Monday through Saturday, 11:30 A.M. to 11 P.M.; Sunday, noon to 11 P.M.

Directions: The Flying Goose is located directly off of I-89 at Exit 11 toward New London. The brewery is located a mile up the road, on the right, near Lake Sunapee Country Club.

Pub-based brewers lead very solitary existences, often toiling for long hours in cramped environs, cast far off from the excitement of the kitchen and the hurried pace of the dining-room floor. The routine involves a lot of unsexy work that drinkers never consider when they dream of working at a brewery. In lugging hoses, cleaning kegs, and scrubbing tanks, brewers understandably feel compelled to bring a little humanity to it all. A touch of humor never hurt, either.

For the young brewmaster at the Flying Goose Brew Pub and Grille, the answer was to name his tanks after famous musicians and writers. As a musician and English major, Kevin Kerner feels better when he can yell at Miles or Nesta for acting up, or shake his fist at Shakespeare or Mahavishnu for giving him some trouble. But secretly, Neil is his favorite. Kerner named this tank, set alone off to one side, after Neil Young because "I like Neil Young much better when he is by himself."

As a student at near Colby-Sawyer College, Kerner started at the Flying Goose doing a variety of jobs, from bussing to waiting tables, before finally getting a chance to work in the brewery. Kerner apprenticed here for six months before his mentor left him with the controls and a stack of brewing books. After learning how to manage the production schedule for the diverse variety of beers Flying Goose offers on a regular basis, Kerner decided to try some new recipes. When other brewers prepare to brew a new style, they often go out and purchase a dozen examples from other breweries to get a better feel for what they want to create. But Kerner decided to make a bock beer—a style he had never sampled—knowing it would be difficult to find good comparison beers due to his rural location. Oddly enough, he saw this as an opportunity to brew a beer completely uninfluenced by any other brewery's beers. After three months of proper lagering, Kerner released the new beer, to the great approval of his local customers.

The Flying Goose is located on the side of the road, right off of I-89. Surrounded by nothing on all sides, the location may seem a somewhat unusual place for a brewpub. From a seat in the back part of the restaurant, you can begin to understand the vision here. Most of the restaurant offers beautiful views of nearby Mount Kearsarge. While the mountain is smaller than its White Mountain brethren to the north, it has always been a popular subject for New Hampshire artists. Sitting in the pub's dining room, surrounded by an assortment of old antiques, fishing poles, glass bottles, and outdoorsy influences of canoes, deer heads, and the occasional flying goose, you can watch clouds swirl around the summit and take in its dark, sloping beauty.

A small beer menu provides detailed descriptions of each of the seventeen beers regularly available on tap. With the regular menu comes a list of Kerner's Brewhouse Specials; namely, the seasonal ales presently available. The beer sampler is a ridiculously large pour of twelve different beers, brought on a large tray. Prepare yourself for looks of concern from fellow customers, many of whom may feel compelled to shield their children's eyes from the guy with a notebook, a pen, and an obvious problem.

Kerner distributes his beers to a handful of other local restaurants and produces growlers for a half-dozen liquor stores in New Hampshire. On a small patch of land behind the brewery, the brewer grows his own Cascade hops; he harvests enough at the end of the growing season to spice up a single batch of the flagship IPA.

Moat Mountain Smoke House and Brewing Company

3378 White Mountain Highway
North Conway, New Hampshire 03860
Tel. (603) 356–6381
www.moatmountain.com

> ★ **Best Beer:** Hoffman Weiss. While I thoroughly enjoy Gilson's lagers, I am quite partial to his version of the classic Bavarian wheat beer style. Named after the Scottish and German restaurant that formerly occupied this space, this wheat beer pours with a medium golden color and has a slightly hazy appearance. The nose offers the customary notes of banana, clove, and a slight yeast bite. The flavor is slightly spicy, with some light, wheat notes, and loads of fruit flavors.

Opened: June 2000.

Type: Brewpub.

Owner: Stephen Johnson.

Brewer: William Gilson.

Brewing system: 7-barrel DME brewhouse.

Amount produced: 700 barrels.

First beer: Hoffman Weiss.

Flagship beer: Bear Peak Brown.

Year-round beers: Moat IPA, Hoffman Weiss, Golden Dog Pilsner, Cathedral Ledge Lager, Iron Mike Pale Ale, Bear Peak Brown, and Smoke House Porter.

Seasonal beers: Double Bock, Liquid Courage Maibock, Fall Bock, Opa's Marzen, Square Tail Stout, Olympic Dunkel Weiss, and Violet Beauregaurde's Blueberry Wheat.

Tours: By appointment.

Beer to go: Growlers and kegs are available for purchase.

Food: Moat Mountain prides itself on creating most of the ingredients on-site; many of the menu items are either smoked or grilled. The kitchen specializes in barbecue.

Amenities: Parking is available in the pub's lot. Full liquor license.

Other attractions: While skiing clearly rules here in the winter, the town of North Conway is a pleasant place to visit in any season. Located in the outdoor wonderland of the White Mountains, the town is filled with shops and restaurants. For those who secretly covet one of those bumper stickers that proclaim that your '87 Corolla huffed its way to the top of Mount Washington, the auto road is open early May through late fall. Route 16, Pinkham Notch 03860, tel. (603) 466–3988.

Pub hours: Closed Mondays. Open Tuesday through Sunday, 11:30 A.M. to close.

Directions: When passing through the village of North Conway on White Mountain Highway, look for the brewery about a half mile past Memorial Hospital.

From the first moment you open the doors at the Moat Mountain Smoke House and Brewing Company, a big, white house just outside of North Conway on Route 16, the wonderful smell of barbecue hits your nose. The atmosphere here fits the natural surroundings, with the bar and dining rooms mainly populated by skiers and vacationers enjoying a casual evening out. With worn floors, a rugged, slab bar, and several small dining rooms, Moat Mountain is a very comfortable place for a meal and some drinks. The house originally functioned as a servant's quarters for the nearby Stonehurst Manor, which was built by Erastus Bigelow, the owner of the largest carpet manufacturing company in the world at that time. After purchasing the building, owner Stephen Johnson gutted it and created a dugout structure to house the brewery. From the bar, you can look down over the entire brewing operation through several large windows. The Mural Room plays host to a series of colorful and unusual paintings done by a set designer from Portland, Maine. Diners can enjoy views of Mount Washington from the enclosed dining area.

Brewer Wil Gilson has been here from the very beginning and helped renovate the old building. In contrast to many other New England brewers, Gilson brings a decidedly German approach to Moat Mountain's beer menu. Applying his German major from college, he attended the prestigious Weihenstephan brewing school before taking his first professional brewing job at the Squatters Pub Brewery in Utah. As the state mandates that all beer brewed within its borders contain not more than 3.2 percent alcohol, Gilson learned to focus on producing very clean, flavorful beers. From there, Gilson spent six years working at the Snake River Brewery in Jackson Hole, Wyoming. While he was at Snake River, the owners instituted a program allowing their brewers to create their own recipes. Gilson immediately set out to brew a full-bodied, massively malty maibock he appropriately deemed the Discombobulator.

In his brewing at Moat Mountain, Gilson splits his efforts between ales and lagers. Though his system is only really designed for the standard single-step infusion brewing process, Gilson tweaks the set-up for several of his lager beers. To perform a decoction mash—a process common in German brewing where part of the mash is removed and boiled in a separate kettle before being returned to the primary brewing vessel—Gilson rigs up a separate, sixty gallon, steam-jacketed kettle, which serves as a cleaning tank when not required in the brewing process. Order a pint at the bar and take a seat high above the subterranean brewhouse for a firsthand look.

Woodstock Inn Station and Brewery

135 Main Street
North Woodstock, New Hampshire 03262
Tel. (800) 321–3985
www.woodstockinnnh.com

★ **Best Beer:** Wassail. Based upon the traditional mold of winter, spiced ales, Woodstock's version nicely balances roasted malt flavors, slightly sweet notes, and a spicy hop presence. The Wassail also offers mild, buttery notes to match an increased level of alcohol.

Opened: March 1995.

Type: Brewpub.

Owners: Scott and Peggy Rice.

Brewers: Butch Chase, head brewer. Mike McKenna, assistant brewer.

Brewing system: 7-barrel Peter Austin brewhouse.

Amount produced: 1,200 barrels. 1,400-barrel total capacity.

First beer: Amber Ale.

Flagship beer: Pig's Ear Brown Ale.

Year-round beers: Pemi Pale Ale, Red Rack Ale, Old Man Oatmeal Stout, Pig's Ear Brown Ale, and White Mountain Weasel Wheat.

Seasonal beers: Lost River Light, White Mountain Raspberry Weasel Wheat, Scotch Ale, Oktoberfest, Cogsman Ale, Autumn Brew, Kanc County Maple Porter, and Wassail.

Tours: Tours available during the summer at noon. By appointment otherwise. Call ahead to confirm.

Beer to go: Growlers for sale in the pub.

Food: The Woodstock Station, which contains the main pub area, is a casual restaurant and offers a very extensive menu of standard pub fare at reasonable prices. The Clement Room Grille offers a more upscale selection of beef, wild game, and seafood dishes and a quieter dining atmosphere.

Amenities: Parking is available in the inn's lot. Full liquor license. The pub offers trivia several nights a week, a massive karaoke challenge on Tuesday evenings, and live music on Friday and Saturday nights. Outdoor seating on the front patio is available during the summer.

Pub hours: Daily, 11:30 A.M. to 1 A.M.

Directions: The Woodstock Inn is located on Route 3 (Main Street) just north of the intersection with Route 112/Kancamagus Highway.

★ ★ ★

For true beer geeks, the experience of working in a brewery is akin to an aspiring parent's first opportunity to babysit a friend's child: while entertaining at first, by the end of the night you're intensely happy to leave it under someone else's control and head home. At the Woodstock Inn Station and Brewery, you can live the crazy life of a brewer, while maintaining a safe harbor at the end of the grueling experience.

On four weekends every year, visitors can enter the brewhouse here, pull on the boots, and start mixing hops and grains for themselves as part of Woodstock's popular brewers-weekend packages. During these events, individuals and couples spend the weekend at the brewpub assisting the brewers in producing beers on the seven-barrel system. The reasonably priced deal includes two nights' lodging, several meals, a reception on the first evening, a brewers' dinner, and a t-shirt or hat. If your significant other or traveling companion would sooner spend their vacation walking over hot coals than shoveling spent grain, the inn is happy to suggest a variety of alternate plans, including outlet shopping and hiking. The program, which draws about twenty participants each weekend, welcomes homebrewers and novices alike. You may even get bitten by the brewing bug, as Dave Wollner did. Before opening his Willimantic Brewing Company in Connecticut, Wollner spent a weekend here checking out the brewer's lifestyle.

Originally occupied by the Clement family, the main house of the Woodstock Inn is more than one hundred years old and offers six guest rooms. The house sat vacant for twenty years before it was restored and decorated to match closely its original design. The owners eventually purchased the house across the street, which provides twenty-one additional rooms.

The brewery takes its name from the Lincoln Railroad Station, which stands behind the inn. From its earliest days in the 1800s, the train station welcomed tourists headed to local luxury resorts and ski vacations on the nearby slopes. In the summer of 1984, a crew sawed the station in half and fused it onto the back of the inn. The present bar area is derived from the old station's freight room, while the lower dining area was once the passenger waiting room.

When customers started asking for Sam Adams and Heineken instead of Budweiser, the inn's owners saw an opportunity. They asked then bartender, Butch Chase, if he would be willing to run a new brewpub annex to the inn. While he admits he was "thrown to the wolves a little bit" due to his complete lack of brewing experience, Chase took up the challenge and quickly learned how to manipulate the "very forgiving" system built by Alan Pugsley's consulting company.

While many visitors flock to the popular upstairs lounge, most miss the inn's true hidden gem. With its low ceiling, stained woods, and peanut shell–encrusted floors, the lower bar area is a warm, welcoming, and refreshingly tranquil place to enjoy a pint. The bar flanks the brewhouse, which runs the length of the room and is open to public view through a glass partition. While many breweries in New England use open fermentation, a system where no lids top the fermenters, few allow visitors to peer into them. The creative brewers at Woodstock have rigged up an angled mirror that allows pubgoers to watch the inner workings of the four fermenters in action. Another window allows visitors to watch the brewing process with the kettles only a few feet away.

Due to the combination of low ceilings and tightness of the space, the lower bar area feels a little bit like one of those display rooms you sometimes see recreated in history museums. Replace the patrons with Old West cowboys and the scene would resemble an old-time exhibit. Far from your average, dry-walled pub, the Woodstock's back bar manages to affect a backwoods, rustic feel without tripping into kitschy grounds.

The Woodstock Inn is also in the process of expanding its brewing operations. The brewpub's two flagship products, the Red Rack Ale and the Pig's Ear Brown Ale, are contract brewed and bottled by Shipyard Brewing Company; they are widely available in New Hampshire bars and package stores. If you enjoy the mainstays and are interested in learning about brewing on a larger scale, or simply want a nice place for a weekend retreat, the Woodstock's got a pair of boots waiting for you.

Portsmouth Brewery

56 Market Street
Portsmouth, New Hampshire 03801
Tel: (603) 431–1115
www.portsmouthbrewery.com

★ **Best Beer:** Old Brown Dog Ale. A winner at the 1989 Great American Beer Festival in the Brown Ale category, the Old Brown Dog is one of the first craft beers I can remember trying. The beer arrived at my doorstep as part of a beer-of-the-month club. Even a decade later, I can still remember its easy-drinking and slightly sweet malt flavor, balanced by a subtle hint of hops. This brown ale is brewed to style and remains a thankful reminder that all beers don't have to smack your palate around to make their presence known.

Opened: 1991.

Type: Brewpub.

Owner: Peter Egelston.

Brewer: Tod Mott.

Brewing system: 7-barrel JV Northwest brewhouse.

Amount produced: 825 barrels.

First beer: Shoals Pale Ale.

Flagship beer: Old Brown Dog.

Year-round beers: Shoals Pale Ale, Old Brown Dog, Weizenheimer, Black Cat Stout, and Amber Lager.

Seasonal beers: The list here is long and ever changing, but includes: Whaddya Smokin Ale, Hophead Ale, Kolsch, Belgian Wit, Dunkelweizen, Porter, Bluebeery Ale, Altbier, Hop's n' Honey Ale, Grand Cru, Wassernixe Blonde Ale, ESB, Murphy's Law Red Ale, Oatmeal Stout, Wood Island Ale, Octoberfest, Razbabby Weizen, Dortmund Lager, Wheat Wine, Imperial Stout, Pumpkinfest, Springfest, Belgian Dubbel, Cranberry Ale, 70 Shilling Scotch Ale, Cream Ale, Belgian Trippel, Blitzen Ale, and Chocolate Brown Ale.

Tours: Tours by appointment. A small store next to the brewery sells a variety of Portsmouth Brewery–branded wares, including t-shirts, hats, and 22-ounce bottles.

Beer to go: Growlers and 22-ounce bottles are for sale.

Food: While the pub fare here is familiar, it's not pedestrian in its presentation. The pub specializes in thin-crusted pizzas and sandwiches.

Amenities: On-street parking is difficult in downtown Portsmouth. An inexpensive municipal parking garage lies directly behind the brewpub. Full liquor license.

Pub hours: Daily, 11:30 A.M. to 12:30 A.M.

Directions: The brewery is easy to locate when driving through downtown Portsmouth on Market Street—look for the mug of beer over the door of the brewery.

Anchoring the heart of downtown, the Portsmouth Brewery is the granddaddy of craft brewing in New Hampshire. Opened in 1991 by the brother and sister team of Peter and Janet Egelston, the brewpub defines Portsmouth for me and is a necessary stop any time I pass by the town. Having sold over three million pints since its inception, the pub is clearly a popular destination for many locals and other lovers of craft beer as well.

The Egelstons originally joined forces in 1987 to open the Northampton Brewery. Peter Egelston handled the brewing operations at the brewpub, the second in all of New England. A homebrewer in his spare time, Egelston developed recipes that would follow him to Portsmouth and eventually led to the opening of the package brewery, Smuttynose Brewing Company. In December 2000, the Egelstons bought each other out, leaving Janet to run Northampton and Peter with Portsmouth.

The laid-back, casual, and friendly atmosphere at Portsmouth reflects the town itself. A mix of locals and tourists, including University of New Hampshire college students and shoppers at the nearby Kittery outlet stores, amble their way down Market Street, stopping into charming shops and waving hello to friends. After soaking up the downtown scene, many of them regroup with a pint and a meal at the brewpub.

The Portsmouth Brewery has one of the great logos in the history of craft brewing. Comprised of a simple, squat mug overflowing with a cascading, white head, the logo appears throughout the pub, including in attractive etchings on the front windows. Inside the pub, the space is very open, with tall ceilings, a raised bar area, a comfortable waiting room, and ample dining space. Two royal portraits hang over the bar, welcoming members of the pub's imperial pint club. In a nod to his former days as a hotel doorman in Manhattan, Peter Egelston dubbed the small, windowless downstairs space the Jimmy LaPanza Room. This was the name of the bar at the hotel where he worked, designated for the diminutive, well-groomed, tuxedoed man who taught Peter how to live the good life.

In December 2003, the legendary brewpub teamed up with another New England brewing icon when it hired Tod Mott as the new head brewer. There may be no more well-traveled brewer in New England than Mott. In the course of his brewing career, he worked at the Catamount Brewing Company, Harpoon, Commonwealth Brewing Company, Back Bay Brewing Company, Quincy Ships Brewing Company, and The Tap Brewpub before finally landing at Portsmouth. While all but two of those breweries have since closed, their failures certainly weren't due to the quality of their beers. Mott won medals at the Great American Beer Festival at nearly all of those locations and his beers are among the most consistently flavorful and well-balanced offerings you will find in New England.

Before finding a home at Portsmouth, Mott earned a master's degree in ceramics and worked as a potter from his studio in Somerville, Massachusetts. His wife changed his professional life when she gave him a homebrewing kit. Mott remains dedicated to the "great combination of art and science" that is brewing, and he is also terribly humble about his past successes. When I ask if he has any plans to resurrect past award-winning recipes, he brushes the thought aside with a wave and suggests that "when you win an award, maybe its time to try a new style."

Egelston gives Mott a great deal of freedom to handle the beer at the pub. When he took over the brewing operations, Mott immediately changed most of the recipes and tweaked the brewing temperatures to achieve his desired results. He is also not afraid to take some controversial steps, including an attempt to phase out the Weizenheimer, a wheat beer popular with patrons and buyers of t-shirts emblazoned with the logo. When Mott considers Portsmouth's cramped, dated brewhouse, which requires much heavy lifting, he laughs and says it's "a lot like brewing in the dark ages." He is in the process of modifying the set-up to make brewing easier on the staff.

The brewing system stands at the back of the restaurant behind tall glass windows that afford diners attractive views of the operations. Whether one sits in the main dining room, the lofted space, or in the bar, the Portsmouth Brewery is a pub for all seasons, and a place I always enjoy.

Redhook Ale Brewery

35 Corporate Drive
Portsmouth, New Hampshire 03801
Tel. (603) 430–8600
www.redhook.com

★ **Best Beer:** Winterhook Winter Ale. First brewed in 1985 as a seasonal, the Winterhook is the marriage of two classic hop varieties, Cascade and Northern Brewer. These hops, including the use of Cascade in dry-hopping, add an earthy, hop aroma and overall balance to the mix of English and Munich malts. At nearly 6 percent alcohol by volume, the Winterhook is no session beer. This deep chestnut-colored beer is well suited to the colder winter months.

Opened: July 1996.

Type: Brewery.

Owner: Publicly traded company.

Brewer: Doug MacNair.

Brewing system: 100-barrel Huppmann brewhouse.

Amount produced: 80,000 barrels. 250,000-barrel total capacity.

First beer: Redhook Ale.

Flagship beer: ESB.

Year-round beers: ESB, IPA (formerly the Ballard Bitter), Blonde, and the Blackhook Porter.

Seasonal beers: Nut Brown (spring), Sunrye (summer), Autumn Ale (fall), and Winterhook (winter).

Tours: Redhook offers a well-constructed schedule of regular daily tours. June 1 through August 31: Monday through Friday at 2 P.M.; Saturday and Sunday at 12 P.M., 1 P.M., 2 P.M., 3 P.M., and 4 P.M. September 1 through May 31: Monday to Friday at 2 P.M.; Saturday and Sunday at 2 P.M. and 4 P.M. The tour costs $1 per person and includes 3 or 4 samples of beer and a souvenir tasting glass. Visit Redhook's website and print out a coupon for a free tour for you and a fellow traveler.

Beer to go: Full off-premise options are available, including 6-packs, single bottles, cases, and kegs.

Food: Straightforward pub fare is offered.

Amenities: Parking is easily available in the brewery's sizable lot.

Pub hours: The Cataqua Public House is open daily. Monday to Thursday, 11:30

A.M. to 10 P.M.; Friday and Saturday, 11:30 A.M. to 10 P.M.; Sunday, 12 P.M. to 8 P.M. The kitchen is open daily: Monday to Saturday, 11:30 A.M. to 9 P.M.; Sunday, 12 P.M. to 6:30 P.M.

Directions: Redhook's sizable Portsmouth brewery is located on Corporate Drive in an office park near Pease International Tradeport. Take the Route 16 / US-4 exit from I-95 and follow the signs to the tradeport.

Formed in the earliest days of the American craft beer movement, the Redhook Ale Brewery was the brainchild of Paul Shipman and Gordon Bowker. After seeing the rise in popularity of imported brands, coupled with the Pacific Northwest's love of draft beer, the pair set up shop in the Ballard section of Seattle, Washington. From humble roots, the company continued to grow, moving to a new facility and then another in nearby Woodinville in 1994.

Redhook is no stranger to taking bold actions in order to grow its business. After more than ten years of brewing, the company reached an inevitable crossroads. The company's directors wanted to continue the brand's expansion in the United States, but they also understood the importance of maintaining fresh product on store shelves. They knew that Boston was a long, sometimes hot, and often bumpy ride from Seattle and that beer bottles hate cross-country road tripping.

With an eye toward expanding without compromising quality, the Pacific Northwest brewery made the enterprising decision to build an entirely new brewery on the East Coast. Unlike many other similarly sized breweries, Redhook decided not to risk leaving stale beer on store shelves and not to brew their beers under contract. It became the first bicoastal American craft brewer when it opened its facility in Portsmouth, New Hampshire.

With this venture coming shortly on the heels of its move from Seattle, Redhook decided to save time and money and simply create a clone of its Woodinville brewery. Visitors to both the Portsmouth and Washington State breweries will notice many similarities. Both of Redhook's breweries are built on a similar scale, with many of the rooms, closets, and toilets built in the same proportion and general location. The design of the Portsmouth brewhouse so matches the Woodinville design that it is even built to withstand the very unlikely event of an earthquake—a much greater concern in the Seattle area.

The structure's steep, sharp, Bavarian-inspired roof lines are quite eye-catching and serve to soften the otherwise ultramodern brewery. During the tour, the sheer scale of the operation puts visitors on notice that Redhook is not your average, cuddly craft brewer. The $30 million facility is fully automated, with six people working the bottling line and only one person manning the kegging operation.

The facility's imposing brewing vessels and its enormous 400-barrel vertical aging tanks skyrocket from floor to ceiling. The tour guides are often full of trivia, offering that at a rate of four pints per day, it would take you sixty-seven years to top off one of the mammoth, stainless-steel tanks. The people at Redhook are welcoming, but asking them to set up a cot for you in the brewhouse might be asking too much.

Accounting for nearly one-third of the company's total production, the Portsmouth brewery distributes Redhook's beers to all states east of the Mississippi. To achieve full distribution across the United States, Redhook entered into a highly criticized strategic agreement with Anheuser-Busch in 1994 (renewed in 2004). Under the agreement, Redhook enjoys the support, clout, and benefits of A-B's vast distribution and sales network. In return, A-B received a 33 percent ownership stake in Redhook. The affiliation with the megabrewer served to damage Redhook's reputation with beer geeks, while seemingly strengthening its business operations. Redhook maintains control over its production, while relying upon A-B's strong distribution network, mainly in the Midwest and East Coast markets.

In contrast to many New England breweries, Redhook's Portsmouth brewery offers a pub for visitors to enjoy. The popular Cataqua Public House, whose name is derived from the nearby Piscataqua River and means "divine waters," is a welcome addition to the usual, scaled-back brewery tour. The rustic pub serves as both a meeting place for the tours and as a fully-functional restaurant showcasing the brewery's beers. Cozy leather couches and old wood tables surround a stone-enclosed hearth at one side, while ample booths and tables are well integrated throughout the great room. Even at six thousand square feet, the pub maintains a pleasant, laid-back atmosphere.

Consistent with its businesslike approach to brewing, Redhook's portfolio of beers remains very constant. The brewery's core offerings have long been in existence and rarely does a new product enter the fold. In recent years, the brewery has phased out several beers, including its Double Black Stout, which was brewed with Starbuck's Coffee. The brewery also dropped its bland American Hefe-Weizen after it signed a licensing agreement to produce the Widmer Hefeweizen.

During the warmer months, the brewery displays the world's largest beer barrel, which, according to the Guinness Book of Records, is capable of holding 7,078 gallons of beer. The enormous wooden keg weighs 2,460 pounds, was built in 1998 in Fremont, New Hampshire, and is used for pouring kegged beer during the brewery's various festivals.

Smuttynose Brewing Company

225 Heritage Avenue
Portsmouth, New Hampshire 03801
Tel. (603) 436–4026
www.smuttynose.com

★ **Best Beer:** Smuttynose IPA. Perhaps the brewery's most memorable beer, the incomparable Smuttynose IPA is loaded with Simcoe and Santiam hops and balanced by the distinctive Amarillo hop. The IPA is a powerfully hoppy beer that remains remarkably drinkable. I first tried the IPA while attending a local beer festival shortly after its release and it stopped me in the middle of the event with its assertive style. The beer has proven wildly popular with beer lovers and its release reenergized Smuttynose.

Opened: 1994.

Type: Brewery.

Owner: Peter Egelston.

Brewer: David Yarrington.

Brewing system: 50-barrel DME brewhouse.

Amount produced: 10,200 barrels.

First beer: Shoals Pale Ale.

Flagship beer: Shoals Pale Ale.

Year-round beers: Old Brown Dog, Portsmouth Lager, Shoals Pale Ale, and Smuttynose IPA.

Seasonal beers: Summer Weizen, Robust Porter, Big A IPA, Barleywine Style Ale, Imperial Stout, Scotch Style Ale, Octoberfest, Pumpkin Ale, S'muttonator (doppelbock), Maibock, and Wheat Wine.

Tours: Tours by appointment.

Beer to go: None.

Amenities: Parking is available at the brewery.

Directions: Take I-95 to Exit 3. Go west and at the second traffic light turn left onto Ocean Road. Travel less than a mile and turn left onto Banfield Road. After the railroad crossing, turn right onto Heritage Avenue.

Nestled in the heart of New Hampshire's seacoast and on the banks of the short, squat Piscataqua River, Portsmouth promotes itself as the America's third-oldest city. Settled in 1623, the town long served as a focal point on the Atlantic seaboard and housed the nation's first naval shipyard. Modern Portsmouth is a charming town boasting an impressive nightlife scene. Portsmouth was also once home to America's largest ale brewery, the Frank Jones Brewing Company. In October 1858, Mr. Jones teamed up with partner John Swindells to form a brewery that distributed its beers from Nova Scotia to Pennsylvania. While the name changed a few times, the brewery stayed open for nearly a hundred years before quietly closing in 1950.

Forty years later, a distant relative of Mr. Jones resurrected his ancestor's brewery and his famous line of ales. The brewery quickly closed and Peter and Janet Egelston, the brother-sister team behind the Northampton Brewery and the Portsmouth Brewery, teamed up with the Ipswich Brewing Company to buy the assets of the failed company at an auction. While the relative retained the rights to the Frank Jones brand, and even continued to brew the India Pale Ale on a contract basis at the now-defunct Nutfield Brewing Company in Derry, the Egelstons opened their first production brewery, named the Smuttynose Brewing Company. Ipswich left the partnership a few months later, and in December 2000, Peter Egelston assumed control of Smuttynose in a deal with his sister, who now solely runs the Northampton Brewery.

Named after a local island in the rugged archipelago of nine small islands known as the Isle of Shoals, Smuttynose started by brewing and bottling recipes from its sister brewpubs, including the Shoals Pale Ale and the classic Old Brown Dog. For me, every Smuttynose beer evokes very vivid memories and feelings. The delightfully hazy Shoals Pale Ale tastes like summer, especially when sampled directly from the bottle. This style-bending English pale ale uses ample doses of both Cascade and Chinook hops to complement its decidedly yeasty flavor. As I've said in reviews for Smuttynose's sister establishments, the Old Brown Dog is one of the first craft beers I can remember trying and loving. With their low bitterness and sweet, malt flavors, brown ales are often a very comfortable, approachable style for beer novices to tackle. The Old Brown Dog remains a classic example of this traditional style.

In 1998, Smuttynose fired one of the earliest rounds in the nascent extreme beer offensive. With the start of its Big Beer Series, Smuttynose dedicated itself to releasing specialty beers with more aggressive flavor profiles. While some releases, including a barleywine and an imperial stout, indeed were big beers, some of the other selections, such as a simple kolsch, seemed wildly out of place in a series dedicated to pushing the limits of beer.

Although Smuttynose's beers were always respectable, the brewery really stepped it up with the addition of brewer David Yarrington in August 2001. A graduate of the master brewer's program at University of California–Davis, Yarrington continually retools Smuttynose's bigger beers, playing with the recipes in simple or substantial ways. The bottles in the series now include vintage dating, and the brewery encourages beer lovers to age the beers.

Smuttynose also distinguishes itself from nearly every other brewery of its size through its dedication to lager beers. Several large, horizontal lagering tanks in the brewery confirm that this brewery is serious about the joys of bottom fermentation. Dedicated to the town's 375th anniversary, the Portsmouth Lager possesses toasted malt flavors balanced by a light dose of Saaz hops. Several of the specialty releases include higher alcohol takes on substantial German-style lagers.

Seven Barrel Brewery

Colonial Plaza
West Lebanon, New Hampshire 03784
Tel. (603) 298–5566

> ★ **Best Beer:** Champion Reserve IPA. Pours with a hazy, deep golden color and offers strong floral hop aromas. The IPA possesses a zesty hop flavor, with slight, earthy notes, and a nice, chewy, malt character as a balancing point. The beer finishes with a nice, sharp, hoppy exit.

Opened: April 1994.

Type: Brewpub.

Owners: Greg and Nancy Noonan.

Brewer: Paul White.

Brewing system: 7-barrel Stainless Steel Specialists brewhouse.

Amount produced: 560 barrels.

First beer: Quechee Cream Ale.

Flagship beer: Quechee Cream Ale.

Year-round beers: Quechee Cream Ale, Ice Rock Canadian, New Dublin Brown Ale, Red 7, Champion Reserve IPA, and R.I.P. Stout.

Seasonal beers: Olde #7 (pale ale), Mick Jack Porter, PNW ESB, 80 Shilling Scotch Ale, Birthday Bock, Sugarhouse Maple Ale, and Spuyten Duyvel (Belgian-style ale).

Tours: By appointment.

Beer to go: Reasonably priced growlers are for sale.

Food: A large menu, laid out in newspaper form, delivers news of typical pub fare mixed with steaks and seafood.

Amenities: Ample parking in the brewpub's lot. Full liquor license. Live music with no cover charge on Friday and Saturday evenings from 10 P.M. until close.

Pub hours: Daily, 11:30 A.M. to 1 A.M.

Directions: Located directly south of I-89 just before the Vermont border at Route 12A and Airport Road in the Colonial Plaza shopping complex.

While there are hundreds of seven-barrel brewhouses throughout America, none is as famous as the one proudly standing at the front windows of this West Lebanon brewpub. Thousands of homebrewers across the country know the Seven Barrel Brewery by name, even if they've never been anywhere near New Hampshire. This is the brewpub that led to the *Seven Barrel Brewery Brewers' Handbook,* a classic guide to the brewing arts, written by owner Greg Noonan and two fellow brewers.

From the highway, it's hard to miss the Seven Barrel Brewery. The long, simple building is abruptly fronted by a vaulted addition containing the brewhouse. Through four large windows, potential visitors can watch brewer Paul White working in the two-story brewery. You have to respect a brewery that puts the name of its brewer on the front door to the brewhouse. White's brewing environs possess an almost medieval character, with touches of brick and a well-worn copper kettle that resembles some sort of dairy mixer. The best seat in the house is the booth overlooking the entire brewing operation.

Anyone who has visited Seven Barrel's sister restaurant, the Vermont Pub and Brewery, will feel a tinge of déjà vu upon entering this pub. From the newsprint menus to the 3-ounce sample glasses with tiny handles to the random décor, which includes two coats of armor, the two pubs share a lot of similarities. This pub is smaller than its Burlington relative and possesses a certain distinguishable charm. Comprised of a mixture of hardwoods and ceiling beams, the raised dining room's décor varies between feeling vaguely English, slightly country western, to that of a roadside, national forest café. It certainly doesn't feel like a pub located in a strip mall parking lot a few hundred feet from a screaming interstate highway.

The square-shaped main bar offers great views of the brewing set-up. The arrangement of eight glimmering serving tanks behind the low-hanging wooden bar is one of the best advertisements for good beer that I can imagine in a brewpub. In great contrast to the dining room, the bar area feels like it was pulled directly from a Magritte painting. Those pubgoers who look directly into their mugs, at the ground, or at the faces of their tablemates, miss the bizarre painting on the ceiling above them. There is Medusa with hop leaves growing from her head, a recessed lighting fixture with puzzle pieces of ceiling missing next to it, and images of the Cheshire Cat, the asp, and the forbidden fruit. Have you long given up looking for Waldo? Stop in for a pint and look up. He's been hiding out here.

Sprinkled with various beer-related quotes, the menu does a good job of providing information about beer and the brewing process. It dedicates two of its four pages to increasing patrons' knowledge of beer, offering descriptions of beer styles, and suggesting food pairings; it also gives histories of beers and a detailed overview of the brewery. The beers here also resemble those available at the Vermont Pub, mainly straightforward representations of classic styles. The list remains pretty constant throughout the year. Cask-conditioned ales are also a house specialty.

Respecting Beer

Beer is a neglected and often-maligned distant cousin of wine in the family of fermented beverages. While it possesses egalitarian charms capable of bringing people together without pretense, beer is often treated as a common, pedestrian beverage. Despite its storied history, rich traditions, and the boundless enthusiasm of modern brewers, beer remains the Rodney Dangerfield of the beverage world.

Battered by stereotypes and a barrage of damaging television commercials, American beer is now represented by a sorry, lifeless, fizzy, yellow substitute. Thanks to the image propagated by the bigger brewers, sadly, 85 percent of the beer consumed in America fits this description, including nearly all of the ten top-selling brands.

After decades of demeaning beer, even the larger brewers are beginning to recognize the dangers of dumbing down beer's image and flavors. The president of the Miller Brewing Company recently worried aloud to a reporter that the single biggest threat to the industry is that people grow bored with beer. Presumably speaking without irony, Miller's executives need look no further than their own boardroom, and those like it in Golden, Colorado and St. Louis, Missouri, for the root causes of the collective, deafening yawn that is the typical response to American beer.

The craft brewers profiled in this guide are fighting a difficult battle against the popular conception of beer. Even twenty years after the dawn of the craft brewing movement, many patrons walk into brewpubs without knowing that the place brews its own beer. Flanked by enormous, shiny brewing vessels, patient bartenders at these establishments deserve awards for the number of times they have to explain why their pub doesn't serve Bud Light.

With the rise of thousands of craft brewers, the American beer scene is experiencing a rebirth. With full awareness of the difficulties ahead of them, upstart, pioneering American craft brewers are rushing forward, full of optimism. Craft beers continue to make inroads into everyday bars and you can usually find at least one flavorful offering wherever you visit. Regional craft breweries, including Harpoon, Long Trail, Magic Hat, and Shipyard continue to grow in size and reputation. While each of these breweries represents only a fraction of beer sold in their home states, they each dream of one day outselling Budweiser in their home markets.

Beer is a wonderfully expressive drink, even more so than wine. Every wine tastes like wine, but not every beer tastes like beer. While wine's flavor is expressive of its unique growing conditions—an impressive feat termed *terroir*—beer results more from the stroke of a brewer's brush. With their sweeping palette, brewers are capable of creating such rich and striking flavors that most drinkers would deny they were actually beers. Fusing their curiosity and skill, enterprising brewers in New England have created beers that look and taste just like iced tea, smell like espresso, and rival the finest cognac. Such things certainly cannot be said about wine.

Away from its wild, experimental side, beer is also remarkable for its ability to be enjoyed in the nearly complete absence of pretense. Ordering a pint will never be as nerve-racking as selecting a glass of wine or as confusing as deciding which bottle to bring to a party. While snobs exist in any area, beer's opinionated minority mainly keeps to itself. The absence of pretense, however, doesn't mean the experience of enjoying beer is a common one. The beers produced by the craft breweries featured here deserve great respect and have earned their rightful places at the table. Enjoy!

Rhode Island

Officially known as the State of Rhode Island and Providence Plantations, America's smallest state also hosts a commensurately small number of breweries. Boasting a total of only five breweries and pubs, two of which are located nearly across the street from one another in downtown Providence, Rhode Island is not particularly well-known for its beer. While the state's beer scene is often overlooked for the offerings of Massachusetts and Connecticut, Rhode Island offers a worthy selection of breweries in an easily traveled stretch.

Comprised of only 1,214 square miles, including 400 miles of coastline, Rhode Island is only 48 miles top to bottom and 37 miles across. For visitors to New England, the state's charms—and breweries—can be experienced in a whirlwind, two-day tour. In Providence, you can walk between the respectfully staid Union Station

Brewery and the delightfully demented Trinity Brewhouse. In Newport, you can enjoy a meal and a beer in the family-friendly Coddington Brewing Company before leaving the kids with a sitter and heading to the Coastal Extreme Brewing Company for its raucous Friday-night tour and sampling session. The next day, travel to nearby Block Island, explore its relatively untouched beauty, and then catch a meal at the ferryside Mohegan Café and Brewery.

Brewing has long been an important industry in Rhode Island, home to one of the first breweries in America: in 1639, Roger Williams placed a communal brewhouse and tavern under the supervision of Sergeant Baulston in Providence. While Rhode Island never possessed a huge brewing scene, it can claim bragging rights to the classic Narragansett Brewing Company, later dubbed the Falstaff Brewing Company. Loyal New England beer drinkers certainly remember the brewery's famous advertising tag line, "Hi, Neighbor . . . Have a 'Gansett." With control over 65 percent of the region's beer market by 1963, this lager beer once reigned as New England's beer of choice, beating out even Budweiser. Narragansett was the last surviving old-guard brewery in New England when it shut its doors in 1981. A new owner is now trying to revive the brand.

When the Rhode Island laws on brewing changed in 1992, a handful of new brewpubs opened across the state. The existing locations are stable, consistent, and have developed their own followings. The addition of the Coastal Extreme Brewing Company in 1999 ended Rhode Island's standing as the only New England state without a production brewery. The young, Newport-based entrepreneurs bring a lot of life and enthusiasm to the local beer scene.

Mohegan Café and Brewery

213 Water Street
Block Island, Rhode Island 02807
Tel. (401) 466–5911

> ★ **Best Beer:** Bock. While not brewed anywhere near to style, the bock is an interesting pint. Filled with wild, fruit flavors and strong malt notes, this beer strays far from the textbook definition of bock. Overall, an interesting extract beer that is enjoyable for a pint.

Opened: 1998.

Type: Brewpub.

Owner: Mike Finnimore.

Brewer: Dave Sniffen.

Brewing system: 10-barrel Specialty Products International extract brewhouse.

Amount produced: 150 barrels. Presently at capacity.

First beer: Mohegan Pilsner.

Flagship beer: Mohegan Pilsner.

Year-round beers: Mohegan Pilsner, Striper Ale, Black Buck Porter, Honey Lemon Pilsner, Bock, and Chili Pepper Ale.

Seasonal beers: None.

Tours: Tours by appointment.

Beer to go: None.

Food: Upscale fare, with a mixture of typical pub food and some more advanced seafood dishes.

Amenities: There is limited parking on Block Island, period. The brewpub is located directly across from the ferry dock. Full liquor license.

Other attractions: A short walk out of town and located on the first floor of the Highview Inn, Club Soda is a popular bar during all seasons. Best experienced in the quieter, off-season months, when it's is entirely populated with locals, the bar offers a variety of events, from live music to team trivia—a show complete with podiums, buzzers, and electronic-scoring displays. The beer selection is above average, including some less widely distributed beers from some of New England's better-known craft breweries. Connecticut Avenue, Block Island, Rhode Island, 02807, tel. (401) 466–5397. For natural beauty, be sure not to miss the Mohegan Bluffs located on the southeastern end of the island. A short walk from the Southeast Lighthouse, these majestic cliffs rise 200 feet from the ocean.

Pub hours: Closed November to St. Patrick's Day (March 17).

Directions: Look for the Water Street Inn across the street from the ferry terminal in Old Harbor. The first floor of the hotel contains the Mohegan Café and Brewery.

Perched on small hill overlooking the Old Harbor and Block Island Sound, the Mohegan Café and Brewery beckons visitors fresh off the ferry to sample her charms. The brewpub is housed in the Water Street Inn, a traditional-looking structure with faded gray siding. The café itself is classic New England in its décor, with a simple nautical theme casually executed. Old photographs on the walls document the history of this beautiful, untouched, natural location.

The café has been a seasonal fixture on the island since it opened in 1990. Owner Mike Finnimore came into the pub one day and found one of his employees, Dave Sniffen, sanitizing his homebrew bottles behind the bar. Intrigued by the sight, Finnimore asked Sniffen some questions about the brewing process. After a brief conversation, the owner posed an unexpected query to his young employee: Could you brew beer here? Sniffen replied that he could, not expecting anything to come of it. He didn't know the conversation would lead Finnimore to research brewing systems, overcome local zoning and licensing issues, and install a system for him, the bartender. By 1998, the brewery was ready to go.

The subject of alcohol has long been controversial on Block Island. One of the island's most famous landmarks is a testament to abstinence. A few hundred feet down the street from the brewpub, in a small traffic rotary, stands a cast-iron statue and fountain erected by the Woman's Christian Temperance Union (WCTU) in 1898. Formed in 1874 by women who were disturbed about the misuse of alcohol by their husbands, the WCTU promotes total abstinence from alcohol as a lifestyle. The group takes as its motto the words of Xenophon, a Greek philosopher, historian, and the original horse whisperer: "Temperance may be defined as moderation in all things healthful and total abstinence from all things harmful."

People on the island have also historically possessed mixed feelings on the topic of moderation versus abstinence, and the statue perhaps best symbolizes that philosophical conflict. The local women's temperance group ordered the statue as a symbol of sobriety and they believed their selection to be a biblical representation of Rebecca at the Well. Instead, the temperance group mistakenly chose a representation of Hebe, a Greek goddess of youth and spring who was known as the wine-bearer to the gods. State officials confirmed the error in 2002, much to the delight of locals, when they renovated the statue and replaced it with a weatherproof replica.

Brewing beer does not come naturally to Block Island, for more than political reasons. As the whole of Block Island is serviced by a single aquifer source, water usage is tightly restricted. Caps exist on the amount of water any business can use, and the fines are substantial for exceeding the limits. The regulations restricted Mohegan's options, leaving only an extract brewing system as a genuine possibility. The use of extract makes double-density brewing possible, a process by which a brewer boils twice the required amount of extract and dilutes it for fermentation. The process produces little to no waste, and reduces the overall amount of water necessary to complete the brewing cycle.

Beer enthusiasts generally consider extract beer as akin to instant coffee (versus that ground fresh from beans). Extract systems resemble large homebrew set-ups, remain relatively easy to use, and require little interaction with the raw ingredient of malted barley. Instead of using grains, extract brewers add malt syrup directly to their kettles. While a skilled brewer who understands the unique properties of malt extract may be able to produce exceptional beers, in reality the brewer often doesn't properly manage the complexities of this type of brewing and the final product suffers.

While companies selling extract brewing systems advertise that their easy-to-use systems do not require the services of a brewmaster, few serious brewpubs employ extract systems except in a pinch for space or, in the case of the Mohegan Café, water. While Mohegan should be praised for perservering in a tough situation, the beers here are sadly not a highlight of a trip to the island. Each beer suffers from a slight flavor tang and often stray far from their intended styles.

The food, however, remains quite a draw at the Mohegan Café and the atmosphere is pleasantly agreeable. Dishes are thoughtfully prepared and flavorful, and the staff is tremendously friendly.

Coastal Extreme Brewing Company

307 Oliphant Lane
Middletown, Rhode Island 02842
Tel: (401) 849–5232
www.newportstorm.com

FROM RHODE ISLAND'S
MICROBREWERY

★ **Best Beer:** The Newport Storm Limited Edition Releases. While each beer in the brewery's regular lineup is solid, Coastal Extreme's limited-edition releases are a step up in terms of flavor. The recipe and intended style change every year and past releases have included barleywines, a doppelbock, and a strong pilsner. They are bottled in distinctive, wine-shaped, cobalt blue bottles and corked. The limited edition releases are meant for aging, and older versions sometimes show up on store shelves.

Opened: July 1999.

Type: Brewery.

Owner: Privately held company. Brent Ryan, president.

Brewer: Derek Luke.

Brewing system: 10-barrel Criveller Company brewhouse.

Amount produced: 5,000 barrels (2,300 barrels draft produced on-site, 2,700 barrels contract brewed). 3,100-barrel total capacity at present location.

First beer: Hurricane Amber Ale.

Flagship beer: Hurricane Amber Ale.

Year-round beers: Hurricane Amber Ale.

Seasonal beers: Thunderhead Irish Red Ale (spring), Maelstrom IPA (summer), Regenschauer Oktoberfest (fall), and Blizzard Porter (winter).

Tours: Tours given Friday evenings at 6 P.M.

Beer to go: Growlers are for sale at the brewery.

Amenities: Parking is available in the industrial park near the brewery. The brewery is tucked away in the back corner of the complex, away from the main entrance.

Other attractions: Located in the heart of downtown Newport, the eclectic Brick Alley Pub and Restaurant is almost a local institution after more than twenty-five years in business. While macro products dominate the selection here, you can usually find a smattering of craft offerings, including a few taps of Coastal Extreme's beers. 140 Thames Street, Newport, Rhode Island 02840, tel. (401) 849–6334, www.brickalley.com.

Directions: Heading through Middletown on Route 114, turn right onto Oliphant Lane along the perimeter of the Newport State Airport and look for the Middletown Tradesman Center. The brewery is tucked around the front corner of the long structure.

Visiting Coastal Extreme is a little like stepping into a college fraternity house. Furniture is scattered about, the smell of beer is in the air, and a bar off to one side is primed with a few taps. The company's Web site is littered with pictures of the young owners promoting their brands at various parties and events, with names such as the Pajama Jammy Jam '00, Easter Kegg Hunt '03, and Derek's Birthday Poker Tourney. Every year the guys personally lead their customers and friends on a pubcrawl around Block Island. You could be forgiven for mistaking the place as a younger version of the movie *Old School*. Beneath the surface, however, Coastal Extreme is far from your typical smash-a-beer-can-on-your-head fraternity. It's more like a brotherhood of business students, where the members maintain a steady balance between partying and achievement.

The four founders—Brent Ryan, Derek Luke, Will Rafferty, and Mark Sinclair, met while attending Colby College in Waterville, Maine. As the date of their collective graduations approached in 1997, the guys considered their respective future prospects. During college, the guys developed the usual affinity for malt beverages, but the group had taken a special shine to craft-brewed beers. Head brewer, Derek Luke, spent some time homebrewing and found he had a talent for it. Together with Brent Ryan, the two considered opening their own brewery. After discussing their idea with Sinclair and Rafferty, they all decided to develop a business plan. After kicking around at other jobs for a year, the four regrouped in 1999, raised money from family and friends, and opened Coastal Extreme.

The legendlike tale becomes even less probable when you consider that among the four founders, not one of them had a single moment of experience in the beer industry. All four of the owners graduated with degrees in science (Ryan also has a mathematical economics degree). What they lacked in experience, however, the founders made up for in sheer pluck. They entered the notoriously capital-intensive beer industry at a time when other breweries were starting to close.

While the whole story sounds like a scenario destined to end badly, Coastal Extreme is no fly-by-night operation. These guys made some smart initial decisions that saved them a lot of troubles. First, they carefully researched where to open their brewery. When they saw that Mainers and Rhode Islanders drank nearly the same amount of beer, they were intrigued: when they found out that Maine had almost twenty microbreweries, while Rhode Island had none, they were sold. Newport was an obvious choice and one that has served the founders well. The young partners knew that consumers loved to sample local products, especially those associated with popular vacation destinations. While the Coastal Extreme name plays off their personal philosophies of living full lives, the Newport Storm brand is the one they push.

Once a week, the team pulls the brewing equivalent of an all-nighter by producing six batches back-to-back. The monster, thirty-six-hour brewing process lasts from Tuesday morning until Wednesday night. Despite this weekly madness and the company's wild name, the brewery's business operation is actually quite measured. Coastal Extreme mainly produces draft beer for their accounts, along with a limited numbers of cans, while contracting out the space-intensive bottling operation to a bigger brewery. Coastal Extreme follows the proven formula of producing a single flagship beer, the Hurricane Amber Ale, supported by four seasonal products. Each of the offerings is flavorful and brewed to session-beer strength for a wide audience of drinkers.

For beer geeks, Coastal Extreme offers a special, high-alcohol release each year, designated simply by the last two digits of the year ('05). Coastal Extreme also created its Cyclone Series of beers, single-batch releases not brewed to any particular style. Similar to the naming of weather disturbances, each new release corresponds alphabetically to its place in the rotational order. The first release, a souped-up brown ale named Alyssa, was released in early 2005.

Coddington Brewing Company

201 Coddington Highway
Middletown, Rhode Island 02842
Tel. (401) 847–6690
www.newport-brewery.com

> ★ **Best Beer:** ESB. In an age of excess, when many brewers have largely abandoned the timeless practice of brewing well-balanced, drinkable beers, Coddington's attractive and mildly hopped ESB stands out as a sober, reserved beer worthy of great praise. The aroma is fresh with simple, earthy hop notes. The ESB is clean flavored, with mild malt notes balancing the initial hop bite. The finish is smooth, with a final kick of hops and a pleasant crispness.

Opened: 1995.

Type: Brewpub.

Owner: William Christy.

Brewer: Marshall Righter.

Brewing system: 7-barrel DME brewhouse.

Amount produced: Figures not available.

First beer: Pale Ale.

Flagship beer: Blueberry Blonde.

Year-round beers: Golden Ale, Blueberry Blonde, India Pale Ale, and Irish Stout.

Seasonal beers: Vienna Lager, Irish Red Ale, Watermelon Ale, Oatmeal Stout, Pumpkin Ale, Hefe-weizen, Winter Warmer, Winter Lager, Summer Wheat, Chocolate Porter, Maibock, ESB, Pale Ale, Porter, Nut Brown Ale, Scotch Ale, European Pilsner, Oktoberfest, Raspberry Wheat, Best Bitter, Dopplebock, Barley Wine, Raspberry Cream Ale, and Lucky Lager.

Tours: Tours not offered.

Beer to go: Growlers for sale at the brewery.

Food: Standard pub fare, with an assortment of pasta, pizza, seafood, and steak dishes. A brief kid's menu is also available.

Amenities: Parking is available in the pub's lot. Full liquor license.

Pub hours: Open Sunday through Thursday, 11 A.M. to 10 P.M.; Friday and Saturday, 11 A.M. to 11 P.M.

Directions: The brewpub is located on Coddington Highway near the intersection of Routes 114 and 138, just outside of Newport proper and a short drive from the Coastal Extreme Brewing Company.

In a delightful instance of historical irony, the Newport area's only brewpub is named after the Puritan who founded the vacation town in 1639. William Coddington originally immigrated to the Massachusetts Bay Colony from England in 1630, seeking freedom from religious oppression. After supporting Anne Hutchinson in her trial for heresy, Coddington and others were banished from the community. Along with fellow Puritans, including Roger Williams, Coddington purchased Aquidneck Island (now known as Rhode Island) from the Narragansett Indians. It is also ironic that this quiet, peaceful pub's namesake was also a notorious rabble-rouser who was run out of nearly every place he ever lived. Coddington was later deposed as leader of the settlement the following year and left to found Newport. He would go on to oppose a union with the mainland settlements of Providence and Warwick and have a serious falling out with Williams, before appointing himself as the first governor of Rhode Island.

Few people would dare call a Newport-area bar "family friendly," but I must say that the Coddington Brewing Company certainly qualifies. From the cozy interior to the separate bar and dining rooms, Coddington is your basic brewpub. I mean this characterization with absolutely no disrespect. The beers here are simple and clean. The food is well prepared and of ample proportions. The booths and tables in the small dining area are well spaced and the environment is quiet and comfortable. The décor is tasteful and uncomplicated. As a package, it's a pleasant if unremarkable place to spend an evening.

Beer is a clear focus of the pub, with the copper exterior of the brewing kettles gleaming through large windows dividing the brewhouse from the main dining room. While brewhouses are often the showcases of their brewpubs, the brewhouse at Coddington truly stands out in the pub's casual, earth-tones design scheme. The tanks and kettles are each marked with letters or numbers that correspond to explanations provided on the menus, so visitors can learn about the brewing process while they dine. The table placemats have designated spaces for taster glasses to fit. Beer-related items, including bags of malt and occasional pieces of breweriana, are design elements used throughout the pub.

The restaurant is broken into two distinct spaces, the smoky, adult bar with television sets and small, raised tables, and the quieter dining room, with a fireplace and comfortable, wooden booths. Brewer Marshall Righter, formerly of Boston Beer Works and the United States Navy, brews a variety of ales and lagers on the 7-barrel system. There is little pretense here, demonstrated by the no-frills names assigned to each of the beers. The beers are all full-flavored, without any overpowering influences or notes. Every offering closely follows the appointed style guidelines so there will be few surprises when you place your order. Along with the pub's relaxed, humble atmosphere, the direct approach is quite refreshing. As Righter says of the pub, "It's just a really nice place to work, have dinner, and relax."

Trinity Brewhouse

136 Fountain Street
Providence, Rhode Island 02903
Tel. (401) 453–2337
www.trinitybrewhouse.com

★ **Best Beer:** Rhode Island IPA. The first IPA available throughout Rhode Island since the demise of the storied Ballantine IPA, Trinity's version is filled with East Kent Goldings hop goodness. With a dull orange color and strong citrus aromas, the IPA is fruity throughout with a nice, malt backbone and a decidedly bitter finish.

Opened: December 1994.

Type: Brewpub.

Owner: Josh Miller.

Brewer: Sean Larkin.

Brewing system: 15-barrel DME brewhouse.

Amount produced: Figures not available.

First beer: Kolsch.

Flagship beer: Rhode Island IPA.

Year-round beers: Rhode Island IPA, PC Pilsner, Tommy's Red Ale, and Brown Ale.

Seasonal beers: Abbey Ale, Belgian Gold, Belgian Wit, Cerveza Lopez, Crump's Chocolate Stout, Dark Wheat, Extra Special Bitter, Foggy Bottom Pale Ale, Imperial IPA, Imperial Pilsner, Larkin's Irish Stout, Mayday (tripel), Oatmeal Stout, People's Porter, Point Break Pale Ale, Prov Bruin Pilsner, Rams Head Doppelbock, RI Ram Light Lager, Russian Imperial Stout, Shark Bite Strong Ale, and Hefe-weizen.

Tours: Tours available by appointment.

Beer to go: Growlers available for purchase. Always a pioneering influence in expanding the rights of Rhode Island's brewpubs, Trinity recently started contract brewing its IPA at the Cottrell Brewing Company in Pawcatuck, Connecticut. 6-packs are not allowed for sale at the pub.

Food: Average pub food with a focus on sandwiches and 12-inch, create-your-own pizzas.

Amenities: Limited street parking available near the brewpub, along with municipal lots. Full liquor license.

Other attractions: Located about a mile from Trinity, near the campus of Brown University, the Wickenden Pub is another attitude-driven beer destination. The

Wick feels like someone converted their cramped basement into a small bar for their friends. It's often packed and noisy, but the pub also offers 13 draft beers served in 16-ounce, 20-ounce, or 34-ounce mugs or half yards. The heart of the bar's beer list is the 99 specialty bottled offerings. 320 Wickenden Street, Providence, Rhode Island 02906, tel. (401) 861–2555.

Pub hours: Open Monday through Thursday, 11:30 A.M. to 1 A.M.; Friday, 11:30 A.M. to 2 A.M.; Saturday, noon to 2 A.M.; and Sunday, noon to 1 A.M.

Directions: Trinity is a short walk from the Providence Civic Center on Fountain Street.

A single glimpse of the Trinity Brewhouse lets you know that the place is far from your standard brewpub. With a black base coat of paint, Trinity's exterior features colorful, hand-painted signs filled with crazy cartoon characters who proclaim that the pub has the best beer in New England. The spectacle continues with your first step past the heavy doors and into the pub itself. Trinity is filled with dark woods, gothic-looking windows, and a long bar overlooking the well-worn, copper-clad brewing system. There are touches of color on the walls, including a circuslike banner in the bar welcoming geeks, bankers, bus drivers, jocks, cross-dressers, and conventioneers. In the dining room, which feels drawn from some creepy old mansion, a large wall mural depicts the Last Supper as it might have been if attended by Kurt Cobain, John Lennon, Biggie Smalls, the Rat Pack, and Elvis.

Split over two levels, including a cool, subterranean bar area, Trinity's atmosphere is part rock hangout, part homey, bohemian pub. You anticipate that the pierced and tattooed staffers are going to act like punk-rock snots, but they warmly welcome you as the newest character in the mad scene. Perhaps sometimes a bit detached, the staff is quite friendly and thoughtful.

Located in downtown Providence, Trinity is a few short blocks from the Union Station Brewery, Providence's other brewpub and Trinity's polar opposite in terms of attitude and design. Named for the repertory theatre next door, Trinity's entire operation centers on the brewhouse, a welcome design choice. While seated at the bar, you can look onto the brewing system, which has clearly taken some abuse over the years. A mix of quirky locals, eager-eyed visitors from the nearby convention center, and theatergoers meld together in the bar's spacious seating area. There is a lot to see at Trinity; it's a fun place to have a beer at nearly any time of the day. And despite Trinity's popularity, the noise level is always manageable and conversation is actually possible.

Brewer Sean Larkin has been here nearly from the start, working in the kitchen before eventually assuming the head brewer job. Trinity features at least six beers on tap at all times and Larkin brews about two dozen different beers throughout the year, including several lagers and high-gravity ales. One beer that clearly stands out from the rest of Trinity's portfolio is the award-winning Russian Imperial Stout. The big, full-flavored, unfiltered beer employs two thousand pounds of malt, boasts 60 IBUs of East Kent Goldings hops, weighs in at 8 percent alcohol, and holds a bronze medal in its category from the 1996 World Beer Cup. While not quite a year-round beer, the brewers don't limit the Russian Imperial Stout's production to cold winter months. You can stop by in the middle of a blazing 90-degree day and order up a ridiculous 23-ounce glass of the thick, roasted liquid courage.

Union Station Brewery

36 Exchange Terrace
Providence, Rhode Island 02903
Tel. (401) 274–2739
www.johnharvards.com

★ **Best Beer:** Cask-conditioned Milk Stout. A bright spot on the beer menu here is the regular availability of real ales. The milk stout possesses a sweet, malty nose with light, oaty aromas. The creamy mouthfeel is set off by slight touches of hop bitterness and light chocolate and coffee flavors.

Opened: December 1993.

Type: Brewpub.

Owner: Boston Culinary Group.

Brewer: Tim Pyne.

Brewing system: 10-barrel Bohemian Brewing Systems brewhouse.

Amount Produced: Figures not available.

First beer: Golden Ale.

Flagship beer: Golden Spike Ale.

Year-round beers: Northern Light Lager, Golden Spike Ale, and Union Station IPA.

Seasonal beers: Milk Stout, Scotch Ale, Jamestown Ale, Belgian Trippel, Harvest Spice Ale, Magnum Red Ale, Maibock, Rusty Griswald (double IPA), and Vanilla Bean Porter.

Tours: Tours by appointment only.

Beer to go: Growlers available for purchase.

Food: The menu is a touch upscale, with few typical pub-fare offerings. While familiar, each of the menu items has an untraditional flair, instanced by their Portabello cheeseburgers and salmon salads.

Amenities: On-street parking can be very difficult in this area. Several pay parking structures are in the area. Full liquor license.

Other attractions: Created by Barnaby Evans in 1994, the WaterFire art installation is a wildly popular public spectacle performed on select Saturday evenings in the summer and early fall. Installed on three rivers in downtown Providence, the display includes sparkling bonfires that contrast with the cool waters. www.waterfire.org.

Pub hours: Open Sunday through Thursday, 11:30 A.M. to 1 A.M.; Friday and Saturday, 11:30 A.M. to 2 A.M.

Directions: The brewery is in downtown Providence, halfway between the Providence Place mall and Kennedy Plaza.

Located a short walk from the sprawling Providence Place mall and across from the famed Biltmore Hotel, the Union Station Brewery is centered in the heart of Rhode Island's capital city. The subterranean restaurant stands on the site of the former home of downtown's main train station. Built in the middle of the nineteenth century, Union Station connected downtown with other parts of the East Coast by rail. The original structure, which burned down in 1896, was considered a brilliant example of Romanesque architecture and was the longest building in the United States. As other modes of transportation grew in popularity, Union Station slowly fell from importance.

Left vacant by the city, the site suffered another devastating fire in 1987. A group of investors sponsored by the Providence Chamber of Commerce helped renovate the site, which now stands adjacent to the cultural and physical center of the city. The brewery opened in 1993 in the lower level of the structure, which is near Waterplace Park. With redbrick walls and textured, beam ceilings, the structure retains much of its original charm. The brewing equipment integrates well into the entire scheme, with gleaming copper kettles shining through picture windows behind the bar. The effect is upscale, while remaining slightly detached and casual.

Although you could walk or drive by the restaurant without even knowing the pub exists, countless numbers of locals clearly have discovered it. The space is tight and fills up quickly. While waits are often considerable in the evening, there is some waiting space available in the small bar area.

Though Union Station doesn't promote it, the restaurant is part of the John Harvard's chain of brewpubs. Unlike the beers available at its sister locations, the offerings here remain average and generally uninspired. This is clearly a restaurant that also happens to have a brewing component. While there are no clear losers on the taps, nothing jumps out demanding the attention of patrons.

Eleven Great New England Beer Bars

A great beer bar is comprised of a combination of rarely achieved elements. Due to the growing popularity of craft beer, even average bars usually offer a few local or nationally available craft beers. The bars listed below set themselves apart as being among the best places in New England for good beer because they excel in the crucial aspects. These noteworthy establishments provide an extraordinary selection of craft beers, respect their clients in terms of keeping prices fair, hold events promoting craft beers (from beer dinners to brewer meet-and-greets), make craft beer key to their business, and also offer true character as pubs.

CONNECTICUT

Delaney's
882 Whalley Avenue
New Haven, Connecticut 06511
Tel. (203) 397–5494

A bit of a sleeper on this list, Delaney's is a nice escape from the soulless clubs that line the streets of downtown New Haven. Made up of three separate rooms—the main pub, an upscale dining room with white tablecloths, and a hole-in-the-wall, dive barroom with scattered tables, dart boards, and pool tables. The Tap Room (i.e., the dive) offers a fine selection of draft beers, including numerous Belgian beers and some rarer offerings. The quality of service varies from night to night, but the beers are almost uniformly served in the proper glassware. Unlike many bars on this list, Delaney's main focus is on imported beers, though local favorites make some appearances. You can often get a good idea of what is available from the board hanging in the Tap Room, but it is sometimes frustratingly out of date, so ask the bartender for late entrants.

 With its sparse décor, scuffed wood floors, and a slight edge to the atmosphere, Delaney's has an odd, Old West feel to it. The pub's clientele is a curious mix of

Southern Connecticut State University students, blue-collar workers, occasional beer geeks, and a cast of colorful, unpredictable characters from this Westville neighborhood. If the Tap Room's ambiance proves too much for you, take your pint and head to the pleasant, quieter, main pub room. Limited parking is available in the pub's lot, but street parking is fairly easy to find.

Eli Cannon's Tap Room
695 Main Street
Middletown, Connecticut 06457
Tel. (860) 347-ELIS
www.elicannons.com
Proprietors: Sue and Phil Ouellette

Eli Cannon's atmosphere, self-described, is a mixture of an Irish/English pub and American Trailer Park Fusion; the pub is also a kaleidoscopic adventure in good beer. An assortment of random debris springs from the walls and hangs from the rafters, including tricycles, barber poles, and an enormous selection of disengaged tap handles. Patrons lounge in old barber chairs, theater seats, and worn leather couches. Throughout the bar, movies ranging from old Bruce Lee flicks, Ed Wood's classic *Plan 9 From Outer Space*, and *Reservoir Dogs* play silently on small, oddly positioned televisions. The motley atmosphere is draw enough for many customers, while others ignore the distractions and resolutely aim their focus on the ample beer list.

Amidst all of the clutter, there are few constants here. The giant boards full of tap handles are not for show. A couple of times per night, the bartenders leave the safe environs of their work-stations to scour the compact but rambling pub for the corresponding tap handle for the latest offering. There is one tap handle you'll never find on the walls, regardless of how hard you look—Eli's has never sold a single bottle, can, or pint of Budweiser. With thirty-two taps, Eli's offers a real focus on local, New England beer, but with a healthy selection of imports. Check out the handy chalkboard hanging above the bar to find out when the beers were tapped, or order something from the pub's extensive bottled-beer list.

On Thursday evenings, Eli's sponsors a meet-and-greet event with local, national, and international breweries ranging from Troutbrook to Rogue to Unibroue. These events allow customers the chance to sample featured products, learn more about the breweries, and to walk away with free pints glasses and other brewery merchandise.

The menu, literally held together by duct tape, is even more dizzying and confusing than the pub's décor. Eli's believes in serving "real meals" and most of the offerings are made on-site from scratch. The Porkies Revenge is an especially troubling but tasty dish, consisting of Eli's fries topped with barbequed pulled pork, cheese, and scallions. While it may not help your ability to taste the beers here, Eli's specializes in hot sauces, providing more than 150 selections.

This motley pub is open Mondays, 4 P.M. to 1 A.M.; Tuesday through Thursday, 11:30 A.M. to 1 A.M.; Friday, 11:30 A.M. to 2 A.M., Saturday and Sunday, 3 P.M. to 2 A.M. The place gets packed with locals after work and with college kids during the weekend evenings, so it is best explored and enjoyed in the off-hours.

MAINE

Great Lost Bear

540 Forest Avenue
Portland, Maine 04101
Tel. (207) 772–0300
www.greatlostbear.com
Proprietors: Dave Evans, Weslie Evans, and Chip MacConnell

A Portland institution since 1979, the Great Lost Bear is one of the true pioneering beer bars in New England. When David Geary opened his brewery in 1986, the Great Lost Bear found new inspiration. As more craft breweries opened in Maine, the Bear slowly started expanding its tap selection, from eight to twenty-four and thirty-six before finally settling at fifty-three lines.

The place is a showcase for the state's brewers and approximately two-thirds of the pub's tap lines are reserved for Maine beer. On Thursday evenings, the Great Lost Bear hosts a different craft brewery. Featured beers cost $1.99 and brewers come to meet and converse with the attendees. These events rank among the best opportunities in New England to sample local beers and meet with the people who create them. Most of the Maine breweries also debut their seasonal and special releases here. The extensive beer list offers three beer engines, with firkins stored in a separate cooler to maintain proper temperature.

To further support Maine breweries and to change things up for consumers, the Great Lost Bear sponsors a variety of events during the year. Every January, the pub gathers beers from Maine's brewpubs for the Annual Brew Pub Cup. At the end of the competition, the Great Lost Bear awards a fan favorite to the brewery with the highest-selling beer. Other events include the Industrial Park Challenge (a battle between several Portland-area breweries), Magic Hat's Mardi Gras party, the Realbeer.com Challenge Cup, and The Summer Ale Rumble.

The Great Lost Bear itself is a trip to visit. Its little rooms and nooks are colored with an eclectic mixture of junk, including numerous pieces of breweriana, license plates, beer promotional materials, foreign currency, and antique beer serving plates. If you find the kitsch overwhelming, retire to the cozy, wraparound bar and spread out. Easily the best place to wait out a snowy, winter's day, the bar at the Great Lost Bear also offers the best vantagepoint for enjoying the pub's steadfast and passionate love of Maine beer. Be sure to take a look at the chalkboard near the front of the pub listing the ten top-selling pints of the month.

The Great Lost Bear is open Monday to Saturday, 11:30 A.M. to 11:30 P.M.; and Sunday, noon to 11 P.M. Parking is sometimes available in the small, often-packed lot off to the left of the pub.

MASSACHUSETTS

Sunset Grille and Tap
130 Brighton Avenue
Allston, Massachusetts 02134
Tel. (617) 254–1331
www.allstonsfinest.com
Proprietor: Marc Kadish

No place in New England offers more lines of draft beer than the Sunset Grille and Tap. With 112 different beers, the selection at this two-floored pub is staggering. Sunset has won so many Best of Boston awards that the magazine had to retire it from competing in the Best Beer Selection category.

Run by owner Marc Kadish, who gained beer experience while working as a chef for Boston Beer Works, Sunset is a staple on the better beer scene in Boston. As the only real multitap in Boston, and the only supertap in New England, there are always some real finds on the menu at incredibly reasonable prices.

The management of so many lines has sometimes proven difficult for Sunset in the past. With 112 offerings and a steady number of customers, the beers sometimes don't turn over as quickly as they should. To help move the beer, the pub drops the price on older beers and sponsors a "Kick the Keg" promotion, where customers can win prizes if they order the last pint in the keg. While this occasionally leads to stale beer going across the bar, the pub publicly pledges on the front cover of its beer menu not to keep a beer tapped longer than thirteen days. Speaking of the beer menu—at fourteen pages in length, this hefty, pamphlet-sized tome is a veritable bible of beers. After perusing the draft list on the back of the menu, be sure to flip through the list of hundreds of bottled beers available. Also check the chalkboard in the front bar to find any newly tapped beers.

The American pub-fare menu here contains a dizzying array of options. The food is acceptable as far as bars go, but the beer is the true star here. Sunset serves beer in sizes ranging from 2 ounces to a full yard. It also provides so-called Randall devices, which contain fresh hops through which beer is drawn to create a hoppier final product.

Due to its location in the heart of Allston, college kids dominate the crowd. The overall atmosphere is much more similar to that of a regular bar than a focused beer bar. Sunset is affiliated with the Big City bar and pool hall located next door.

The Moan and Dove
460 West Street
Amherst, Massachusetts 01002
Tel. (413) 256–1710
www.themoananddove.com
Proprietor: Daniel Lanigan

Easily one of New England's top beer bars for two simple reasons: the owner works hard to bring in rare offerings you aren't likely to find elsewhere and the atmosphere is unapologetically brash and in your face. If you prefer a little attitude with your beer, welcome home.

Oddly located off by itself in a small, roadside mall on the outskirts of Amherst, the Moan and Dove is a true prize for beer-loving souls in the western half of the commonwealth. With its hardwood booths, limestone tabletops, and concrete floors, no one would ever describe the Moan and Dove's décor as warm or welcoming. But add the colorful staff and bountiful beer list to the mix and the space feels simultaneously cold yet comfortable, which is a bit unsettling.

Grab one of the enormous, oversized, beer-stained menus and start narrowing your choices. The offerings are generally broken down by style, with insightful, typed style descriptions and entertaining, handwritten editorial comments ("yeast bomb" or "for booze hounds only"). The staff and the owner take their beer very seriously. If a keg kicks, you can spend an hour watching the bartender meticulously hand print the next beer in stylish script on the chalkboard hanging off to the side of the bar.

The beer menu on my visit announces a recent change in the pub's offerings. "You'll notice we've gotten rid of about 50 beers," it offers. "These are largely beers in the middle ground of decency (call them training wheels) that I feel, after a year of trying to educate your palates, you no longer need to rely on, and I am happy to no longer sell (i.e. Sam or Newcastle or Czech Rebel)."

The beer list is heavy on obscure Belgian beers, including nearly the entire line of Cantillon beers. Local importers and distributors Dan and Will Shelton befriended owner Daniel Lanigan when he opened the pub and they often provide the proprietor some unique offerings sold only at the Moan and Dove. The bottled-beer list is dominated by imported beers and rounded out by a smattering of higher-alcohol American beers.

The pub sponsors a series of special events for American craft brewers throughout the year, including dinners with Dogfish Head and special release nights for Stone Brewing and Heavyweight Brewing. The Moan and Dove also sponsors a hard-core take on the ordinary mug club concept. As opposed to those wussy operations where you can simply buy your way in, regulars here have to drink their way through a list of 144 bottled beers in a single year in order to secure membership. Upon consumption of your final beer, you then have to stand on the bar and recite a poem while wearing the ceremonial Guinness hockey jersey before receiving your 26-ounce mug.

Beyond the bin of peanuts, food is not available for purchase here, but the staff is more than willing to provide recommendations and menus for places that will deliver. Look for a second Moan and Dove location coming soon to the Boston area.

The Publick House Brookline
1648 Beacon Street
Brookline, Massachusetts 02445
Tel. (617) 277–2880
www.anamcarapublickhouse.com
Proprietors: David Ciccolo and Ailish Gilligan

A relative newcomer to the Boston-area beer scene, the Publick House Brookline has certainly made a strong first impression. Cofounded by a former brewer at the now-defunct Tremont Brewing Company, the place mixes a healthy dose of beer geekism with another part neighborhood bar. Formerly named the Anam Cara Publick House, the pub is one of the area's premier beer bars. Considering the upscale nature of the Washington Square neighborhood of Brookline in which the pub is located, most people assume it's just another prefab Irish bar. A quick review of the beer listings on the chalkboard across from the bar should disabuse them of any such notion.

The selections break down into three simple categories: Belgians, Here, and There. Beers in the Here category include domestic craft beers, while There includes all foreign-made products not brewed in Belgium. With twenty-six total draft lines, the Publick House Brookline dedicates more than half of its list to American craft beers, while reserving about eight slots for Belgian offerings. The beers are priced and sized in part by alcohol level, with those weighing in at 8 percent alcohol and above seeing a reduction in size to a 10-ounce pour. While the prices are not cheap, they are certainly fair, unlike some other Boston-area so-called beer bars that did not make this list. A publican certainly has the right to make an honest return on his investment, but a true beer bar does not seek to gouge its customers for the experience.

Ciccolo takes great efforts to ensure the beers are served in proper glassware and at the correct temperatures to maximize both the experience and the enjoyment of the individual beers. The owners integrate beer throughout the pub's menu to create a unique opportunity to sample cuisine *à la biere*. The offerings include a selection of artisanal cheeses from Chimay and Orval, clam chowder made with Pabst Blue Ribbon, and littleneck clams sauteed in an Allagash White broth.

The pub sponsors occasional events throughout the year, including its popular HopHead Throwdown, a charity event showcasing some of the region's most tongue blisteringly bitter beers.

The Publick House Brookline is open Monday through Friday, 5 P.M. to 2 A.M.; Saturday and Sunday, 12 P.M. to 2 A.M. The pub is open for lunch on Saturdays and brunch on Sunday, from Labor Day to Memorial Day, 12 P.M. to 3 P.M. Dinner is served year-round: Sunday through Wednesday, 5 P.M. to 10 P.M.; and Thursday through Saturday, 5 P.M. to 11 P.M.

Horseshoe Pub and Restaurant
29 South Street
Hudson, Massachusetts 01749
Tel. (978) 568–1265
www.horseshoepub.com
Proprietor: Nick Pizzimento

Running seventy-five flowing lines of craft beer outside of the bustle and foot traffic of a major metropolitan area is no easy task. Tucked just inside the Boston side of the I-495 belt, the Horseshoe Pub is a beacon of good beer in a sometimes-bleak sea of macro bottles and flavorless lagers in this area.

The pub is owned by the Pizzimento family, who purchased the present building in 1980; the youngest son, Nick, took over the reins in 1991. The pub recently emerged from some substantial renovations, which included a sizable expansion of the structure, which dates to 1832. The updates and additions offer a fair amount of architectural charm, with vaulted ceilings in the dining room, beer-related, stained-glass skylights, and an additional, lofted dining area.

Mixing "99 Bottles of Beer on the Wall" with the spirit of Jules Verne, the Horseshoe gives drinkers the opportunity to circumnavigate the world of beer through its Beer Safari Club. To encourage participation in the challenge, every time an explorer completes a sampling of twenty-five beers, the pub offers a host of prizes ranging from a pint glass to a party of free appetizers for twenty or more people. The pub's motto is, "There are many beers in the world, the experience is not equal to the expense." As far as adventures go, this is not exactly a big-game hunt in the African plains but I give the pub points for creativity.

For those who don't feel the urge to add a competitive component to their beer drinking, you are still encouraged to journey through the enormous draft list. The list does indeed cover much of the globe, but its most rewarding pleasures are the local offerings, which include up to six beers from the Wachusett Brewing Company.

Though the audience is decidedly local, the staff is attentive and welcoming to all. The pub is open Monday through Saturday, 11:30 A.M. to midnight (kitchen closes at 10:00 P.M.). Parking is available in the adjacent lot.

Redbones
55 Chester Street
Somerville, Massachusetts 02144
Tel. (617) 628–2200
www.redbonesbbq.com
Proprietors: Robert Gregory and Caryn Whitney

As a long-standing force on the better-beer scene in the Boston area, Redbones mixes savory barbeque with a laid-back atmosphere to provide you a breather from cookie-cutter, Irish-themed bars. Opened in 1987, Redbones is perhaps the granddaddy of New England's beer bars. The twenty-four rotating taps offer only a few mainstays, including such familiar draft lines as Newcastle, Bass, Guinness, and, of course, Pabst Blue Ribbon. Beyond these four staples, anything is fair game. The beer menu changes daily, if not every few hours, as new, interesting beers replace kicked kegs. Redbones specializes in local New England beers, but also offers a smattering of hard-to-find American craft and imported beers.

With three distinct rooms, Redbones provides a place for everyone from families to lone drinkers. The narrow, upstairs bar is usually packed with people waiting for seating in the main room or watching the Red Sox play on the bar's two televisions. You can spend a lot of time in this bar looking up at the hanging beer menu, perusing a written beer list, or trying to figure out what that big, wooden spinning arrow is on the wall. A spin of the bar's Dial-A-Draft wheel allows uncertain pubgoers to leave up to fate the decision of which beer they will enjoy. The highlight of the main dining room is the small counter-seating area that gives diners a front row seat to the action heating up in the kitchen, where pit masters toil against flames in the name of smoky, tender barbeque goodness. The chefs are also likely to offer you free samples of their wares. Be sure to tip accordingly by leaving a few dollars in a clothespin above you. Downstairs lurks Underbones, a lair of additional seating and bar space festooned with the funky, cartoonish works of a local artist.

Many members of the bar- and waitstaff have worked here for a long time, a testament to the bar's hip, welcoming environs. With all of its subtle charms, the attitude at Redbones remains relaxed and unpretentious. While Redbones is one of the undisputed kings of good beer in the Boston area, it couldn't seem to care less. Good beer, as well as good barbeque, is just a way of life here. The menu offers a tantalizing mix of barbeque offerings from a wide variety of schools, ranging from Memphis pork ribs to Texas beef ribs.

Redbones does outwardly acknowledge its role as a Boston-area beer pioneer a few times each year. For more a decade, Redbones has dedicated November to celebrating the splendors of American beers from the Pacific Northwest. In a testament to the good beer reputation of Redbones, brewers small and large not only send a keg or two of their beers—most of which are not otherwise available in Massachusetts or even on the East Coast—but many of the brewers themselves fly across country to meet, greet, imbibe, and speak at the beer dinners that cap off the celebratory month.

NEW HAMPSHIRE

Barley Pub
328 Central Avenue
Dover, New Hampshire 03820
Tel. (603) 742–4226
www.barleypub.com
Proprietor: Scott Mason

For craft beer lovers who sometimes feel lost in the wilderness trying to track down suitable offerings in New Hampshire, the good news is that the Dover-based Barley Pub continues to fight the good fight. Opened in July 2000, New Hampshire's top beer bar runs sixteen draft lines, with a rotating selection of local and regional craft offerings, including Smuttynose, Moat Mountain, and Long Trail.

Walk into the unpretentious barroom from the street and you could easily mistake the Barley Pub for just another small-town, Budweiser-loving tavern. The room is long and dark, a bit dank and divey, with wood-paneled walls adorned with various pieces of brewery signage. A small stage toward the back of the bar also looks suspiciously like a place where late-nighters might dance to sappy Garth Brooks songs.

Refusing to put on airs, the Barley Pub takes a refreshingly unpretentious approach to the promotion of good beer. The staff shuns fancy glassware in favor of classic, sixteen-ounce pint glasses (even for Smuttynose's powerful barleywine). While the place is mainly filled with locals, the tap selection makes it clear that pubgoers here are not thoughtless members of Budweiser nation. So a warning to snooty beer geeks: before visiting the Barley Pub, be sure to check your attitude at the door.

After taking a seat, you may notice a rooster tethered to the end of the bar. When asked about the bird's confinement, the bartender glances to the side and says, "Oh, you mean Larry." He promptly turns on his heel, retrieves a photo album from the other end of the bar, and drops it in front of me. Inside, a regular relates the history of the imprisoned rooster. It turns out that one night a couple of young men stopped by the bar for a few drinks. When the bartender turned his back, one of the kids ran off with the rooster. Owner Scott Mason raced outside, caught the plate number, and called the cops. The responding officer took the crime very seriously, asking a series of unintentionally humorous questions seeking descriptive information about "the wayward cock." After several hours of investigation, the cops tracked down the thief, recovered Larry, and brought him back home. Since that day, Larry remains forever chained to the Barley Pub's bar.

There are few staple beers here and the lineup changes frequently. The only seeming consistency is that Mason tries to secure specialty releases, including aged barleywines and other vintage strong ales. Fans of the Smuttynose Brewing Company can often find a couple of rare draft offerings from the brewery's portfolio on tap. The pub also lobbied hard to bring Sierra Nevada to New Hampshire and rewards that brewery's interest with two tap handles.

The pub offers live music several nights a week, with a bluegrass jam on Tuesday evenings. Dogs are welcome (the bar is named after a friendly Newfoundland who is depicted, with pint glass in hand, on the pub's logo) and you can bring your own food and snacks or order from the pub's very limited menu (panini sandwiches). Open daily, 3:30 P.M. to 1 A.M.

RHODE ISLAND

Mews Tavern
456 Main Street
Wakefield, Rhode Island 02879
Tel. (401) 783–9370
www.mewstavern.com
Proprietor: Dan Rubino

Boasting sixty-nine draft beers, two hundred single-malt Scotches, thirty tequilas, forty rums, and thirty varieties of vodka, the Mews Tavern is an adult playground for barflies. Simply walking around the place is an adventure, as the pub meanders up and down stairs, through a series of distinctly decorated rooms and nooks. The dark bar on the left side of the Mews is the destination for beer enthusiasts. A long line of tap handles runs the length of the bar. As there is no real signage promoting the available beers, grab one of the handy beer menus for quicker consideration. Many of the draft beers, including Amstel Light, Heineken, and Foster's, will be familiar to those who lack even a passing interest in the subject. Keep reading. There are always some true gems available that you are not likely to find elsewhere, including rare kegs of Samuel Adams Chocolate Bock.

The tavern is split into several rooms that cater to every form of drinker. There is a martini bar, a main dining room for families, and of course the darker pub for beer drinkers. Every time I visit, the pub has added some new dimension, be it a new room or a refinished deck. The clientele here is decidedly not full of snooty beer snobs. The atmosphere is quiet and the pubgoers remain focused on consuming their drink of choice. The Mews allows patrons time for contemplation while watching a baseball game or other sporting event on one of the bar's televisions.

The Mews also respects the pocketbooks of its beer-loving customers. On the first Wednesday of every month, the pub offers Pint Night, where customers keep the pint glass in which the featured beer is served.

Mr. Pickwick's

433 Mountain Road
Stowe, Vermont 05672
Tel. (802) 253–2106
www.englandinn.com
Proprietors: Christopher and Linda Francis

I have a theory about why it is so hard to find a true beer bar in Vermont. After much searching, asking various beer geeks and brewery owners, I found few who could name a Vermont bar that really focuses on good beer. For some states, the lack of a true beer bar is emblematic of a general lack of enthusiasm for craft beer. Nothing could be further from the truth when it comes to Vermont. Vermonters are notoriously supportive of their locally made products, be it cheese, maple syrup, or beer. Craft brewers enjoy wide support here from locals who have helped create and sustain the state's many breweries and brewpubs.

Now to the theory. If you go into nearly any bar in Vermont, you can probably find a half-dozen locally made beers, a situation that does not exist in any other New England state. Dedication to local products and love of craft beer is so well integrated into the defining character of Vermonters that every bar is a good beer-bar. With their fanatical dedication to locally made products, it never really dawned on Vermonters that a bar might distinguish itself from competitors by specializing in craft beer. It's just a given that a Vermont bar would carry Vermont beers. Nearly every bar you enter in Vermont is guaranteed to offer a healthy selection of beers crafted in the state. Local package and convenience stores are the same way.

With this theory in mind, Mr. Pickwick's in Stowe is as close to a great beer bar as you will find in Vermont. I mean no disrespect to this well-appointed, British-style pub at the Ye Olde England Inne. Replete with plaid carpeting, slanting rock archways, and exposed-wood beams, Mr. Pickwick's boasts plenty of great nooks for both dining and drinking. Be sure to take special note of the collection of silver and pewter tankards hanging above the bar area.

The service at Mr. Pickwick's is impeccable, with ultra-informed bartenders who can guide you through the pub's well-considered tap and bottled beer list. If you're unsure which local or imported beer to choose, the staff happily inquires about your tastes and will aid in your decision making. The pub's extensive beer menu takes pains to explain cask-conditioned ale, which is always available. The bartenders are also just as happy to converse with you about the worlds of wine and spirits, especially that delightful first-cousin of beer, single-malt Scotch.

Vermont

Locally crafted beer is truly a way of life here. From Burlington to Brattleboro, the Vermont beer scene vibrantly teems with excellent opportunities to sample great beers and meet a cast of colorful characters. Vermont also boasts some of the best beer culture in America, with craft beer flowing through the veins of informed local beer lovers. Craft beer is so well ingrained in Vermont culture that a half-dozen breweries legitimately vie for the crown of making *the* beer of the Green Mountain State, including major players such as Long Trail and Magic Hat.

Vermont's spirit of promoting its own products causes outside breweries to have difficulty competing here. While Vermonters love craft beer, they're more likely to buy Switchback than Smuttynose. One major brewery recently fled from

the state in the face of such determined parochialism, returning to the friendlier confines of its home state. Vermonters figure that they have enough good beer at home, so why bother buying beer from some pesky Mainer? The locals even treat Harpoon, which bought the Windsor-based Catamount brewery out of bankruptcy and attempted to continue its line of ales, as a bit of a carpetbagger.

It is a pleasure to drive around this beautiful state, with its wonderfully diverse topography. From the mountains in the Northern Kingdom to the flatlands of the south, Vermont is home to some of the most colorful characters in the New England brewing industry. From the bedazzling Alan Newman to the opinionated Ray McNeill, the passionate owners define the breweries and pubs profiled here.

The Queen City of Burlington, on the shores of picturesque Lake Champlain, is the perfect destination for a beer vacation. Within a short drive of the city limits, you can experience a half-dozen quality breweries and brewpubs. Burlington is also the only place in New England where you can walk to three brewpubs in less than five minutes. Anchoring the downtown dining and drinking scene, the stalwart Vermont Pub and Brewery looks onto the building containing one of New England's newest brewpubs, Paul Sayler's crunchy American Flatbread, while the Three Needs Brewery and Taproom dances to its own drummer a few blocks away.

Beyond the excellent craft breweries, Vermont's true beer treasures can be discovered in its superb brewpubs, including McNeill's in Brattleboro, the Jasper Murdock Alehouse at the Norwich Inn, the Bobcat Café in Bristol, and the Alchemist Pub in Waterbury. More than simple brewpubs, these places are destinations worthy of their own road trip. The collective and continued strength of the state's brewpubs is an exciting development in the New England brewing scene. Regardless of the season, there is simply no excuse needed to spend a weekend slowly winding your way through the state and enjoying its unique beer culture.

Madison Brewing Company

428 Main Street
Bennington, Vermont 05201
Tel. (802) 244-BREWS
www.madisonbrewing.com

★ **Best Beer:** Willoughby's Scottish Ale. I admit this is an entirely reluctant choice because of the overall poor quality of the beers available at this brewpub. This beer is mildly representative of the broad category of Scottish ales, with a simple malt profile and an unexpectedly strong, and not particularly enjoyable, hop finish. The buttery characters often associated with the Ringwood yeast are sometimes at play here, along with the brewpub's characteristic off-flavors.

Opened: February 1996.

Type: Brewpub.

Owner: Michael Madison.

Brewer: Michael Madison, Jr.

Brewing system: 7-barrel Peter Austin System.

Amount produced: 270 barrels. 1,000-barrel total capacity.

First beer: Old 76 Strong Ale.

Flagship beer: Old 76 Strong Ale.

Year-round beers: Old 76 Strong Ale, Willoughby's Scottish Ale, Buck's Honey Wheat, Crowtown Pale Ale, and Monument Light.

Seasonal beers: Sucker Pond Blonde, Vermont Special Porter (VSP), Benny's Brew Pale Ale, Squirrel's Breath IPA, Oktoberfest, Winter Warmer, and Stark Hose #1 Raspberry Ale.

Tours: Tours are not offered.

Beer to go: The pub sells both bottles and growlers to go.

Food: The spacious pub specializes in sandwiches at reasonable prices and offers a special, reduced-price menu for kids and seniors. I believe it is without irony that the pub offers beer-battered chicken tenders smothered in cheese as a "Lite Fare" offering.

Amenities: On-street, metered parking is available. Full liquor license.

Pub hours: Open Sunday through Thursday, 11:30 A.M. to 9:30 P.M.; Friday and Saturday, 11:30 A.M. to 10:30 P.M.

Directions: The brewpub is on Route 9 in the center of Bennington, close to the intersection with Route 7.

Owned and operated by three brothers and their father, the Madison Brewing Company is a no-nonsense pub in the heart of downtown Bennington. From its simple, brick exterior to its open-air, lofted dining space with exposed duct work, Madison is a pleasant-enough environment in which to enjoy a meal. The open brewhouse sits off to one side of the pub's main dining room, ready for all to see. The family's crest also hangs in various places throughout the pub, including on the shield of a coat of armor.

For Mel Madison, the brewpub concept started with a chance business class in college. Mel's professor was a former brewer with the Miller Brewing Company. From that experience, Mel admits, grew "a college project gone out of control." When the family decided to open a restaurant, the youngest Madison, a home-brewer, suggested adding a brewery element.

After researching potential brewing systems, the family settled upon the comprehensive, one-stop-shop of services offered by Alan Pugsley's consulting company. The family purchased a seven-barrel, Peter Austin system from Pugsley and his team helped the Madisons navigate the entire range of brewing hurdles, from recipe design to system to installation. In August 1994, the three Madison brothers and their father took the ultimate family vacation, spending several days working at Pugsley's Shipyard Brewing Company in Maine.

After the Madisons opened their own pub, members of Pugsley's consulting team visited and supervised the first brew days. During the process of crafting the pub's own recipes, the family selected a beer called Old 76 Strong Ale as its flagship brand. A self-described "rich English Yorkshire style ale," the Old 76 is incorporated as a design element throughout the pub. Its logo is imprinted attractively on a Revolutionary flag, along with a coat of arms painted on a brick wall adjacent to the pub's entryway, and it greets diners on the front page of the menu.

While there is lip service paid to the beer in terms of decoration and in the marketing concept, the family willingly acknowledges that beer is not the top priority here. "We focus more on the dining room," says Mel Madison. "We just also happen to make beer." Along these lines, tours are "rarely given," even by appointment.

Unfortunately, beer's low place in the pub's pecking order shows in the finished product. It's certainly never enjoyable to criticize a brewery or pub, but sometimes it's necessary. Served on a helpful sheet explaining the individual beers, each of Madison's housebrewed beers has a certain slightly sour and bitter off-flavor. These off-putting flavors are common to all of the beers, regardless of the individual style presented. This is not a criticism of the often-maligned Ringwood yeast character, which is often described as possessing butterscotch or buttery notes (technically referred to as diacetyl). This familiar flavor—usually the end result of many breweries using the well-aged yeast strain provided by Pugsley—is curiously absent from Madison's beers, something I doubt was an intentional achievement.

To create the brewpub's Stark Hose #1 Raspberry beer, the bartender simply and sadly pours a syrupy, raspberry extract into a pint of Buck's Honey Wheat at the bar. And, voila—a new beer is born. The raspberry beer, with tell-tale purple syrup droplets polluting its head, is then served to the awaiting customer. The pub's flagship beer, the Old 76, doesn't fare much better. The beer is a mess of sweet and bitter notes that engage in an unpleasant and futile battle for control of the beer's flavor profile. Neither wins and only the drinker loses in the process.

There are signs that a love of beer once existed in this large space. A creative, if ill-executed, mural detailing the brewing process from start to finish dovetails across an expansive dining-room wall. Signs on the bathroom doors denote separate entrances for "mALES" and "femALES." An attractive and unusual half-moon–shaped nook built into a distant corner of the upstairs dining space announces that the nook is reserved for a "Stammtisch." This Bavarian idiom, which roughly translates as a "table for the regulars," is sometimes seen on little signs in German beer halls and pubs. If you sit there, the waitstaff will probably usher you away in order to welcome the pub's regular and much-appreciated clientele.

With its attractive, welcoming pub, open and ample dining space, and great downtown location, I raise a glass in hopes that the Madisons can rekindle a lost love for beer and brewing.

McNeill's Brewery

90 Elliot Street
Brattleboro, Vermont 05301
Tel: (802) 254–2553

★ **Best Beer:** Dead Horse IPA on cask. Despite the unappetizing name, McNeill's Dead Horse IPA on cask is as powerful as the Corleone family's signature warning shot. McNeill's specializes in cask ales, usually running three separate offerings. The aroma is playful and full of alcohol and sharp hop notes. Coarse over all, the Dead Horse is raw from start to finish. Bitterness mixes with fruit and toasted-malt notes to finish as a big take on the traditional English style.

Opened: June 1991.

Type: Brewpub.

Owner: Ray McNeill.

Brewer: Otis Rogers.

Brewing system: 10-barrel brewhouse of local origin.

Amount produced: 1,500 barrels. Presently at capacity.

First beer: Unknown.

Flagship beer: Duck's Breath Bitter.

Year-round beers: Dead Horse IPA, Duck's Breath Bitter, Alle Tage Altbier, Champ

Ale, Extra Special Bitter, Firehouse Amber Ale, Slopbucket Brown, Pullman's Porter, and Ruby Ale.

Seasonal beers: McNeill's brews a wide range of seasonal offerings, including the 80 Shilling, Big Nose Blond, Bucksnort Barleywine, Exterminator Doppelbock, Imperial Stout, Kolsch, Oatmeal Stout, Old Ringworm, Professor Brewhead's Brown Ale, Scotch Ale, and Summer IPA.

Tours: By appointment.

Beer to go: A wide selection of the house specialties are available in 22-ounce bottles from a cooler across from the bar.

Food: Don't visit McNeill's expecting to eat much more than simple nachos, hummus and pita chips, or peanuts. The kitchen is simply a hot plate off to the side of the bar. McNeill does, however, make an excellent salsa.

Amenities: Limited on-street parking is available around the pub, or simply park in the enormous lot that now blocks the views from the pub's back windows. I don't remember if there is any liquor served here and it shouldn't matter. You're not coming here for margaritas.

Other attractions: If you're settling in for a long night at McNeill's, something I highly recommend, you may want to consider staying at the nearby Latchis Hotel. One of only two Art Deco buildings in the entire state, the stylish if slightly worn four-story hotel opened in 1938. In 2003, a local group purchased the entire building, which is on the National Register of Historic Places and includes three movie screens, a 750-seat, grand movie palace with balcony, a restaurant, and several shops. The Brattleboro Arts Initiative and the Preservation Trust of Vermont plan to renovate the structure and create a center for the arts in downtown Brattleboro. There is also late word that Chris Lalli of the Berkshire Brewing Company and his partners plan to renovate and reopen the defunct Windham Brewery in the Latchis Hotel's basement. 50 Main Street, Brattleboro, Vermont 05301, tel. (802) 254–6300, www.latchis.com. A full range of McNeill's beers, along with many other Vermont-brewed craft beers, can also be found at the excellent Brattleboro Food Coop. 2 Main Street, Brattleboro, Vermont 05301, tel. (802) 257–0236. Open Monday through Saturday, 8 A.M. to 9 P.M.; and Sunday, 9 A.M. to 9 P.M.

Pub hours: Daily, 4 P.M. to 2 A.M.

Directions: From Main Street in Brattleboro, turn west onto Elliot Street. The brewpub is located near the center of town.

Behind the façade of the little red house on Elliot Street lurks the lair of Ray McNeill. Watch your step as you pass through a door off the main barroom, down a rickety metal staircase—pause to note the bitterly cold wind whistling through sizable gaps in the exterior siding—and you find yourself in the scariest brewhouse in America. The brewhouse at McNeill's Brewery is a freezing cold dungeon that, in a testament to the free-spirited, laissez-faire nature of Brattleboro, has not been condemned. God bless the poor brewers who have toiled in this evil, inhumane environment to produce flavorful ales and lagers.

The owner of McNeill's Brewery is an intriguing mix of personalities—alternately brash, kindly, brusque, and passionate. Early in his ownership of the pub, McNeill, with his frizzy black hair, was commonly seen dressed in brightly colored Zuma pajama pants, a tie-dyed t-shirt, and no shoes. With hair cropped short and lightly graying at the temples, the modern Ray McNeill now sports a simple knit sweater and jeans. A classically trained cellist, the bohemian spirit and pub owner has turned into a respectable Brattleboro businessman.

When he first considered opening a brewpub, McNeill approached the task by reading every brewing text he could find. He would select a technical brewing manual, read it cover to cover, and then start all over again. After spending time training at the Catamount Brewery in White River Junction, he eventually opened his own place in a rundown building in downtown Brattleboro, a structure that once served as a police station, a town office hall, and a jail. "I was trying to create a sort of social meeting house for the town. . . . You know that stupid television show *Cheers?* That actually happens here. That's what this bar is like."

From the start, McNeill focused on brewing traditional beer styles. "I'm really interested in beer styles, in what makes 'pilsner' pilsner," he says. "And what makes pilsner different than Budweiser. Then going a little further, what makes north German pilsner different from south German pilsner, different from Czech pilsner. And I became a pretty serious student of that."

McNeill is not shy about his approach. "To some degree, I know this sounds a little egotistical, but to some degree with some beer styles, I define them, at least in the Northeast." He points to his Alle Tage Altbier, a beer widely praised among beer enthusiasts and in beer competitions as being one of his best accomplishments as a brewer. "My alt beer is one of the best anywhere," he flatly states.

Beyond the hype, the beers on tap at McNeill's Brewery are worth a special trip in their own right. Cask-conditioned ales are a house specialty and something I highly recommend. The prices are downright cheap and make for a very affordable evening, and sometimes a painful following morning. There is something special about the variety of ales and lagers available in this quirky pub setting. Consisting of a small room with well-worn floors and filled with long communal, wooden tables, McNeill's feels very much like the local bar that it is. This is a beer hall in a classic sense, a place to enjoy a pint with strangers and friends alike.

McNeill's always boasts local color, often with the owner himself playing a large role. During my visit, I watch McNeill play genial host to guests of his pub, myself included. He floats between tables, talking with regulars, hugging friends, buying rounds, and sitting down to talk with complete strangers. Watching him in his own environment, it is clear that few pub owners in New England are so closely identified with their establishments. The pub is perfectly named. It is indeed McNeill's place.

Long Trail Brewing Company

Junction Route 4 and 100A
Box 168
Bridgewater Corners, Vermont 05035
Tel. (802) 672–5011
www.longtrail.com

★ **Best Beer:** Double Bag. While I enjoy each of Long Trail's well-built selections, the gloriously malty Double Bag combines the best of German
brewing. The strong ale includes a substantial malt base, followed by a
healthy dose of noble hops to make a very drinkable, warming beer.

Opened: November 1989.

Type: Brewery.

Owner: Andy Pherson.

Brewers: Joe Schinella and Dan Gore.

Brewing system: 60-barrel locally fabricated brewhouse.

Amount produced: 47,100 barrels. 75,000-barrel total capacity.

First beer: Long Trail Ale.

Flagship beer: Long Trail Ale.

Year-round beers: Long Trail Ale, India Pale Ale, Double Bag (strong ale), and Hit
The Trail Ale (brown ale).

Seasonal beers: Blackbeary Wheat (March through August), Harvest Ale (September through early November), and Hibernator Ale (October through March).

Tours: Tours are not given, though a viewing platform allows visitors to check out
the brewhouse.

Beer to go: 6-packs, mixed cases, and kegs are available for purchase at the brewery.

Food: A small menu of pub fare and snacks is available.

Amenities: Ample parking is available in the brewery's lot.

Pub hours: Daily, 10 A.M. to 6 P.M. Kitchen closes at 5 P.M.

Directions: The brewery is situated at the crossroads of Routes 4 and 100A in
Bridgewater Corners.

During his global business trips as an electrical engineer, Andy Pherson drank a
lot of beer. As any good adventurer knows, the true purpose of travel, even business travel, is to explore and sample your destination's local culture and fare. After
his meetings adjourned, Pherson would seek out beers from a wide variety of

styles. When he engaged the locals in discussions about beer, they often teased him over the dreadful state of American brewing.

While on a trip to California, Pherson stumbled upon the nascent craft beer movement. After watching West Coasters enjoy bold new American beers, including Anchor Steam, Pherson called his wife from Santa Clara and asked her to buy some books on brewing if she had a chance. "Why?" she asked. In his mind, Pherson wanted to show those laughing foreigners how good American beer could be. He returned home to southern New Hampshire and wrote a business plan for a brewery, whose straightforward mission remains in place to this day: "To handcraft locally brewed alternatives to the imports."

A few months later, Pherson quit his stable job and decided to start a brewery near his vacation home in Vermont. From the beginning, Long Trail Ale has been the flagship product. Though not true for many beers in New England, the German school of brewing heavily influences Long Trail's beers. Despite his love for German beer, Pherson knew from the start it was not economically possible for his small craft brewery to produce lagers. He loved the crisp, clean ales of Dusseldorf and Cologne and loosely based his flagship product on the classic altbier style.

While the atmosphere here is laid-back and friendly, Pherson and his team remain very serious about running a business. In trying to expand the distribution for his products back in 1993, Pherson sent a letter to Anheuser-Busch proposing a distribution agreement. When word spread in 1995 that Long Trail had outgrown its original brewery, which was located in the basement of the old Bridgewater Woolen Mill, Pherson suddenly received a response from St. Louis. After a few months of negotiation, a deal was nearly finalized for the purchase of Long Trail by America's largest brewer. As the details were being hammered out, Pherson determined that he could only focus on one major project at a time. With great trepidation, the owner decided to concentrate on building a new brewery, walked away from the deal, and Anheuser-Busch went on to form a similar deal with Redhook.

Long Trail is a very focused operation, from the brewery's line of consistent, flavorful ales to its environmentally conscious business practices. The company remains heavily involved with draft beer, which accounts for three-quarters of its production. The flagship Long Trail Ale comprises about 65 percent of beer production. Pherson prides himself on being a hands-on owner who enjoys messing with the machinery more than doing public relations events. As we walk through the brewery, he proudly points out various innovations designed by his staff, including a malt-cleaning unit and a vacuum system to remove grain dust. Though they brew several times a day, four days a week, you'll never see any steam billowing from the structure. In order to save energy typically lost during the brewing process, the staff built a heat exchanger to capture steam and recycle it in the form of hot water for the next boil.

The former hay field where the new brewery sits is a beautiful place, but a logistical nightmare for an industrial business. In the small town of Bridgewater Corners, there is only a general store, a post office, and a brewery. Beyond the natural beauty, it's hard to see what Pherson saw in the place. The staff had to install three power poles to provide electricity to the site and drill two bedrock artesian wells two hundred feet deep to secure brewing water.

Even in the absence of regularly scheduled tours, a visit to the Long Trail brewery is a rewarding experience. When the brewery moved here, Pherson also added a new pub. Picnic tables are scattered across the pub's two large, open rooms. A busted canoe, dubbed the *S.S. Fermentation,* hangs above the comfortable bar; Pherson's beer can collection stands on display against a far wall. Relics from the brewery's history line another wall. The vibe remains decidedly low-key, as locals enjoy sipping on a twenty-three-ounce "Vermont pint" of the state's most popular craft beer.

Bobcat Café

5 Main Street
Bristol, Vermont 05443
Tel. (802) 453-3311

★ **Best Beer:** App Gap IPA. A wonderful mix of malt and hops creates an impeccably well-balanced beer. The substantial malt backbone is the key pillar of this beer.

Opened: June 2003.

Type: Brewpub.

Owner: Robert Fuller.

Brewer: Ron Cotte.

Brewing system: 10-barrel Criveller Company brewhouse.

Amount produced: Figures not available.

First beer: Bobcat Bristol Pride.

Flagship beer: Bobcat Bristol Pride.

Year-round beers: Mud Puddle Porter, Bobcat Bristol Pride, South Mountain Stout, App Gap IPA, and Deerleap Lager.

Seasonal beers: Octoberfest and Hogback Bock.

Tours: Tours available by appointment

Beer to go: None.

Food: The menu is a mix of upscale offerings and upgraded old favorites, including baked macaroni and cheese, lamb bolognese, and a particularly nice pulled pork dish. The portions are ample and well presented. Reservations for dinner are an absolute necessity. You can also sit at the bar for dinner, but that fills up quickly as well.

Amenities: Limited on-street parking. Full liquor license.

Pub hours: Open daily at 4:30 P.M. Dinner starts at 5 P.M. Kitchen closes at 9:30 P.M. No set time for bar close.

Directions: The brewpub is on Main Street in the heart of Bristol, nestled among shops and restaurants.

The Bobcat Café is one of the great, little-known brewpubs in this guide. Tucked away behind a simple storefront in the quiet town of Bristol, this charming little bistro is remarkably popular with residents from all across Vermont. With friendly, thoughtful service, solid cuisine, and superior beers, it's easy to see what makes the place so popular.

Even though the Bobcat Café's doors don't open for dinner until 4:30 P.M., I arrive at 4:10 P.M. to find people already waiting out front. As I join the line, I immediately begin to worry about not having a reservation. After confirming my poor planning, the smiling hostess suggests I take dinner at the bar. I pull up a seat at the one-hundred-year old bar and am greeted by another pleasant employee, the bartender Dana. His attention to detail is obvious as he deftly offers advice on the available beers while supplying me with samples to illustrate his suggestions. While most of the staff appears to be younger, local women, Dana has worked exclusively at brewpubs for many years before landing at the Bobcat. Through his experiences tending bar at the Vermont Pub and Brewery and the Alchemist, Dana is able to provide many valuable insights about the brewpub and its beer.

The Bobcat came into existence through a unique sponsorship program introduced by principal owner Robert Fuller. The shrewd businessman, who owns several other restaurants in Burlington, Shelburne, and Bristol, wanted to find twelve investors in order to demonstrate that there was sufficient local support to justify the venture. In return for a five-thousand-dollar investment, each of the contributors would receive a 25 percent discount on meals for themselves and a friend and the loan would be repaid, in full with interest, within five years. While Fuller initially sought twelve local investors, his presentation successfully won over thirty-two.

One of the initial investors was Paul Sayler, the well-traveled former brewer at the Catamount Brewing Company. Soon thereafter, plans were laid to add beer made on-site to complement the restaurant concept. Licensing and legal issues waylaid the brewing component of the operation for the first year; Sayler began plying his trade here in the summer of 2003. To complement the bistro's menu, Sayler designed a series of subtle, yet stylish, ales. Despite splitting time between numerous other projects, Sayler remained the head brewer here until leaving to open his own brewpub, the American Flatbread Burlington Hearth.

Whereas many brewpubs load their walls with various kitschy adornments, the pleasant, minimalist design at work at the Bobcat Café keeps distractions to a minimum and the focus on the quality food and drink. Beyond the two glass-encased fermenters anchoring the restaurant's back wall, there are few hints that the place is actually a brewpub. The brewing equipment is located down a hidden flight of stairs in the basement, removed from public view due to the obvious space limitations of the room. The most noticeable quality is the light buzz to the atmosphere as family and friends come together in a true community meeting place.

American Flatbread— Burlington Hearth
115 St. Paul Street
Burlington, Vermont 05401
Tel. (802) 861–2999
www.americanflatbread.com

★ **Best Beer:** Extra Stout. Possessing rich, deeply roasted aromas and matching flavors with a light, residual sweetness, this offering portends good things for Sayler's future releases.

Opened: April 2005.

Type: Brewpub.

Owners: Paul Sayler and Rob Downey.

Brewer: Paul Sayler.

Brewing system: 10-barrel Newland Systems brewhouse.

Amount produced: Figures not yet available.

First beer: Extra Stout.

Flagship beer: Not yet determined.

Year-round beers: Villier's Special Bitter.

Seasonal beers: The regular and seasonal beer menus are still under development and the pub will eventually offer 8 to 12 of its own beers. The list will include the Extra Stout and the India Pale Ale.

Tours: By appointment.

Beer to go: None.

Food: The menu is as straightforward as they come: several varieties of flatbread pizza and one salad. The pizzas are made at a preparation station in the main dining room and fired in an enormous, 50,000-pound brick and concrete oven in the corner.

Amenities: Street parking is tough in downtown Burlington, especially on the weekends. Additional parking is available in municipal lots. Live music, including small jazz outfits, play on the weekends with no cover. Full liquor license.

Pub hours: Daily, 11:30 A.M. to 2 A.M. The kitchen is open for lunch Monday through Saturday, 11:30 A.M. to 2:30 P.M. Dinner is available daily, 5:30 P.M. to 9:30 P.M.

Directions: This brewery and pizza restaurant is located on St. Paul Street in downtown Burlington, just around the corner from College Street.

Forming the final corner of Burlington's downtown good beer triangle, the American Flatbread Burlington Hearth offers a relaxed, homey environment in which to celebrate hearty food and drink with friends. As part of the American Flatbread chain, the Burlington Hearth builds upon the successful model of offering wholesome, filling flatbread pizzas by adding a brewing operation to the mix.

Though it is the newest brewpub in this guide, American Flatbread's owners have a deep résumé filled with noteworthy restaurant and brewing ventures. Co-owner Paul Sayler is one of the most well-regarded brewers plying his craft in New England. A former brewer at the now-closed Catamount Brewing Company, Sayler has worked in a staggering range of breweries across New England. After home-brewing for six years, Sayler worked for Catamount, Back Bay Brewing Company, the Commonwealth Brewing Company in Rockefeller Center, and the Colorado Brewing Company in Connecticut, before partnering with a local businessman to bring beer to the delightful Bobcat Café in nearby Bristol, Vermont.

For his part, the quiet and thoughtful Sayler is happy to finally set down permanent roots with the completion of this long-planned project. Sayler teamed with Rob Downey, an environmental lawyer and green-business consultant, to develop the new brewpub in Burlington. The pair originally had hoped to open the pub in a new development near Lake Champlain. When that project became ensnared in a local planning and zoning controversy, Sayler and Downey started shopping for a new location. When the historic Carbur's Restaurant closed, the pair scored a choice location right on the main square in downtown Burlington, a hundred feet or so from the long-time home of the Vermont Pub and Brewery.

The small American Flatbread chain is remarkably popular throughout Vermont. At the original location attached to the Lareau Farm Country Inn in Waitsfield, it is not uncommon to meet diners who have traveled an hour or two to wait another 90 minutes for a slice of the restaurant's pizza. Attracted to the company's social mission and sense of corporate responsibility, Sayler initially started working with American Flatbread to help develop a restaurant in Middlebury. Sayler speaks of the power of whole food and the important role such nourishment plays in people's lives. He also respected the company's dedication to its local community.

American Flatbread's environmental consciousness manifests itself in design elements throughout the new Burlington pub. Each menu is accompanied by a written "dedication" in which one of the owners or staff members writes a sort of blessing or welcome message for the week. The messages are sometimes personal, often passionately relating a desire to create a friendly, safe, community meeting place.

The chain's whole concept may at times feel a bit too earthy-crunchy and touchy-feely for some—hand-drawn prayer flags thread across the bar area—or even a little bit staged and inorganic—the sloganeering banners exclaiming truisms such as "Good Food Helps" strike an oddly corporate tone. Putting aside these minor points, the owners did a fantastic job renovating this building, constructed in 1884, into such a welcoming, familiar place. The pub is awash in red brick, from the tall, imposing walls to the gently sloping archway dividing the dining room and the pub. The giant brick oven anchors the dining room and warmth emanates from its flaming core.

After working in a mélange of brewing operations over the last fifteen years, Sayler has a clear vision of the role he wants beer to play at his pub. While creating the pub's concept, Sayler sought to address Vermont's lack of a genuine beer bar. The Burlington Hearth location offers an excellent selection of craft beers from across the state, along with some hard-to-find imported drafts and a dedicated Belgian beer tap line. With so many other brewpubs and breweries already open in Vermont, Sayler makes it plain that he wants to help support their operations, not just compete with them. The beer menu board hanging off to the side of the bar is a testament to this desire. Among the eighteen draft beers and three cask engines, Sayler's own beers are humbly buried in the middle of this list, with no fanfare to announce them as having been made on-site. When I ask why he doesn't give them greater play, Sayler simply remarks that Vermont beer consumers have evolved to a point where they simply enjoy good beer and the pub doesn't need to differentiate its beers from the other quality offerings.

Even while balancing multiple projects, including this substantial operation, Sayler is still hoping to create a farmhouse brewery under the Zero Gravity brand name. As a sister operation to the Burlington Hearth pub, the package facility would produce a variety of bottle-conditioned beers in an environmentally friendly manner.

Switchback Brewing Company

160 Flynn Avenue
Burlington, Vermont 05401
Tel. (802) 651–4114

> ★ **Best Beer:** Switchback Ale. As the guys at Switchback love to note, their flagship ale tends to defy categorization by style. With a hazy, reddish gold hue, the beer simultaneously offers a light wheat body while possessing some sizable underlying malt strength. Brewed with four different specialty malts and a touch of wheat, the beer finishes with a light bitterness.

Opened: October 2002.

Type: Brewery.

Owners: Bill Cherry and Jeff Neiblum.

Brewer: Chris Dooley.

Brewing system: 15-barrel Pico Brewing Systems brewhouse.

Amount produced: 1,600 barrels. 2,400-barrel total capacity.

First beer: Switchback Ale

Flagship beer: Switchback Ale

Year-round beers: Switchback Ale.

Seasonal beers: None.

Tours: By appointment. Make sure to call in advance.

Beer to go: None.

Amenities: Limited parking available in front of the brewery.

Directions: Turn off Route 7 in Burlington onto Flynn Avenue, heading west toward Lake Champlain, and look for the brewery right after crossing over the railroad tracks. Note that there is no sign for the brewery, so park on your left when you see the lot. The brewery is located through the doors on the far left, though you may have to ask around for it.

Hidden away in the middle of a warehouse structure, the Switchback Brewing Company is nearly impossible to find. There are no signs announcing its existence and even the neighbors don't seem to know they're working next to a functioning brewery. One or two of the local workers know the secret and they frequently stop by for samples.

As far as quirky start-up stories go, the history of the relatively undiscovered brewery is right up near the top. With a microbiology degree in hand, owner Bill

Cherry decided that he wanted to be a brewer. Before applying for any jobs, Cherry wrote to executives at Anheuser-Busch, Coors, and Miller asking for advice. To his surprise, he received some very detailed responses, including a long, single-spaced reply from an executive at Coors who encouraged him to attend brewing school. Emboldened by the response, Cherry entered University of California at Davis.

After graduating with his brewing degree, Cherry found that there were no brewing jobs available. His encouraging contact at Coors unfortunately had passed away prior to his graduation. With the doors to the brewing world closed to him, Cherry started making baloney. Literally. Before becoming the owner of this curious brewery, Cherry used to work in this very building when it was a food-processing plant. Instead of mixing malts and hops, he processed hot dogs, pickles, and various other products.

Cherry eventually returned to the brewing world, spending time with Anheuser-Busch in Fort Collins, Colorado, and working a five-year stint at the Boulevard Brewing Company in Kansas City. It was at Boulevard that Cherry fell back in love with brewing and learned the industry's practical side, helping guide that brewery from 7,000 barrels to 38,000 barrels in annual production. While he enjoyed working for Boulevard, Cherry missed spending time in the outdoors. The brewer began to consider a plan that would allow him to return to the outdoors.

After considering several locations, Cherry moved to Burlington, Vermont, and took the food-processing job. When Cherry's employer closed in late 2000, his college friend and now partner, Jeff Neiblum, convinced him to open his own brewery. Cherry credits his partner for having the entrepreneurial spirit to jumpstart the operation. On the strength of their business plan and Cherry's extensive brewing experience, the partners secured a rare Small Business Administration loan and opened Switchback Brewing Company.

Beyond his polite and slightly reserved exterior, Cherry remains steadfastly dedicated to running his little brewery his own way. The brewery produces only one beer and it is specifically designed not to compete with existing products in the highly competitive Vermont beer market. Cherry's style-bending Switchback Ale, which he is only willing to describe as "eclectic," generally defies description. This unclassifiable character gives the beer a certain cachet with local beer lovers, who appreciate that it's not just another IPA or brown ale. Cherry also adamantly refuses to filter his beer, bottle his product, artificially carbonate his kegs, advertise, or even put up a sign out front. While others question his refusal to brew a wider variety of offerings, Cherry smartly recognizes that competition for tap handles is fierce and that while bar owners might be willing to add one of his beers, two or more requires a much bigger fight.

Cherry laughs when asked about the origins of the brewery's name. Switchback refers to a zigzag trail up the side of a steep ridge or hill that allows a biker or hiker to take a more gradual ascent. While the word clearly references his love of the outdoors, Cherry also thinks Switchback serves as an apt metaphor for his intriguing career path from meat processor to master brewer.

Three Needs Brewery and Taproom

207 College Street
Burlington, Vermont 05401
Tel. (802) 658–0889

> ★ **Best Beer:** Peat Smoked Altbiere. A nice attempt at a difficult, elusive German beer style. The pub's version includes a touch of smoke—likely a leftover influence from the owner's days working at the Vermont Pub. With a noble hop aroma, the Altbiere offers a light malt base and some assertive hop notes to balance out the final flavor.

Opened: October 1995.

Type: Brewpub.

Owner: Glenn Walters.

Brewer: James Tierney.

Brewing system: 3.5-barrel self-fabricated system.

Amount produced: 285 barrels. 520-barrel total capacity.

First beer: Not known.

Flagship beer: None.

Year-round beers: None.

Seasonal beers: The Three Needs produces more than 140 different beers during the brewing year, including a full range of styles.

Tours: By appointment or ask at the bar.

Beer to go: None.

Food: None.

Amenities: On-street parking and municipal structures are available. Full liquor license. Seasonal outdoor seating in the alley next to the brewpub.

Pub hours: Open daily, 4 P.M. to 2 A.M.

Directions: The Three Needs is just off Church Street in downtown Burlington.

Burlington's troika of downtown brewpubs couldn't be more different in terms of style, approach, and attitude. While all three make smart, well-crafted beers, their respective atmospheres attract and satisfy vastly different audiences. The Vermont Pub and Brewery is the old stalwart—family-friendly and pleasing a wide audience—while newcomer American Flatbread is the crunchy, mildly political, environmentally conscious type. Further down College Street, the Three Needs is the brewpub for hipsters, rogues, and loners.

You can sense the attitude here before you even open the door. A pack of twentysomethings stand in front of the building smoking cigarettes, banished to the outdoors since the Man outlawed indoor smoking. Once inside the bar's small environs, the song remains the same, with ample opportunities for people watching. The Three Needs is comprised of a single dimly-lit barroom, with a handful of tables, two great window booths, a small bar, and a pool table anchoring the back of the space. Back in the day, smoke clouds filled the room, adding to the ooze of attitude and cool. The environment was a bad place to sample beer, but a great place to enjoy one. That vibe remains true today, but the absence of cigarette smog has vastly improved the beer scene.

The Three Needs is an experience, best considered as a whole package rather than by isolating its individual parts. Despite the seemingly too-cool-for-you attitude, the staff is quite friendly and attentive. Simce the Three Needs is often busy in the evenings, it may take a minute or two for the servers to provide your chosen flavor, but they'll eventually get to you. A lone chalkboard sign on the wall invites you to enjoy a Catamount, the now-defunct brand that once defined Vermont beer. The pub usually runs five of its own beers and a matching number of guest taps from other local craft breweries, including Long Trail and Switchback.

With all of the brewing equipment tucked away in the basement, far from public view, you could be forgiven for failing to ever notice that the Three Needs is a brewpub. The décor occasionally relates to beer, but generally remains simple and unobtrusive. The basement, however, is all about beer. Filled with stainless-steel tankage, including seven conditioning units, the brewery is the laboratory of brewer James Tierney. Over the course of the year, Tierney produces more than 140 kinds of beer from a wide range of styles. He draws from several influences, including Belgian, German, English, Irish, and American beer styles. "I'm doing beer for beer's sake," he says. Due to the small size of the system, the beer at the Three Needs turns over quickly, allowing Tierney greater freedom than a brewer working on a seven- or ten-barrel system.

While each beer possesses genuine quality and flavor, Tierney is most proud of his unusually large stable of lager beers. "I brew lagers because no one else does," he says. Lagers account for nearly half of Tierney's eight or ten batches every month and include a schwarzbier, rauchbier, maibock, and a Vienna-style offering. Before starting at Three Needs, Tierney was a prolific homebrewer whose grandfather introduced him to homebrewing when he was young. When Tierney's home system was full of beer—he made an astounding five hundred gallons of beer every year at home—he sometimes helped brew batches on the three-and-a-half-barrel system here. While Tierney was working next door as a bartender, the owner of the Three Needs (who once brewed for the Vermont Pub and Brewery just up the street) popped into the establishment and asked Tierney if he wanted to be the pub's new brewer. That was the extent of Tierney's job interview and he excitedly accepted the position. Although the brewpub has always offered a rambling list of beers, Tierney took the concept to the extreme and continues to add a few new beers to the roster every few months.

The origins of the pub's intriguing name remain much in dispute and everybody here tells a different story. For his part, Tierney suggests that at any one time, each person has three needs. If that postulate doesn't suit you, the bartenders have a little yellow notebook in which you can write your own three needs. If you're seated at the bar, the need for a good pint and some voyeuristic entertainment aren't likely to make your list.

Vermont Pub and Brewery

144 College Street
Burlington, Vermont 05401
Tel. (802) 865-0500
www.vermontbrewery.com

★ **Best Beer:** Wee Heavy Scotch Ale. This beer is a cellared Scottish-style strong ale. Served in a small snifter, the strength of the Wee Heavy's aroma is so powerful as to be noticeable from ten feet away. The aroma is part alcohol, part enticing malt sweetness. On first sip, the beer washes over the tongue with a thoroughly full mouthfeel. Big alcohol flavors balance the sweet, caramel malt, with a slight hop backbone to prevent the beer from becoming cloying. This beer is a hearty meal in itself.

Opened: November 1988.

Type: Brewpub.

Owners: Greg and Nancy Noonan.

Brewer: Greg Noonan.

Brewing system: 14-barrel handcrafted brewing system.

Amount produced: 1,000 barrels.

First beer: Dogbite Bitter.

Flagship beer: Burly Irish Ale.

Year-round beers: Bombay Grab IPA, Burly Irish Ale, Dogbite Bitter, Handsome Mick's Irish Stout, Rock Dunder Brown Ale, Uber Alt, and Vermont Smoked Porter.

Seasonal beers: Ethan Alien Lager, Forbidden Fruit, Sputyin Devil Tripel, and Wee Heavy Scotch Ale.

Tours: By appointment.

Beer to go: Growlers available for purchase.

Food: Typical pub food with predictable offerings of nachos, fries, calamari, and burgers, alongside some notable British offerings, including cock-a-leekie pie and bangers and mash. The pub also prepares beef from locally raised and well-treated Black Angus cattle.

Amenities: A limited amount of free parking is available next door to the restaurant or on-street.

Pub hours: Open daily from 11 A.M. to 1 A.M.

Directions: Located on College Street, the brewpub is across from the town center.

Located in a nondescript bank building in downtown Burlington, the Vermont Pub and Brewery is one of America's oldest and finest brewpubs. Founded by noted author and brewing authority Greg Noonan and his wife, Nancy, the Vermont Pub has stayed close to its roots in this activist city. In 1985, Greg and Nancy took note of the growing craft-brewing movement and considered opening a place of their own. The couple quickly learned that Vermont law prohibited pub brewing in the state. Instead of giving up, the couple petitioned the Vermont Legislature to change the law. After three years of hard lobbying work, the legislation passed in May 1988 and the brewpub opened in November.

As they began converting the space, Greg created a hodge-podge brewery using a maple-sap boiler, a stockyard feeder, and a former commercial ice cream–manufacturing vessel. This Yankee ingenuity has served the Vermont Pub well; quickly gaining honors for its solid lineup of beers, the pub remains strong more than fifteen years later.

Located a few hundred feet from the beautiful shores of Lake Champlain, the Vermont Pub produces a variety of high-quality ales and lagers. Among its offerings, the Smoked Porter stands above others in terms of its reputation. In the early days of brewing, the warmth of the sun and the air dried the malt. Because brewers quickly used them, the malts didn't have to dry to the levels modern brewers require for storage and transportation. With the development of kiln technology, malts were eventually dried over open fires. While more effective in the drying of the malt, this direct heating process resulted in beers possessed of acrid, foul smoke flavors. With the dawn of the Industrial Revolution came the flavor-clarifying benefits of better, indirect kilning procedures and less-offensive fuel sources.

Although many earlier brewers fled from smoke flavors, a posse of modern craft brewers has embraced the unique contributing essences of fire and heat. To produce its Smoked Porter, the pub's brewers smoke their own malt every three months in a grueling eight- to ten-hour operation. The brewers employ a mix of maple, hickory, and apple wood chips during the smoking process. The smoked malt makes up 15 percent of the malt bill in the Smoked Porter, which gives the beer a consistent, smoky flavor. It has a pleasant, almost sweet malt bill with a big, bitter hop bite at the finish. Patrons have varied reactions to the smoke in the beer. Some love it, while others negatively associate it with other smoked foods. Whatever you do, please don't tell the brewer that his beer tastes like smoked ham (though you might be right).

While the Smoked Porter is an excellent offering, it is actually not the pub's most notable beer. A few years back, I stopped off at the pub after visiting a Montreal beer festival. After ordering a sampler of a limited release offering, I began to smell an enticing mixture of sweet malt and alcohol. As I looked up, my server brought me what I still consider to be the finest beer I have ever enjoyed: the Wee Heavy Scotch Ale. The brewers cellared this beer for two years before releasing it to the public. The beer's balance was magical and its powerful malt flavors simultaneously soothed and enticed my palate. It's a beer that I will never forget and always hope to catch when I visit the Vermont Pub and Brewery.

Trout River Brewing Company

Route 5
Lyndonville, Vermont 05851
Tel. (802) 626–9396
www.troutriverbrewing.com

★ **Best Beer:** Boneyard Barleywine. This beer clearly stands out among Trout River's offerings. A very full-bodied ale, the hops are muted, giving full stage to sweet, portlike malt notes and fruity flavors. A very complex and enjoyable beer the owners hope to bottle in the future.

Opened: December 1996.

Type: Brewery.

Owner: Dan and Laura Gates.

Brewer: Dan Gates.

Brewing system: 20-barrel brewhouse.

Amount produced: 3,000 barrels. 6,000-barrel total capacity.

First beer: Rainbow Red Ale.

Flagship beer: Rainbow Red Ale.

Year-round beers: Rainbow Red Ale and Hoppin' Mad Trout (pale ale).

Seasonal beers: Scottish Ale, Bullpout Stout, Whitewater Wheat Ale, and Boneyard Barleywine.

Tours: Available by appointment.

Beer to go: Growlers, 6-packs, cases, and kegs available for purchase.

Food: The brewery has a tiny pub that serves food, including hand-tossed gourmet pizzas, as well as 6 to 8 tap beers.

Amenities: Parking is available next to the brewery.

Other attractions: The annual Vermont Brewer's Festival is one of the most idyllic gatherings in all of America. Held right on the banks of Lake Champlain in Burlington's Waterfront Park (with awe-inspiring views of the Adirondack Mountains), the festival provides beer lovers a terrific opportunity to sample beers from across the host state. The festival is the longest-running outdoor beer festival on the East Coast and usually inspires brewers to bring special releases and open a few hard-to-find offerings. Vermont Brewers Association, 607 Crossett Hill, Waterbury, Vermont 05676, tel. (802) 244–6828, www.vermontbrewers.com.

Pub hours: The pub is open Friday and Saturday, 11 A.M. to 9 P.M. Food is served from 4:30 P.M. to 8:30 P.M. The brewery closes in April and November, so call ahead to confirm hours.

Directions: From I-91 take Exit 23 and head north on Route 5 for about a mile. The brewery is on the left.

Trout River is a little like a transient college kid who keeps packing up and moving from place to place at the end of each term. After spending two years writing their business plan and securing financing, owners Dan and Laura Gates first opened in East Burke with a simple 4-barrel system. Looking back, Laura Gates admits the tiny system was grossly undersized. They quickly doubled the system size and almost as quickly outgrew the space. Trout River moved a few miles down the road to its present Lyndonville location. After several years here, the couple is again preparing to move to a new space.

Nestled in the Green Mountain State's Northeast Kingdom, the brewery produces a substantial amount of beer in its cramped facility. The owners jumped from a 4-barrel system to a 20-barrel outfit with matching double-batch, 40-barrel fermenters. After working between the Burke and Lyndonville facilities, Laura looks forward to settling down in a better-sized brewery sometime in 2007. Due the seasonal nature of Trout River's trade, the Gates family closes the brewery and takes two extended vacations in April and November. The brewery also hosts a small, thirty-seat pub and retail shop that opens for visitors a few days each week.

Brewer Dan Gates started as a homebrewer who enjoyed substantial success at his craft. When he won a gold medal for his Scottish ale in a prestigious national homebrewing competition, Dan gained the confidence to start his own operation. Trout River continues to produce a Scottish Ale, which is a distant second to the popular flagship Rainbow Red Ale. You may notice that the labels look crooked on every bottle of Trout River. Your eyesight is fine. As a result of a truck accident on the way to the brewery, Trout River's bottling line, lovingly dubbed "Cybil" by its handlers, has never been quite right.

Otter Creek Brewing Company

793 Exchange Street
Middlebury, Vermont 05753
Tel. (800) 473–0727
www.ottercreekbrewing.com

★ **Best Beer:** American Amber Ale. This special-release offering embarrasses most weak-kneed attempts at this broadly defined style. Possessing a sweet, almost cotton candy–like aroma, the beer's flavor is explosively malty but with a perfectly assertive, bitter hop balance, followed again by a final wave of malt sweetness. Available only in draft at the brewery and in limited quantities.

Opened: March 1991.

Type: Brewery.

Owners: Robert and Morgan Wolaver.

Brewer: Steve Parkes.

Brewing system: 40-barrel Century Manufacturing brewhouse.

Amount produced: 30,000 barrels. 40,000-barrel total capacity.

First beer: Copper Ale.

Flagship beer: Copper Ale.

Year-round beers: Otter Creek: Vermont Lager, Stovepipe Porter, Pale Ale, Copper Ale. Wolaver's: Pale Ale, Brown Ale, and India Pale Ale.

Seasonal beers: Otter Creek: Middleberry Ale (summer), Octoberfest (fall), and Alpine Ale (winter). Wolaver's: Wit (summer) and Oatmeal Stout (late fall to spring).

Tours: Closed Sundays. Tours are offered from Monday to Saturday at 1 P.M., 3 P.M., and 5 P.M. The brewhouse shop is open Monday through Saturday, 10 A.M. to 6 P.M.

Beer to go: A whole variety of offerings from both the Otter Creek and Wolaver's lines of beer is available for purchase, including 6-packs, mix-and-match cases, and freshly filled growlers.

Amenities: Parking is available in the brewery's lot. The brewery's shop sells an assortment of branded items, including backpack coolers, frisbees, and beer bread in a bottle. If you can't make up your mind, try purchasing a gift basket filled with a variety of Otter Creek paraphernalia.

Other attractions: The Two Brothers Tavern in downtown Middlebury serves many beers from Otter Creek and other Vermont craft brewers. The pub is the invention of Beal and Holmes Jacobs, who are the sons of an American history professor at nearby Middlebury College. In the white tablecloth restaurant, the creative, well-priced menu includes pizzas, sandwiches, cheap tapas-style starters, and an excellent tomato soup. 86 Main Street, Middlebury, Vermont 05753, tel. (802) 388–0002. Open daily, 11:30 A.M. to 2 A.M. Jazz brunch on Sundays.

Directions: From Route 7 in Middlebury, go west onto Exchange Street. The brewery is set off by itself next to the enormous Hood milk plant.

Comprised of two very different beer brands acting in concert, the Otter Creek Brewing Company was originally founded by passionate homebrewer Lawrence Miller. During his time at Reed College in Portland, Miller watched firsthand the rise of American craft brewing. After researching German-style beers in Europe, he returned with a precise recipe in mind for his flagship Copper Ale. He selected the town of Middlebury as his headquarters, not so much for its sleepy, congenial atmosphere and built-in base of collegiate patrons, but for the qualities of its water. The pH levels of the town's water met the exact criteria Miller had set for his altbier yeast strain.

Starting as a one-man operation, Miller released his signature Copper Ale on March 12, 1991. By year's end, Otter Creek was primed for its first expansion. The brewery quickly outgrew its space, and after several expansions, Miller built an entirely new, fifteen-thousand-square-foot facility down the street on a ten-acre parcel of land in 1995. Though it's located in an industrial office park, and across from a major Cabot cheese plant, the compact brewery at Otter Creek is attractively surrounded by trees and blends well into the environment.

In 1998, Otter Creek struck an important business deal to begin producing the Wolaver's line of certified-organic ales in partnership with the Panorama Brewing Company. Founded by the Wolaver family in 1997, the two principal owners of Panorama, Robert and Morgan Wolaver, wanted to fuse together a family history of farming, a dedication to environmentally friendly business, and a passion for brewing. In order to limit the start-up costs, Panorama chose to contract its recipes out to seven regional breweries across the country rather than build its own facility. The business plan worked and the beers found a niche in the marketplace.

In May 2002, the Wolaver family purchased the Otter Creek Brewing Company, keeping its name and products. The mix of the two brands seems to work well; not much has changed since the brewery merger. Otter Creek remains mainly a regional product, while the Wolaver's line is distributed in select markets around the country. The Wolaver's line is certified organic by the Vermont Organic Farmers; the brewery is likely the largest purchaser of organic malt in the country.

While organic malt is plentiful in the United States and abroad, organically grown hops are much harder to come by. Very few farmers are willing to grow organic hops; the biggest producers are found far away—in New Zealand. Another constant problem is the limited range of available hop varieties. Otter Creek remains conscious of these problems and continues to work with hop farmers in Yakima Valley to sponsor the expansion of organic hop agriculture in that region.

The company's first offering was the Wolaver's Pale Ale, a beer whose malt body is more noticeable than its hop character. While the beer has more in common with less hoppier products than it does with more typical versions of the style, it is a pleasant, refreshing beer. The brewery's Brown Ale, which relies less on hops, is more representative of its intended style. It boasts a slightly sweet, creamy malt base, a deep, reddish amber hue, and a very mild hop balance. The Wit and Oatmeal Stout also allow the brewers to focus more on the flavors of available organic malts than on hops.

With their clear German influence, Otter Creek's beers stand in contrast to many other ales brewed in New England. The flagship Copper Ale takes its inspiration from the altbiers of Dusseldorf and Northern Germany. Brewed with a blend of six different malts and three hop varieties, the Copper Ale balances biscuity flavors with solid, but not overpowering, hop bitterness. The beer remains a classic forerunner of New England craft brewing. Though brewed as an ale, the Oktoberfest uses two classic German noble hop varieties, Hallertau and Tettnang, to add a slight hop edge to the traditional, malt-enhanced Bavarian classic.

Rock Art Brewery

254 Wilkins Street
Morrisville, Vermont 05661
Tel. (802) 888–9400
www.rockartbrewery.com

★ **Best Beer:** Ridge Runner Ale. At 7.5 percent alcohol by volume, the Ridge Runner Ale is a butt-kicker of a flagship product. Though it is labeled as a barleywine, the beer is very light for the style and more closely resembles a strong American red ale. The Ridge Runner is brewed with a complex mixture of pale, dark crystal, Munich, flaked barley, black and chocolate malts, and liberal doses of Cascade, Crystal, Challenger, and Perle hops. The result is a pleasing mix of fruitiness and playful malt flavors.

Opened: November 1997.

Type: Brewery.

Owners: Matt and Renee Nadeau.

Brewer: Matt Nadeau.

Brewing system: 20-barrel Stainless Steel Specialists brewhouse.

Amount produced: 2,000 barrels. 3,500-barrel total capacity.

First beer: Whitetail Golden Ale.

Flagship beer: Ridge Runner Ale.

Year-round beers: Whitetail Golden Ale, Ridge Runner Ale, American Red Ale, Brown Bear Ale, and Stock Ale.

Seasonal beers: Blonde Ale (summer), India Pale Ale (summer), 80 Shilling Export Lager (fall), Vermont Maple Wheat Ale (fall), Midnight Madness Smoked Porter (winter), Mountain Holidays Bock (winter), and Stump Jumper (stout).

Tours: By appointment or just stop by during business hours.

Beer to go: 6-packs, cases, and growlers for sale.

Amenities: Limited parking available next to the brewery.

Directions: Starting in the center of Morrisville, travel north on Route 100 and turn left onto Wilkins Street. The brewery is located at the end of the road in a big red barn.

During my visit to the Rock Art Brewery in northern Vermont, owner Matt Nadeau beams like a brand-new father. With the smile on his face, he hardly seems to notice that anyone else is around. Nadeau's full attention is drawn to the gleaming new 20-barrel brewhouse on which his brewer has just finished the first batch of Ridge Runner Ale. The owner and brewer are both amazed at some of the new system's bells and whistles. Instead of their having to rake out the spent grain manually after each brew, the brewhouse does most of the work for them. When I try to interview him, Nadeau can sometimes only manage a simple "Wow," followed by bigger smiles, in response to a question.

Rock Art stands in a long, red, wooden barn just outside of downtown Morrisville. With its tall ceilings, the space is vastly different from the brewery's original home. For its first three years of existence, Rock Art operated as a cottage brewery, producing about twenty-five thousand gallons of beer a year out of Nadeau's basement. The owners talk of adding a pub to this location, but nothing is yet planned. As the staff settles in with the new system, Nadeau also hopes to add some specialty release beers.

Matt, a native Vermonter, and Renee were living and working in Colorado when inspiration struck. While river rafting, Matt saw a Kokopelli figure carved into a rock formation. An image familiar to all, even if the name doesn't immediately resonate, Kokopelli is a figure drawn from ancient Anasazi Indian mythology. With his signature hunchback posture, the stick-looking figure dances happily around, playing his flute. To his followers, Kokopelli symbolized fertility, replenishment, dance, music, and mischief. The image immediately intrigued Nadeau and he later recalled it when trying to think of an original name for his brewery. The owner didn't want to choose a boring, regional descriptor; he wanted a standout name. From this desire, and with the help of Kokopelli, Rock Art was born.

Kokopelli's life-loving spirit continues to provide inspiration for the brewery, which integrates his distinctive image in all of its wares, including bottles, growlers, hand-carved tap handles, and bottle caps. The figure's trademark hump was often considered to be a sack of gifts, including seeds of plants and flowers he would scatter every spring. From the look of it, I imagine he may have had some room in that bag for a growler or two as well.

Rock Art's beers generally tend toward the malty side of the flavor wheel. The brewers also produce a few lagers, including the special release Mountain Holidays Bock. Bottled in a cream-colored label and topped with gold foil, this beer tastes of slight fruit and alcohol notes and offers a mild malt balance. While lighter in terms of the style, the bock is an enjoyable seasonal release.

Jasper Murdock's Alehouse

The Norwich Inn
325 Main Street
Norwich, Vermont 05055
Tel. (802) 649–1143

The NORWICH INN

ESTABLISHED 1797

★ **Best Beer:** Jasper Murdock's Private Stock. This is akin to picking favorites among your children. Tim Wilson's excellent English-style ales are all well-rounded, but the Private Stock really is something special. A very limited-edition strong ale made with hops from the Inn's own hop garden, this beer is a wonderful mastery of malts and hops.

Opened: May 1993.

Type: Brewpub.

Owners: Sally and Tim Wilson.

Brewer: Tim Wilson.

Brewing system: 4-barrel Elliott Bay Metal Fabricating brewhouse.

Amount produced: 220 barrels. 250-barrel total capacity.

First beer: Whistling Pig Red Ale.

Flagship beer: Whistling Pig Red Ale.

Year-round beers: Whistling Pig Red Ale, Old Slipperyskin India Pale Ale, Stackpole Porter, and Second Wind Oatmeal Stout.

Seasonal beers: Fuggle & Barleycorn, Dr. Bowie's Elixir Amber, Oh Be Joyful Mild Ale, Last Pick Pale Ale, and Jasper Murdock's Private Stock.

Tours: "If the lights are on and the dogs are out front, come on in," Tim Wilson says. Tours otherwise by appointment. You can also simply look through the brewhouse's glass doors to take in most of the operation.

Beer to go: Wrapped in antique-looking labels, only 3,000 bottles of the year-round beers, along with a few choice bottles of the Private Stock, are offered for sale every year in the inn's bottle shop.

Food: Far from typical pub food, the Alehouse's incredibly well-considered menu is a welcome reprieve. Co-owner Sally Wilson, a graduate of the Johnson and Wales Culinary Arts Institute, oversees the pub and dining-room menus. The selections criss-cross the globe with no hint of self-consciousness, offering flashes of Cajun, Indonesian, southwestern, and even staples of New England seafood. While lesser establishments would make a mess of such a diverse medley of dishes, the Alehouse always impresses. The menu changes three times during the year and more formal dining is also available in the Inn's main restaurant. The kitchen in the Alehouse is open daily from 2 P.M. to 9 P.M.

Amenities: Parking is available behind the inn. Full liquor license.

Pub hours: Closed Mondays. Tuesday through Sunday, 11 A.M. to 2 A.M.

Directions: From I-91, take Exit 13 and head into Norwich on Route 5. Look for the striking Norwich Inn on the left side after the road becomes Main Street.

There are few more pleasant ways to spend a chilly winter's evening than in the warm comfort and care of genial hosts, fortified with good food and classically brewed ale. In the earliest days of our republic, New England innkeepers provided more than a place to sleep for their customers. The clientele were treated more like guests in their homes and the innkeepers were responsible for supplying quality meals and victuals. While this tradition long ago disappeared from fashion, one couple has revived the concept in a beautiful Victorian manse in Norwich, Vermont.

Before the Norwich Inn entered his life on a full-time basis, Tim Wilson worked as a senior loan officer at a local bank and the inn was simply one of his accounts. During a visit to Vermont in 1990, Sally passed by the inn and noticed it was starting to fall into disrepair. Instead of simply shrugging off the unfortunate condition, Sally asked around to find out who owned the place. Her friends couldn't tell her, so they referred her to the friendly banker who kept tabs on the inn. Sally called Tim, who was impressed with the young lady's enthusiasm. After their meeting, Tim decided keep the lady's number around.

By the fall of 1990, the inn's owners were in financial trouble and the inn's condition continued to degenerate. When the owners missed their loan payments, the bank foreclosed on the property. Tim lined up a local caretaker to run the inn while the bank prepared it for sale; the man left Tim's office and promptly died before he could take over the position. In a panic, Tim suddenly remembered the pleasant, eager woman who had visited him earlier that year.

For her part, the Norwich Inn still occupied Sally's thoughts even while she worked as a manager for another property out-of-state. As Sally prepared to close the Kennebunkport Inn in Portland, Maine, she received a life-changing phone call. The nice banker Tim Wilson was on the line, and he told her he needed someone to run the inn. On New Year's Day, Sally packed her things and headed to Norwich to oversee the inn for the bank.

After running the place for eight months, Sally was convinced of its numerous charms and great potential. In August 1991, Tim and the bank listed the property for auction, and Sally placed the highest bid with the help of much-needed loans from the SBA and her father. The inn was now hers, but the story only begins at this point.

After purchasing the Inn, Sally and Tim's friendship continued. They worked closely on the inn as Tim shared Sally's passion for the place and her vision for its renewal. In 1994, the pair married and today reside in a newly built home a short walk from their twenty-seven-room inn. The Wilsons have now spent more than ten years renovating the inn; the place is a true testament to their dedication and passion. The once-lost, architectural flourishes have been recovered, and every inch has been scraped and repainted; floors, ceilings, and walls torn out and rebuilt. The Wilsons even replaced the inn's signature towers, which were inexplicably removed by prior owners. The handsome Victorian structure, painted with its distinctive, original color scheme, has been faithfully restored to its former splendor.

If you love history, thoughtfully prepared and well-executed cuisine, or classic, flavorful beer—or any combination thereof—the Norwich Inn is simply not to be missed. In 1993, the Wilson's revived another old innkeeping tradition by brewing and serving beer for their guests. After homebrewing for a few years, Tim took a modest two-thousand-dollar investment and converted a former chicken coop into a tiny brewery. He originally made small, five-gallon batches on a three-keg system and fermented them in standard glass carboys. When the kegs were ready to be served, he'd wheel them over to the bar on a wagon.

After a few batches, word spread and the inn played host to people from as far away as Colorado who had come to try the beer. The couple immediately saw an opportunity and started planning to build a bigger brewery. Two years later, Tim finished renovating an old livery barn across the courtyard from the pub. With his small, 4-barrel brewing system (built by inmates at a maximum-security prison in Washington State), Tim produces a line of ales under the Jasper Murdock label—a nod to the man who built the original Norwich Inn. In 1996, Tim started hand-bottling his beers in 22-ounce bottles for sale in the inn's bottle shop. He also grows about twenty pounds of his own Norwich Inn hops on the property and uses them to dry-hop some of his beers.

Wilson exclusively brews English-style ales, which are fermented in the brew-house before being pumped to conditioning tanks in the basement. The beer is then pumped underground to the pub across the way. The brewer prefers easy-drinking, session ales, and it shows. Each of his offerings, minus the powerful Private Stock ale, are brimming with flavor, but with a manageable alcohol level that allows you to enjoy a few pints. The stable of beers rotates occasionally, but otherwise remains very consistent. The ale is best enjoyed on a stool at the seven-seat bar in the inn's small pub, called the Alehouse.

While there is a great deal of history here—including a visit from sitting president James Monroe on July 22, 1817, guest registries on display dating back to the 1800s, and reports of a resident ghost—it is the story of the Wilsons that I like the best. I hope to return soon to enjoy the treasure they brought back to life.

Magic Hat Brewing Company

5 Bartlett Bay Road
Burlington, Vermont 05403
Tel. (802) 658-BREW
www.magichat.net

★ **Best Beer:** Chaotic Chemistry. With its distinctive sloping, smoky-hued bottle, Chaotic Chemistry is part of Magic Hat's Humdinger special release series. This barleywine is aged for three years in oak bourbon casks before release. The aroma of vanilla, wood, and maple syrup starts as soon as the cork disgorges from the bottle. The alcohol level of 10.8 percent is perceptible and presents itself similarly to the aroma of dark rum. With a huge mouthfeel, the lightly carbonated beer possesses a slightly nutty flavor, mixed with hints of butter and a distinct fruitiness. At nearly $20 a bottle, this beer is priced for special occasions.

Opened: November 1994.

Type: Brewery.

Owners: Alan Newman and Bob Johnson.

Brewer: Todd Haire.

Brewing system: 50-barrel JV Northwest brewhouse.

Amount produced: 47,110 barrels. 70,000-barrel total capacity.

First beer: Magic Hat Ale (renamed Humble Patience).

Flagship beer: #9.

Year-round beers: #9, Blind Faith (India pale ale), Heart of Darkness (stout), and Fat Angel (pale ale).

Seasonal beers: Hi.P.A., Ravell (vanilla porter), Braggot, Chaotic Chemistry (barleywine), Thumbsucker (imperial stout), Nailbiter (imperial stout), Mother Lager, Jinx (smoked ale), Hocus Pocus (American wheat ale), and Single Chair Ale.

Tours: Magic Hat avidly encourages visitors to "come watch our spores dance and play." The brewery's funky company store, dubbed the Artifactory, is open Monday through Saturday, 10 A.M. to 6 P.M. (until 7 P.M. in the summer) and Sunday, noon to 5 P.M. Entertaining and informative tours are available year-round. From Memorial Day through Superbowl Sunday, tours operate Thursday and Friday at 3:30 P.M. and 4:30 P.M.; and Saturday at noon, 1 P.M., 2 P.M., and 3 P.M. From Superbowl Sunday through Memorial Day, Magic Hat offers tours Wednesday through Friday at 3 P.M., 4 P.M., and 5 P.M.; and Saturday at noon, 1 P.M., 2 P.M., and 3 P.M.

Beer To Go: Growlers filled directly from the taps are very popular here.

Amenities: Parking is available in the brewery's parking lot. The Artifactory offers a wide assortment of Magic Hat goodies, from soap to t-shirts to glassware. The growler backpack, which allows you to carry safely two growlers full of beer, is an especially handy item.

Directions: From Route 7 in South Burlington, turn onto Bartlett Bay Road and look for the Magic Hat sign on the right. The complex is a big, black building.

Alan Newman has a proven knack for being in the right place, with the right idea, at exactly the right time. The man the *Wall Street Journal* described as a "serial entrepreneur" and who confesses to being an "unemployable insubordinate," has scored a string of successful businesses. In 1988, Newman founded Seventh Generation, a company that has grown to become the nation's leading brand of environmentally safe household products. After taking over a failing catalog business, Newman renamed the company and helped save the entire operation. After leaving the company on less-than-friendly terms in 1991, Newman took a break from business life and settled in with his family.

Fate winked at Newman when a chance meeting with a former employee on Burlington's popular Church Street led to the creation of one of the largest regional breweries in America. Newman ran into Bob Johnson, a former warehouse manager at Seventh Generation. An avid homebrewer, Johnson announced his intention of moving to Martha's Vineyard to run a microbrewery. Having enjoyed Johnson's homebrewed beer in the past, Newman suggested the pair team up and build the brewery in Burlington. After a whirlwind tour of thirty-three breweries in ten days, the pair knew they wanted to do things differently from other craft beer companies. Setting the stage for the follies to come, Newman and Johnson dubbed their new business the Magic Hat Brewing Company and Performing Arts Center, Inc. Although he no longer works at the brewery, Johnson still remains on tasting panels.

It's hard to believe that Newman isn't actually a native Vermonter, but instead moved here in 1970 after living on a commune in Oregon. With his flowing, white beard and flamboyant, carefree sense of personal style, Newman has become something of a local celebrity. Every year, the brewery sponsors a Mardi Gras party in downtown Burlington that draws thousands of free spirits. Festooned in a wild, purple coat with gold garland and sparkling top hat that would make the Mad Hatter proud, Newman leads a parade through the city's streets.

While Magic Hat may appear possessed with an insouciant spirit, the colorful Newman is serious about succeeding in the highly competitive brewing industry. Though the brewery has taken a more creative and less traditional approach to spreading brand awareness, Magic Hat has grown to become the largest brewery in Vermont. Newman and his brewery are compelling figures, befitting vintage Tom Wolfe characters. Not *Bonfire of the Vanities,* mind you—more like *The Electric Kool-Aid Acid Test.*

As Magic Hat lives up to its full name, a visit to the actual brewery is a must for beer and theatre lovers alike. The brewery is a gallery of oddities, beginning with discarded implements of brewing technology exhibited in the parking lot like pieces of industrial, outdoor artwork. The brewery shop and tasting rooms are decorated in wild style, with plenty of eye-catching curiosities on display for ogling, including a fermenter cut in half and turned into a display rack for Magic Hat merchandise. In contrast to the industrial cement floors, the wacky tasting-bar is a pleasure-inducing, tactile wonder that mixes corrugated-steel siding and twisted copper.

Around the corner from the Artifactory, a tour guide leads you through a curving entrance to the brewery and into a minigallery of Magic Hat–related marvels. The very popular, unconventional tour details the brewery's peculiar history and highlights the eccentricities of its owners and staff. The best touch is a multimedia presentation, which includes Newman's face projected on a small, round video screen embedded in a life-sized, costumed version of himself. Newman narrates a short film chronicling the history of craft brewing in America, in which he rails against the homogenization of American brewing. In the film, Newman equates the bland, soulless products of the country's big three breweries with Twinkies, McDonald's, and Wonder Bread. Showing a much-appreciated camaraderie with his fellow brewers, he publicly thanks Anchor Brewing Company founder Fritz Maytag for his pioneering role in American craft brewing, and highlights Sierra Nevada and other small breweries.

The brewery produces a variety of off-beat ales packaged in exceedingly creative ways. Magic Hat's curiously named flagship ale, the #9, is an apricot-infused, "not quite pale ale." Lore has it that the beer is either named for the Beatles' song, "Revolution No. 9," or for the classic oldie by the Clovers, "Love Potion No. 9." The brewery reports that it was originally named the X19 Prototype and when the beer proved popular enough to justify a wider release, they had to choose a new name due to trademark issues. Among flagship ales, #9 clearly stands out not only in New England, but in the country. The ale's distinctive flavor pleases beer snobs and novices alike. #9 accounts for 75 to 85 percent of the company's production.

The brewery continues to work from the original Ringwood strain, purchased from Shipyard's Alan Pugsley. Most brewers capture and repitch their yeast a handful of times before tossing it out to guard against off-flavors. Along with a few other users of this hardy strain, Magic Hat's brewers simply repitch the yeast time after time, thus developing a unique house character. While the majority of Magic Hat's beers, including the Ravell, the juicy Hi.P.A., and its specialty releases are excellent, others are overpowered by the Ringwood house yeast. These beers, including Hocus Pocus, Fat Angel, Humble Patience, and the most recent release of the Braggot, are possessed with an overabundance of diacetyl esters and buttery flavors.

Shed Restaurant and Brewery

1859 Mountain Road
Stowe, Vermont, 05672
Tel. (802) 253-4364

★ **Best Beer:** Spring Stout. One of Hill's first creations, the brewer adds oak and maple chips along with Mount Gay Rum to create a uniquely flavored beer. Among a mix of roasted malts and an ever-so-slight hint of Ringwood yeast, the light, oaky flavors imparted by the chips complement the distinct rum notes.

Opened: December 1994.

Type: Brewpub.

Owners: Ken and Kathy Strong.

Brewer: Shaun Hill.

Brewing system: 7-barrel Peter Austin brewhouse.

Amount produced: 1,700 barrels. Presently at capacity.

First beer: Mountain Ale.

Flagship beer: Mountain Ale.

Year-round beers: West Branch Golden, Shed Amber Ale, National IPA, Smugglers Stout, and Mountain Ale.

Seasonal beers: Maple Brown Ale, Raspberry Wheat, Pumpkin Ale, Spiced Christmas Ale, Irish Red, Scottish Ale, and Porter. Also look for one of the brewer's rotating selections, often his stout of choice.

Tours: Tours by appointment.

Beer to go: 64-ounce growlers are very popular here and go quickly. Kegs in a variety of sizes are also available for order.

Food: The typical pub fare on the menu seems a little out of place in some of the Shed's nicer dining rooms. The menu specializes in a series of low-calorie, low-fat items. The Shed's Kid's Corner menu offers hot dogs, burgers, and grilled cheese, with French fries and a milk or soda for little skiers. Late-night dining after 10 P.M. is available in the pub.

Amenities: Parking is available alongside the restaurant and behind it. Outdoor seating in warmer months. Full liquor license.

Pub hours: Daily, 11:30 A.M. to late.

Directions: Head west from the center of Stowe on Route 108, and look for the Shed after a mile and a half.

★ ★ ★

From the seasoned look of the place, you would never guess that the substantial, barn-looking structure housing this brewpub is only slightly more than a decade old. In fact, some patrons who used to visit the original Shed hardly notice that the place was entirely rebuilt following a devastating fire on January 26, 1994. The colossal red building, whose roots go back to 1830 when it was a cider mill, was lost due to a careless cigarette in the bar. Due to the uncommonly cold temperatures that evening, which dipped well below zero, the firemen's equipment froze during their attempts to save the burning building. The temperature was so cold that a giant ice sculpture located near the building didn't even melt.

Friends of the Shed were devastated, but the owners remained undaunted. When staffers received a phone call from owner Ken Strong the next morning telling them to report to work, they thought he was crazy. While the building continued to smolder, Strong declared his intention to rebuild the Shed.

Before the year ended, the Shed was reborn from the ashes, reflecting much of its original architecture and design. While walking through the pub, stop to peruse the various pictures of the fire. When you compare the old structure to the new Shed, the similarities are eerie. The owners simply added a natural stone fireplace to the Vermont Room, a vaulted cathedral ceiling to the Garden Room, and a new greenhouse room with a bar on the side. With all of its character and rustic charm, it's hard to believe the front bar area is so new. The wooden bar is actually a bank teller's station taken from a closed branch of the Northfield Savings Bank. (That the pub still allows smoking is hard to believe, but that's another matter entirely.)

The 7-barrel brewhouse was actually a last-minute addition to the plans, as the original Shed didn't contain a brewery. During a chance meeting at a college reunion, an old acquaintance suggested the owners add a brewing system to their pub. Even with the plans finalized and construction already under way, Ken Strong returned to Stowe determined to add the brewhouse.

From the look of it, the architect barely managed to fit the brick Peter Austin kettles into the comically small brewhouse. Customers in the pub area can sit under the hand-hewn, native timber beams and watch the young brewer, Shaun Hill, twist himself around the equipment in creation of their future pints.

Hill is also a new addition to the Shed, having been the brewer for a mere two months at the time of my visit. He was previously working odd jobs around the restaurant when the Shed's former brewers decided to leave to open their own business. With some limited homebrewing experience, Hill threw himself into the opportunity. He apprenticed under the former brewers for a week before taking over the production himself. In a testament to the trust of the owners, Hill has pretty much unfettered discretion to run the brewing operations. While he continues to follow the long-standing recipes for the pub's standard offerings, he has recently started branching out with the release of his tasty Spring Stout.

The addition of the young and enthusiastic Hill portends good things to come for the Shed. The brewer hopes to reconnect with the local beer scene and spread the brewpub's name beyond the local ski environs. The Shed also continues to promote its flagship Mountain Ale to accounts outside of the brewpub, which account for approximately one-third of all production. With a hectic, five-day-a-week brewing schedule, the young brewer's on-the-job training looks like it will continue at a breakneck pace for the foreseeable future.

Alchemist Pub and Brewery

23 South Main Street
Waterbury, Vermont 05676
Tel. (802) 244–4120
www.alchemistbeer.com

PUB & BREWERY

> ★ **Best Beer:** Sterk Wit. Less than a year after it opened, the Alchemist won a gold medal with this so-called double white ale in the Belgian-style Strong Specialty Ale category at the 2004 Great American Beer. Delightfully full-bodied, the Sterk Wit abounds with coriander and orange aromas. The flavor offers muted tropical fruit flavors ranging from coconut to pineapple.

Opened: November 2003.

Type: Brewpub.

Owners: John and Jennifer Kimmich.

Brewer: John Kimmich.

Brewing system: 7-barrel locally fabricated brewhouse.

Amount produced: 336 barrels. 700-barrel total capacity.

First beer: Light Weight (pilsner).

Flagship beer: Donovan's Red.

Year-round beers: Light Weight, Donovan's Red, Sterk Wit, Pappy's Porter, Holy Cow IPA, and Blackout (stout).

Seasonal beers: Zommer Bier (summer), Thatcher Brook Blonde, Shtupulator (doppelbock), Heady Topper (double IPA), Broken Spoke (pale ale), Solstice (Belgian-style ale), Bolton Brown, Charlie (brown ale), HellBrook (double red ale), Dunkler Stern, El Jefe (IPA), Grote Bruin, Onion River Rye, O Positive (Belgian-style fruit beer), Piston Bitter, and Harvest Ale.

Tours: Tours not available.

Beer to go: None.

Food: Jen Kimmich, a former food and beverage manager at several restaurants, directs the food side of the business. The pub is a member of Vermont Farm Fresh and the menu features a variety of local ingredients, including organic produce and dairy products, along with vegetarian offerings.

Amenities: Limited on-street parking is available. Full liquor license. Pool table.

Other attractions: Before getting your beverage fix at the Alchemist, you can throw your low-carb diet out the window with a visit to the Ben and Jerry's factory, about a mile away from the pub. No longer owned by the irreverent pair, but by corporate giant Unilever, the folksy tour is still a hit with both adults and kids. Route 100, Waterbury, Vermont 05676, tel. (866) BJ-TOURS. The Cold Hollow Cider Mill in nearby Waterbury Center is New England's largest producer of fresh apple cider. Come see the cider press in action and sample a few handfuls of delicious cider donuts. Route 100, Waterbury Center, Vermont 05677, tel. (800) 3-APPLES.

Pub hours: Monday through Thursday, 4 P.M. to midnight; Friday through Sunday, 3 P.M. to 1 A.M.

Directions: From I-89, head toward Waterbury on VT-100 at Exit 10. Take VT-100 until it hits Route 2, then go south. The pub is on South Main Street just north of the Vermont State Hospital a few blocks down the street.

Nestled prominently on Main Street in downtown Waterbury, the Alchemist offers a quiet, hospitable environment in which to enjoy a few pints of quality beer. The idea for the Alchemist was born in another Vermont brewpub located a few miles to the northwest of Waterbury. The owners, John and Jen Kimmich, first met at the Vermont Pub and Brewery in 1996, where he was brewing and she was waitressing and helping to manage the pub. The pair knew they wanted to open a place of their own and they conducted a wide search to find the right location. The Kimmichs scouted places in nearby Stowe, and almost opened a location in Boston—a decision John admits would have been disastrous.

When the couple walked into this space in downtown Waterbury, John says they knew immediately it was the right location. They set to renovating the building, which was formerly a post office, a sporting goods store, and a blacksmithery. After several concentrated months of work, the Kimmichs opened the Alchemist on the day after Thanksgiving in 2003. They didn't have long to contemplate the new addition to their family: the day after opening the Alchemist, they learned that soon their family was going to grow even larger with a little brewster of their own, a son named Charlie.

It's hard to picture the Alchemist existing in another location, let alone a sprawling city environment. The atmosphere is simultaneously convivial and contemplative. The friendly staff interacts with locals and other pubgoers, but gives you enough room to concentrate on your own pint or conversation. The attractive, colorful mosaic bar top was created by a local artist with tiles she collected from around the world. Against the muted, earthy colors of the walls and bar, another local artisan has created custom mobiles and metalworks, including the large piece hanging over the pool table. In keeping with the pub's occult name, a local painter created a sparkling gold and silver mural of the alchemic wheel on the back wall. Even the curving, metal French fry containers are the work of a Waterbury artist.

This small storefront abuts the street with large, floor-to-ceiling bay windows. The cartoonish engravings on the pub's windows are worth some examination. With its twisted, cursive lettering, the Alchemist's name slopes across the pane over the pub's distinctive icon. The sharply slanted emblem, which is the alchemic symbol for fermentation, looks like a disfigured candle.

The word *alchemy* once described the suspect practice of trying to turn simple, base metals into shining gold; the modern incarnation at play here connotes the practice of transforming common grains and hops into something special. Though there remains little that is inexplicable or mysterious about the brewing process, a talented brewer can mix an enigmatic potion that leaves your curiosity aroused. With good beer, however, you should never feel left with fool's gold.

John Kimmich constantly scrutinizes his shiny new brewpub, rethinking design schemes, and constantly tweaks his own recipes. Kimmich is a man who knows what he likes and is not afraid to share his thoughts. He offers that New England beer leaves him entirely underwhelmed. His qualities of self-confidence and singular vision border on arrogance but also push his beers to new heights.

Kimmich is proud of his brewing system, a mish-mash of beat-up kettles. He admits the system it isn't particularly easy on the eyes but it makes some nice beers. "I wanted the ugliest system possible," he says with a laugh. Kimmich confesses that he doesn't follow style guidelines too closely, but instead prefers to brew outside of traditionally drawn lines. With that said, the beers available at the Alchemist generally don't stray too far from their represented styles. They distinguish themselves with their clean flavors and carefully crafted nuances. In a short time, Kimmich has scored great success on this homely system. While attending the 2004 GABF with his brothers, he patiently watched from the audience while organizers announced the winners in the Belgian-style Strong Specialty Ale category. As the bronze and silver medals came and went, he looked at his brothers and said, "Well, it's gold or nothing." The medal for this heady brew now proudly hangs on display behind the pub's bar as notice of the quality beers brewed on-site for the Sterk Wit.

Maple Leaf Malt and Brewing Company

3 North Main Street
Wilmington, Vermont 05363
Tel. (802) 464–9900

★ **Best Beer:** Bombshell Blonde. A very drinkable Kolsch-style ale filled with old-school German hops. The beer possesses a very pleasant fruitiness throughout and nicely showcases the Perle hop.

Opened: 1999 (new ownership in 2003).

Type: Brewpub.

Owners: Darren Fehring and Mark Marchionni.

Brewer: Darren Fehring.

Brewing system: 3-barrel New World Brewing Systems brewhouse.

Amount produced: 300 barrels.

First beer: Wee Heavy (under new ownership).

Flagship beer: Hopadelic IPA.

Year-round beers: Hopadelic IPA and Bombshell Blonde.

Seasonal beers: A rotating selection of up to fifty offerings.

Tours: By appointment or simply ask someone at the bar. Fehring is often at the location and is always willing to give tours.

Beer to go: The brewery sells both growlers and kegs.

Food: As the operation remains in flux, the menu is subject to change.

Amenities: Limited street parking is available. Full liquor license.

Pub hours: Open Sunday through Thursday, noon to midnight; Friday and Saturday, noon to 1 A.M. or 2 A.M.

Directions: The brewery is located on North Main Street at the crossroads of Routes 100 and 9.

Only the fulfillment of a dream could drive a person to leave the pleasures of Key West for a small, slightly dilapidated pub in a town where the previous owners openly discouraged locals from visiting. When Darren Fehring found the Maple Leaf Malt and Brewing Company, he did just that. Formerly the head brewer at the now-closed Key West Brewing Company, Fehring met his partner, Mark Marchionni, at another brewpub gig, where the latter was the bar manager. Both eventually moved on to other places, with Fehring working with regional powerhouse Frederick Brewing Company in Maryland. Though the two were happily employed in the beer business, they constantly thought about going off on their own. After several years apart, both separately decided to take the plunge into self-employment, but only if the other was also willing.

After reconnecting, the partners traversed the Western Hemisphere on a three-year search for a location to open a new brewpub. Their travels took them from the Caribbean to the Pacific and through various Mid-Atlantic states before they found their inspiration in a small, three-story, green and yellow dwellinghouse in downtown Wilmington, Vermont.

From the outside, it's hard to see how this two-hundred-year old structure could be the end result of anything but a set redesign for *The Money Pit*. After purchasing the existing brewpub, the partners learned that several accounts remained outstanding, including that of a major hop producer who refused to work with them despite their plea of new ownership. They also undertook the difficult task of reaching out to locals who had felt unwelcome at the pub under the previous ownership; Fehring even managed to strike up a few friendships across the bar.

Initial hurdles over, Fehring and Marchionni view the place as the foundation on which to build their brewpub vision. The owners plan some serious changes for the old brewhouse on Main Street, including a renovation of the building and retiring the Maple Leaf name. In its present well-worn state, the ridiculously small twenty-five-seat dining room has tables that push right up to the glass windows of the cramped brewhouse.

The owners are also in the process of building a new dining room on the second floor, complete with a bar, fireplace, and outdoor seating on the structure's street-side balcony. The pub will expand to eight-five seats in order to fully accommodate the overflows from the seasonal visitors. Fehring also hopes to drop the small brew house down into the basement in order to gain some much-needed vertical space for a larger, 7-barrel system.

Despite the owners' good intentions, at least one local businessman does not care to see the pub expand and succeed. After the partners secured unanimous go-aheads from the planning, zoning, and historical commissions, a local restaurateur served Maple Leaf with a lawsuit. A judge granted a preliminary injunction, which stopped the owners from further renovating the structure. The second floor now sits in tatters, torn down to the studs, awaiting the final court result and the attention of contractors and electricians.

The partners hope to soon rechristen the awkwardly named brewpub as the humorous Grumpy Gnome brewpub. While Fehring admits the iconic and whimsical name is more a marketing concept than a serious pub name, he hopes the change will encourage visitors to stop by for a pint. "I want people to say, 'What the hell is that? We have to go there,'" Fehring remarks about the name.

Enjoined from directing his energy to the structure itself, Fehring instead fiddles with the pub's beers. Working from a list of fifty staple recipes, he clearly enjoys the luxury of small-batch brewing. Born of his desire to experiment, the brewer changes each batch, even the core beers. "I haven't brewed the perfect batch yet," he notes.

With so much changing at the Maple Leaf, the adage of "only time will tell" is unavoidably appropriate. Although the process remains stalled, Fehring and Marchionni enjoy interacting with their customers and new friends. And if you see Fehring in the fishbowl brewery yelling at his little three-barrel system, he just asks that you not call him the Grumpy Gnome.

Harpoon Brewery

336 Ruth Carney Drive
Windsor, Vermont 05089
Tel. (888) HARPOON
www.harpoonbrewery.com

> ★ **Best Beer:** 100 Barrel Series. Brewed on site here at the Windsor facility, these specialty releases are bottled in 22-ounce packages and appear only once. The brewers take turns designing and brewing the beers, which have included a Smoked Porter, Barleywine, and Maibock. The beers are brewed from two 50-barrel batches that are combined and fermented in a single unitank.

Opened: 2000.

Type: Brewery.

Owner: Privately held corporation. Richard Doyle, CEO.

Brewer: Al Marzi, vice president of brewing operations.

Brewing system: 50-barrel Santa Rosa Stainless Steel brewhouse.

Amount produced: 28,000 barrels. 35,000-barrel present capacity, soon to expand to 60,000 barrels.

First beer: Catamount Pale Ale.

Flagship beer: Harpoon IPA.

Year-round beers: Harpoon IPA, Harpoon UFO, Harpoon Ale, and Harpoon Munich Dark.

Seasonal beers: Harpoon Summer Beer, Harpoon Winter Warmer, Harpoon Hibernian Ale, Harpoon Octoberfest, and 100 Barrel Series.

Tours: The Windsor facility is open year-round and offers tours and a sizable brewery store full of Harpoon-related merchandise. You can take a self-guided tour by walking out of the store into a roped-off section of the brewery floor, which is surprisingly close to the boiling kettles. In between making sandwiches and pouring free, 2-ounce samples, the staff also informally rounds people up for comprehensive and highly informed tours of the small brewery. The brewery's café overlooks various parts of the brewing and bottling operation.

Beer to go: The whole range of Harpoon products are for sale at the brewery, including kegs, 64-ounce growlers, cases, 12-packs, and 22-ounce bottles. You can even pick up selections from Harpoon's line of handcrafted sodas, including root beer, orange and cream, and vanilla cream.

Food: The Harpoon Beer Garden Menu celebrates its local Vermont surroundings, focusing on excellent, grilled panini sandwiches such as the Vermonter, which includes Green Mountain Smokehouse–smoked turkey breast and bacon, Granny Smith Apple slices, and Cabot sharp cheddar topped with locally made spicy mustard.

Amenities: Plenty of parking is available in the brewery's lot.

Other attractions: The Windsor brewery hosts two popular events during the year. Forty teams compete in late July during the New England Barbeque Championship. In early October, the brewery celebrates the release of its seasonal beer with a traditional Octoberfest celebration, complete with German music, food, and dancing.

Pub hours: May through August: Sunday through Wednesday, 10 A.M. to 6 P.M.; and Thursday through Saturday, 10 A.M. to 8 P.M. September through October: closed Mondays; open Tuesday through Sunday, 10 A.M. to 6 P.M. November through April: closed Sundays and Mondays; open Tuesday through Saturday, 10 A.M. to 6 P.M.

Directions: From I-91, take Exit 9 (US-5/VT-12) south and turn left at Ruth Carney Drive.

Nestled at the base of the eastern flank of the Green Mountains, Harpoon's brewery in Windsor is a beautiful place to visit. Surrounded by a mix of trees and open space, the brewery is a far cry from the cramped, industrial Boston facility. As the Connecticut River quickly flows nearby, only the gentle rising of steam from the center of the cream-colored structure gives notice that a mechanized operation lies within.

In 1997, the iconic Catamount Brewery was busy trying to keep up with demand, while simultaneously overextending itself with a five-million-dollar loan to open the beautiful new Windsor brewery. Soon thereafter, Catamount's sales went downhill, fueled in part by the brewery's lack of marketing support behind its products. As sales slipped, Catamount started missing payments on its loan and soon surrendered its assets to the local lending institution. In March 2000, the bank closed the Windsor brewery and sought a buyer.

As Harpoon's popularity increased during the nineties, its owners knew it would soon hit capacity at its home brewery. Due to space restrictions, expansion possibilities were extremely limited. Catamount's tragic loss was Harpoon's lucky gain. Harpoon stepped in and purchased the Windsor brewery and its brands for the fire-sale price of one million dollars. In a conscious move to appease the notoriously provincial Vermont market, and to comfort them after losing such an identifiable brand, Harpoon announced it would continue to brew a line of beer under the Catamount label.

Sadly, Harpoon's olive branch soon withered as a result of several considerations beyond its control. In light of the derelict condition of the brand, and Harpoon's understandable desire to focus on growing its own brands, the brewery's eventual decision to stop production of the Catamount line was its only realistic course of action. The permanent retirement of the Catamount brand was a terrible loss for New England, as it was one of the true pioneers of the craft beer movement here.

The spirit of Catamount lives in Windsor, and you can see some of the old brewery's bottles lining the shelves of the facility's collection of craft beer bottles. Raise a glass to the departed brand and to Harpoon for bringing this beautiful facility back to life for the local community to enjoy.

Alcohol by volume. A by-product of fermentation that occurs when yeast eats the sugars in the wort. Expressed as a percentage of volume (ABV) or by weight (ABW). A misunderstanding of these two measurement tools underlies the common misconception that Canadian beer is stronger than American beer. Canadian brewers generally use the ABV designation, while larger American brewers have traditionally relied upon ABW. Craft brewers most often use the ABV standard for alcohol measurement. A beer with an ABV of 5 percent has an ABW of 3.98 percent, as alcohol weighs slightly less than 80 percent as much as water.

Alan Pugsley. The head brewer and part-owner of the Shipyard Brewing Company. Pugsley once worked for Peter Austin at the Ringwood Brewery in Hampshire, England. After coming to America to help David Geary open his pioneering brewery in the early 1980s, Pugsley opened a very influential consulting company. With his sample of the Ringwood house yeast, Pugsley helped dozens of breweries open in New England, including many profiled in this guide.

Adjunct. A fermentable element substituted for cereal grains. These ingredients include rice and corn, both of which are often used by larger breweries to lighten the bodies of their beers. Adjuncts comprise between 30 and 40 percent of the ingredients found in many popular American beers. Viewed with great disdain by beer geeks who believe their use cheapens the final product.

Ale. One of the two main families of beer. Ales are distinguished from lagers by their use of *Saccharomyces cerevisiae,* an aerobic yeast that settles at the top of a fermentation vessel. Ale yeasts generally prefer warmer temperatures, which contribute their signature fruity, estery flavors.

Barley. The most traditional cereal grain used in the mash of the brewing process after malting. Brewers use dozens of varieties of malt, kilned to different temperatures, in order to achieve different flavor profiles. Barley typically makes up the majority of the fermentable materials found in beer.

Barrel. A unit used to measure amounts of beer. The amounts found in a barrel differ between the American and metric systems of measurement. In the metric system, a barrel contains 36 imperial gallons or 163.7 liters, while an American barrel holds 31.5 gallons, or 119.2 liters. An American barrel contains approximately two traditionally-sized kegs.

Beer. Any beverage alcohol produced by the fermentation of cereal grain, usually malted barley.

Beer geek. An avid enthusiast of all things beer-related. Beer geeks run the gamut from respectfully passionate to disturbingly obsessesed. Beer geeks will take a stroll past the tap handles upon entering any restaurant, disappear into nearby liquor stores to peruse their offerings, and generally take an interest in beer as a hobby. The term is sometimes used in a derogatory fashion about someone who takes beer too seriously.

Bottle-conditioned. A process of secondary fermentation by which brewers add live yeast to, or allow live yeast to enter, the delivery vessel, typically a bottle, to feed upon remaining sugars. The practice creates new aromas and flavors and can help carbonate the final beer by trapping carbon dioxide in the bottle. You can sometimes distinguish a bottle-conditioned beer if there is sediment in the bottom of the bottle.

Brewhouse. The physical location, including the brew kettles, where a brewer makes beer.

Brewpub. A pub or restaurant that produces its own beer on-site and sells at least 25 percent of its production on the premises. The beer is often dispensed directly from the pub's storage tanks. Where allowed by law, brewpubs sell beer to go and even distribute it to off-site accounts.

Brewery. A facility that mainly brews beer for sale off-premise at restaurants and package stores.

Cask-conditioned. Similar to the process of bottle-conditioning, but taking place in a cask or metal keg.

Contract brewing. The arrangement whereby one brewery produces beer on behalf of another brewery or company. Some smaller breweries contract out the production of their beer, often in bottles, to larger breweries that have the benefit of scale brewing. Considered a controversial practice among beer geeks, who inappropriately criticize such beers as being of inferior quality.

Craft Brewer. A brewery that generally produces beers with 100 percent malted barley. Where appropriate for style, a craft brewer may substitute a percentage of malted wheat, rye, or other ingredients to improve the flavor profiles of their beers. A company qualifies as a craft brewer if the majority of its sales consist of craft beer.

David Geary. The founder of the D. L. Geary Brewing Company, in Portland, Maine—the first craft brewery to open in New England.

Diacetyl. A compound in beer that contributes buttery aromas and butterscotch-like flavors. A by-product of some yeast strains, including the Ringwood strain. Acceptable as part of the flavor profiles of some styles, while inappropriate and evidence of a defect in other styles.

Dry-hopping. The addition of hops to fermenting or conditioning beer; used to increase hop character and aroma.

Extract brewing. A brewing process similar to most homebrewing where brewers use a condensed wort, often in the form of a syrup, as a substitute for actual cereal grains. While disdained by beer geeks as a sign of an inferior brewery, extract brewing actually gives the brewer more consistent results. Because of the perceived ease of use, however, many extract brewers do not employ skilled brewers to produce their beers, resulting in substandard beers.

Extreme brewing. The name given to a recent brewing trend toward unusual, experimental, and often high-alcohol or highly hopped beers.

Fermentation. The conversion of sugars into alcohol and carbon dioxide, created through the addition of yeast.

Great American Beer Festival (GABF). Held annually since 1982, this event is one of the largest and oldest beer festivals in America. Hosted by the Brewers Association (BA) in Denver, Colorado, the GABF offers 1,600 beers on tap from 350 American breweries. The BA also holds a well-regarded, blind-tasted competition, awarding highly coveted medals for the top finishers in more than 65 style categories.

Growler. A container of beer, traditionally a half gallon (64 ounces) in size, in which brewers bottle and sell their products. Growlers are popular methods for selling beer at brewpubs, yet are not legal in all states. Many brewpubs charge a small deposit for the bottle and will refill it at discounted rates upon return. Depending on how the containers are filled, the beer usually should be consumed within a short time after purchase. A great device for sharing beer with friends.

Hops. A flowering plant (*Humulus*) used as a flavoring agent in beer. Often added to boiling wort or fermenting beer in order to impart bitter flavors or aromas. There are many varieties of hops and each possesses distinctive characters and contributes different influences to beer. Hop resins contain two main acids, called *alpha* and *beta*. Alpha acids act as preservatives and contribute bitterness early in the boil, flavor in the latter part of the boil, and aroma in the final minutes of the boil. Bitterness is determined the by the degree to which the alpha acids are isomerized during the boil; they are expressed in International Bitterness Units (IBUs). Beta acids do not isomerize during the boil, have a negligible effect on beer flavor, but contribute to the aroma. So-called noble hops are low in bitterness and high in aroma. They traditionally come from European hop regions, including Hallertauer Mittelfrueh, Tettnanger, Spalter, and Saaz.

International Bitterness Unit (IBU). A standard system for calculating and expressing the hop bitterness in beer. An IBU is one part per million of isohumulone. The higher the number, the greater the level of bitterness. American light lagers generally have 5 IBUs, while souped-up India Pale Ales can exceed 100. Some experts believe that people cannot differentiate between beers with more than 100 IBUs.

Homebrewing. The small-scale brewing of beer for personal consumption. Allowed by a law signed by President Jimmy Carter in 1978. Homebrewers are generally allowed to produce between 50 and 100 gallons of beer per year without taxation. Many craft brewers started as homebrewers before stepping up to commercial-scale production.

Lager. The second of the two main families of beer. Lagers are distinguished from ales by their use of *Saccharomyces uvarum* or *carlsbergensis,* anaerobic yeasts that settle to the bottom of the fermenter. Lager yeasts generally prefer cooler temperatures, which tend to soften the edges of the resulting products and provide crisper beers.

Mash. A mixture of hot water and crushed cereal grain, usually barley or wheat, which is produced during the early stage of beer production.

Malt. A process by which cereal grains, often barley, are steeped in water, then allowed to germinate. The germination process is quickly stopped when the resulting product (malt) is kilned to convert the starches to sugars. Maltsters dry beers at various temperatures in order to create different types of malted barley.

Macrobrewery. A large brewery that produces more than 2 million barrels of beer per year. The name given to larger breweries, including Anheuser-Busch, Miller Brewing, and Coors. Beer geeks often refer to the beers produced by these breweries as "macro brews" or "macros."

Microbrewery. Technically, a brewery that produces less than 15,000 barrels of beer per year. The phrase was popularized in the early days of craft brewing and now generally refers to all craft breweries. Larger craft breweries that produce more than 15,000 barrels per year, but less than 2 million barrels, are called regional breweries.

Peter Austin. Founder of the Ringwood Brewery in Hampshire, England, and mentor to Shipyard Brewing Company's Alan Pugsley. He is the main cultivator of the Ringwood yeast strain. He started his brewery in the late 1970s when Britain's larger breweries started abandoning cask-conditioned ales.

Prohibition. The long national dry spell, when the production of most beverage alcohol was banned by the federal government. Achieved by the ratification of the Eighteenth Amendment on January 16, 1919, and the signing of the Volstead Act on October 28, 1919, Prohibition officially began on January 16, 1920. The Eighteenth Amendment was repealed in 1933 with the ratification of the Twenty-First Amendment. Many states, following an example set by Maine, had already passed prohibition laws by the time the federal government took action.

Reinheitsgebot. The so-called German Purity Law, adopted in 1516 by William IV, Duke of Bavaria. The law once applied to all German brewers and limited their ingredients to grains, hops, and water. When scientists discovered the role of yeast in beer, it was added to the list of ingredients. An exception was also later added for wheat beers. One of the oldest existing food regulations, the law has been severely undercut by Germany's involvement in the European Union. Many brewers voluntarily comply with the law out of a sense of tradition.

Ringwood. The yeast strain cultivated by Peter Austin at the Ringwood Brewery and spread throughout New England by Alan Pugsley. A fast-working ale strain, Ringwood cuts down on production time and flocculates and attenuates quickly. Used by many breweries in New England, the Ringwood strain sometimes contributes diacetyl notes to its beers. Some beer geeks criticize the flavor profiles created by the Ringwood strain, which they refer to as buttery or butterscotchy.

Session beer. A beer with a relatively low alcohol level, usually 3 to 4 percent alcohol by weight, which allows the drinker to enjoy several pints in one sitting without becoming intoxicated. Many English-style ales set the standard for such beers.

Siebel Institute of Technology. Founded in 1868 by Dr. John Ewald Siebel as the Zymotechnic Institute, this brewing school is one of the most prestigious in the world. Based in Chicago, Illinois, the school offers many different courses and degree programs in tasting and brewing studies,

University of California–Davis. Located near San Francisco and Sacramento, California, America's other main brewing school offers a well-respected Master Brewers Program through its extension school.

Wort. The liquid solution created when sugar water is strained from the spent cereal grain in the mash tun. Through fermentation, wort turns into beer.

Yeast. A fungus found in the genus *Saccharomyces*, the microorganism feeds on the sugars found in wort, creating alcohol and carbon dioxide as by-products. Some yeast strains contribute distinct flavors to beer and are used to brew specific styles.

★ Index ★

Andy Crouch is an award-winning freelance writer whose articles have appeared in the *Boston Phoenix, American Brewer, Celebrator Beer News, Ale Street News, Yankee Food News, Beverage Magazine,* and on his Web site at www.beerscribe.com. He travels on beer-related adventures as often as possible when he's not practicing criminal law in downtown Boston. This is his first book.